INTROSPECTIONS

EDITED BY

Robert Pack
Jay Parini

Introspections

American Poets on One of Their Own Poems

Middlebury College Press

Published by University Press of New England

Hanover and London

MIDDLEBURY COLLEGE PRESS

Published by University Press of New England

Hanover, NH 03755

Printed in the United States of America

5 4 3 2 1

CIP data appear at the end of the book

CONTENTS

	Introduction	I
Sandra Alcosser	The Autumn Courtship of Surface-Feeding Ducks ("By the Nape")	6
Julia Alvarez	A First Step with "Dusting"	14
A. R. Ammons	One More Poem ("Coming Round")	19
David Baker	Critical Disobedience: Nine Ways of Looking at a Poem ("Still-Hildreth Sanatorium, 1936")	23
Peter Balakian	Falling Into a Rug: Some Notes on "The Oriental Rug"	35
Marvin Bell	About the Dead Man Poems ("The Book of the Dead Man #70")	42
Philip Booth	Speaking for the Speechless Kid ("Hot 5th of July")	48
Rosellen Brown	About Cora Fry	52
Teresa Cader	About "Wind, Horse, Snow"	57
Carl Dennis	Poetry and History ("Sarit Narai")	62
Mark Doty	Souls on Ice ("A Display of Mackerel")	70
Rita Dove	Writing "Parsley"	78
Stephen Dunn	"The Guardian Angel"	86

John Engels   "The Silence": Life Through the Lens
                   of Structure   92

Carol Frost   Starling Eggs ("Scorn")   98

Alice Fulton   A Descant on "Echo Location"   104

Pamela White Hadas Dressing Up Naked: A Life Class in
                   Revision ("Woman with Gardenia")   111

David Huddle   About My "Basket": Looking for Closure 119

Richard Jackson   Talking Poetry at the *Cafe Tazza* ("Do Not
                   Duplicate This Key")   126

Erica Jong   Gestations ("The Buddha in the Womb")   132

X. J. Kennedy   About "B Negative"   138

Maxine Kumin   Word for Word ("Poem for My Son")   145

Gary Margolis   Perhaps Before We Both Must Leave
                   ("To the Young Woman Looking for the
                   Eating Disorder Workshop Who Found
                   a Poetry Reading Instead")   150

Paul Mariani   Quid Pro Quo   155

William Matthews   "People Like Us"   161

J. D. McClatchy   On "My Mammogram"   167

Lynn McMahon   "For Gabriel, Falling Through Glass
                   and Ice"   171

Christopher Merrill Seaglass: Notes on "The Hurricane"   177

Joyce Carol Oates "Edward Hopper's *Nighthawks, 1942*"   182

Carole Simmons Oles Merely Dead, Not Absent ("Her Story,
                   My Daughter Beatrice")   186

Robert Pack   Naming the Animals ("The Trees
                   Will Die")   193

Jay Parini   Conversing in Oxford with Sir Isaiah
                   Berlin ("A Conversation in Oxford")   203

Robert Pinksy   Notes on a Poem: "Desecration at the
                   Gravestone of Rose P. (1897–1924)"   208

Stanley Plumly   Sleeps ("Nobody Sleeps")   213

Wyatt Prunty	Perspectives ("The Ferris Wheel")	219
Lawrence Raab	Elegiac Problems ("Years Later")	225
Bin Ramke	Homage ("Sad Stories")	229
Hilda Raz	A Vision ("Sarah Fledging")	232
Ira Sadoff	On the Composition of "Solitude Étude"	237
Robert Siegel	An Alien and Silken Intelligence ("Silverfish")	243
Dave Smith	"Making a Statement"	247
W. D. Snodgrass	"Lifelong"	252
Katherine Soniat	On Reading Histories: "The Captain's Advice to Those Headed for the Trees: 1609"	259
Mark Strand	Beginning to End ("I Will Love the Twenty-First Century")	264
Dabney Stuart	Good Nature ("The Tapawera Raspberry Festival")	267
Thomas Swiss	Rilke Unplugged ("On a Stanza by Rilke")	274
Sue Ellen Thompson	Writing the Unspeakable ("What Happened After")	280
Eric Trethewey	Cutting to the Bone ("Scar")	284
Chase Twichell	"To Throw Away"	290
Ellen Bryant Voigt	Kyrie	294
Richard Wilbur	Becoming Subtropical ("Bone Key")	299
Nancy Willard	The Dialogue of Question and Answer ("Questions My Son Asked Me, Answers I Never Gave Him")	304
Miller Williams	The Writing of "Adjusting to the Light"	307
Clara Yu	A Destitute Time ("Little Purple")	313
Paul Zimmer	Apples ("In Apple Country")	321
	Notes on Contributors	325

INTRODUCTION

The relationship between writers of poetry and critics of poetry has not always been easy, although the major critics of the past four centuries, from Ben Jonson through Dr. Johnson, Pope, Coleridge, Arnold, and T. S. Eliot, have themselves been practitioners of the art. In this century, Eliot has defined the role of the poet-as-critic, noting that "The nearest we get to pure literary criticism is the criticism of artists writing about their own art." In saying this, Eliot was echoing a famous line of his own mentor, Ezra Pound, who wrote more bluntly: "Pay no attention to the criticisms of men who have never themselves written a notable work."

This may sound exclusive, rather extreme, especially in a time when poet-critics seem few and far between and the province of criticism has been almost wholly absorbed by the academy. Literary theory itself has raised questions about artists writing about their own art, wondering if there were not always something a little unreliable about writers' accounts of their own writing. How, for example, can they really know what went into the making of their works? Aren't there a thousand things that writers cannot possibly know about their own motivation? Do we dare trust writers to appraise their own performances? The questions multiply, making this anthology seem—at first glance a dubious (or at least anachronistic) enterprise in the poststructuralist era of criticism.

There is certainly some truth here, in that poets in particular have a vested interest in promoting their own aesthetic principles. Eliot, again, put the matter succinctly:

I believe that the critical writings of poets, of which in the past there have been some very distinguished examples, owe a great deal of their interest to the fact that the poet, at the back of his mind, if not as his ostensible purpose, is always trying to defend the kind of poetry he is writing, or to formulate the kind that he wants to write. . . . He is not so much a judge as an advocate. . . . What he writes about poetry, in short, must be assessed in relation to the poetry he writes.

If one were to judge by what gets written on this subject by literary theorists in the wake of Deconstruction, one could well imagine that poets are the least to be trusted among readers of their own work. Nevertheless, few critics will deny that there remains something irresistible in any account of the creation of a poem by a poet. What the poet chooses to dwell on, as well as to occlude or avoid altogether, may well illuminate the poem under the spotlight and will surely reveal something about the process of creation itself.

This volume can be thought of as a companion to our previous anthology, *Touchstones: American Poets on a Favorite Poem* (1996). In that book, we asked fifty-nine poets to choose a poem from the canon, well known or obscure, and to write about it from their own viewpoint, *qua* poet. The results were heartening. While many of the essays were idiosyncratic (which is to say that they did not look exactly like the kind of criticism one normally sees within the academy), they were almost all fascinating and provocative. In *Introspections* we invited a similar number of poets—all writers with considerable records of publication, including Rita Dove, A. R. Ammons, W. D. Snodgrass, Joyce Carol Oates, J. D. McClatchy, Mark Strand, Mark Doty, and Richard Wilbur—to write about the genesis or making of one of their own poems.

As you will see, our contributors take many different tacks. Some write about the circumstances in which the poem was conceived, or filled in the background to the poem—often revealing the invisible scaffolding that was present while the poem was itself under construction. Others offer a close reading of their own work, teasing out meanings that lie just below the surface. Julia Alvarez, for instance, writes a deeply autobiographical piece about her own struggles to become a poet, while Rosellen Brown returns to a favorite poem to offer a close textual account. Erica Jong ponders the mysterious process of gestation, wondering about the sources—conscious and unconscious—of poetry. William Matthews presents a detailed examination of the linguistic turns of one of his witty, recent poems, while Ira Sadoff considers the idea of "writing strategies," looking closely at one of his own. Ellen Bryant Voigt takes an autobiographical excursion in her account of the writing of *Kyrie*, and Richard Wilbur takes us back to his own childhood in New Jersey.

One could not hope to classify the different approaches taken by the fifty-five poets included here. The one thing these essays have in common is a commitment to the craft of poetry, a belief in the power of language to "summon a vision and declare it pure," as Theodore Roethke once wrote. That dedication shines through the work included here. Our hope is that *Introspections* will interest readers and writers alike, taking them on a precious journey into the heart of creation itself. This has certainly been our experience in editing them.

SANDRA ALCOSSER

By the Nape

Though sun rubbed honey slow
down rose hips, the world lost
its tenderness. Nipplehaired, joint swollen,
the grasses waved for attention.
I wanted a watery demonstration for love,
more than wingpaper, twisted stalk of heartleaf.
Squalls rushed over pearling the world,
enlarging the smallest gesture, as I waited
for a drake in first winter plumage
to stretch his neck, utter a grunt whistle
begin his ritualized display.
I'd held a wild mallard in my palm,
hoodlum heart whooping like a blood balloon.
I'd watched a woman suck coins
between her thighs and up inside her body.
How long she must have trained to let the cold world
enter so. The old man said his neighbor asked him
to milk her breasts, spray the walls, bathe in it.
That was his idea of paradise.
Sometimes I don't know who I am—
my age, my sex, my species—
only that I am an animal who will love
and die and the soft plumage of another body
gives me pleasure as I listen for the bubbling
and drumming, the exaggerated drinking
of a lover rising vertically from the sedges
to expose the violet streaks inside his body
the vulnerable question of a nape.

The Autumn Courtship of
Surface-Feeding Ducks

It was that time in autumn when the sun, riding close to the horizon, enlarges everything. Migrations had not yet begun. We hiked a flood-plain between the Sapphires and Bitterroots in a wildlife refuge near Stevensville, Montana. We tiptoed around the back ponds, blond grasses crackling above our heads. The water flicked and spun with birds, but because of our orientation, all movement appeared in silhouette.

Pattiann Rogers and I were walking together, discussing form in poetry. She was leaving in a month for the University of Arkansas and I was going to the University of Michigan; we would both be teaching workshops in experimental form. We talked about a shared desire to dis-cover new variations in rhetorical structure. I mentioned Alice Fulton's essay, "Formal, Free and Fractal Verse," in which she writes: *It's time we as poets, readers, and critics, begin to discern and analyze the subtle, governing structures of free verse and to talk more about its operative tropes. Dissect the poem's larger governing organization: its rhetorical questions, conceits, virtuoso listings, registers of diction and lineations.* Studying poems by various modernist and postmodernist writers (the Oulipos, for instance), I hoped to encourage students to conceptualize, to welcome accidental discovery. Pattiann Rogers and I considered ways that one could apply the laws and patterns of nature (random branching, explosions, meanders) to the creation of form. We were both courting surprise.

Have you noticed how many grasses there are, she asked? We spend so much time identifying birds, mammals, while we're surrounded by grasses, by insects we cannot name. Millions of bodies brush against us, register in our brains. The idea of being swallowed up by the unname-able always delights me. The poet's work, like the detective's, is surely epistemological, often incomplete. In the second century of life, after soils, stars, and water currents, I wanted to learn the complex families of grasses. That night I cracked a *1948 Yearbook of Agriculture on Grasses* and let the text romance: *lanate—covered with soft, tangled long hair; erose; mouse gnawed; papillose; glaucous. Bee grasses, trefoils, lucernes, fleabanes, thirty species of poa alone. Rice root. Bashful dicebox. White wool of ghost lariat.*

As I listed names, I found them more suggestive than anticipated. I often invite the language of science, Latinate and colloquial, into poems; I like the way it ambushes one's focus. *Science and poetry,* wrote May Swenson, *are alike, or allied it seems to me in their largest and main target—to investigate any and all phenomena of existence beyond the flat surface of appearances. . . . The poet's material has always been nature—human and otherwise—all objects and aspects of our outer environment as well as the climate of the soul and the theater of the emotions.*

Years ago I worked in Central Park following the plans of writer and landscape designer Frederick Law Olmsted. It was in Central Park I learned the history and aesthetics of landscape architecture—how boldly and foolishly the physical world could be graded for its darkness, its vastness, its irregularity. I have been called a surrealist, and though I am tempted by the social critique and brilliant, playful conceptualism, it seems that reality is slippery and whimsical enough. My prosody is governed less by tradition than curiosity. I like what Charles Simic has to say about the dialectics of composition: *(one) no longer has the option of being a surrealist or an imagist fifty years after and to the exclusion of everything else that has been understood since . . . (all the same) not to subject oneself to their dialectics and uncertainties is truly not to experience the world we have inherited.*

I returned to the refuge the next day to get a closer look at the grasses, noting their plume and scratch, their diffusion of wind and light. *An artist works like a nervous system, selecting significant details of the environment and synthesizing from them an excitatory complex,* said Rebecca West. But alone and dwarfed, weedy thoughts surfaced that were irritating, unpleasant. As a child, I had crossed a field daily that had the same texture as the one in which I stood now; in memory, I was escaping a gang of boys who waited to pummel small girls on their way to and from school. I remembered other grasses—as an adult I had made love along a riverbank only to discover we had curled in nettles, our skin stinging with pink welts. Actually when I thought about it, I did not even like the smudge of sage and sweetgrass.

Like most poets, I browse distractedly when I write. Skim books. Deadhead flowers. Scan the Web. That night I slipped *Field Studies in Natural History* from a bookshelf, fingered an essay by zoologist Paul Johnsgard, "The Evolution of Duck Courtship," and something else we saw in the wildlife refuge floated to the foreground. The shadow play we witnessed on the ponds had actually been the autumn betrothals of surface-feeding ducks. We had been watching a mating dance: *a complex sequence of postures, beginning when the male suddenly whistles while stretching his neck vertically, at the same time raising the tail and lifting his folded wings, thus exposing the purple wing-speculum pattern. . . . He terminates the sequence by raising his head and simultaneously directing his blackish nape feathers toward the female.* These pair-forming displays are so instinctive that downy, inexperienced ducklings, given hormone treatments by scientists, will perform the nuptials without a single mistake. Hormone treatments for ducklings? Surely science, in the act of study, produces its own surrealism.

Perhaps the zoological description would have been less engaging had I not recently been a volunteer in San Diego for Project Wildlife, a group that nurses and releases 7000 wild animals a year, many of whom have lost their habitat to development. I knew the urban soap operas of ducks. I assisted the leader of the seabird team whose home lifted and lofted with pewter feathers: a pelican sat politely in the corner of the living room on his towel; a green heron with a yellow ring around its eye shivered in the kitchen next to a pelagic northern fulmer. *Poetry is a kind of psychic fossil fuel,* says Seamus Heaney. For the time that I worked with Project Wildlife, birds came to me, collapsed at my feet in the Home Depot parking lot, leaped off telephone wires, stared down from their leafy billboard nests. What a privilege it is to become tender with or even respectably close to another life.

In the essay "Waking Up the Rake," Linda Hogan, a member of the Chickasaw tribe, shares the words of a traditional Native American healer who tells her: *Our work is our altar.* Hogan, a poet and prose writer, who leads workshops at the University of Colorado, has also raked and cleaned the cages of eagles, owls, and hawks. She describes it as *the smoothing over of broken ground, the healing of the severed trust we humans hold with earth. It is work at the borderland between species, at the boundary between injury and healing.*

When I wrote the first draft of "By the Nape," it was a formal, traditional argument between the birds and the grasses. It had stanzaic, metrical integrity. Walt Whitman said: *Do I contradict myself? / Very well then I contradict myself.* If anyone had asked me to speak about my poetics that year, I would have told them that I had moved far away from the transcendental nature poem, that I was reading the notes of John Cage and Robert Wilson, considering how modern and avant-garde musical composition might be applied to poetry.

I meet with a small group of writers every few weeks when I am in Montana, and after dinner we read new work to each other. The reception for an early draft of "By the Nape" was mild; I could sense no shared current between the erotic, interspecial exchange that I described and the poem that my friends heard. Obviously, ducks did not have the mythological weight of swans; I would need a bridge to lure readers across the watery expanse, to bring them to a correspondent place.

The year I worked with Project Wildlife, I rented living space in a friend's condominium in San Diego. A prose writer and collector of strange tales, I could tell she found my volunteer effort with seabirds eccentric. *Thanks Sandra*, she'd say, as we drove through the smoke of wieners burning on a barbecue grill. *Friday night. Other women are out on dates. We're driving around Campland, chasing a duck with an arrow through its chest.* We parked on Avocet Way and walked up to a trailer. Inside was a Mexican family, a young man on a bed, his mother in the kitchen, his father in a recliner, all watching television. The boy was getting medical treatment in San Diego. His walker stood outside the trailer. The family had reported a duck near their trailer with an arrow through its breast. Together in the dark, we netted and held the duck while the seabird leader clipped its bloody feathers. Even a common mallard has the most intricate markings, a perfect tweed breast, enamel green head, and strong, scaled orange feet. Its thick blood dropped on our wrists. Though my roommate never could figure out why we cared for one of ten million ducks in the world, her pleasure in a single thing— the mallard's heart beating against her fingertips, for instance—often clarified a reason for the work.

Of course I know this physical connection to nature, to wild animals, is something not all people share. As John Berger points out in "Why Look at Animals," commerce has marginalized and broken our mediations with animals: *yet to suppose that animals first entered the human imagination as meat or leather or horn is to project a 19th century attitude backward across the millennia. Animals first entered the imagination as messengers and promises. . . . Animals are born, are sentient, and are mortal. In these things they resemble man. With their parallel lives, animals offer man a companionship which is different from any offered by human exchange. Different because it is a companionship offered to the loneliness of man as a species.*

At the same time, I knew I was in an audience of gentle and generous readers when I read the early version of the poem. If they did not respond, there was a good chance I was writing something no one shared, yearned toward. Writers grow from an erotic engagement with the land: *eros*, the principle of attraction, union, involvement which binds together. Some writers. As Paul Shepard points out: *hairlessness developed with the increased sensuousness of human body surface.* And readers share this as well, but how could I engage a reader who cared nothing about ducks or grasses. How could I convey that curious and erotic moment when a body is attracted to another body for nothing more than its vitality, its beauty, the intricacy of its ritual.

Most people know the story of the sixteenth-century Jesuit who carried a memory palace from the Greeks to the Chinese, an elaborate palace one constructed inside the head, a mental architecture that became impossible to erase. When a person wanted to recall an image, she would enter the front door of the palace and wander from room to room until she found where the image had been placed. Neurobiologists speculate that memory, like pain, does not reside in a single place, but floats like smoke through the body. And yet by slicing the neural tissue of a poor rat less than a micron thick and photographing that tissue with an electron microscope, researchers have found constellations of events.

A reader can hear Wallace Stevens walking the corridors and grounds of the memory palace in this passage: *One cries out to a living name, a living place, a living thing, and in crying out confesses openly all the bitter secretions of experience. This is why trivial things often touch us intensely. It is why the sight of an old berry patch, a new growth in the woods in spring, the particular things on display at a farmers' market, as, for example, the trays of poor apples, the few boxes of black-eyed peas, the bags of dried corn, have an emotional power for us that for a moment is more than we can control.*

Though the brain feels more often like a filing drawer than a palace, if I ask myself in what room or folder does the beautiful wild mallard reside, and if I follow the synaptic map, I do indeed find other events lodged in the same constellation. Every image in this place is skewed, positioned at a rakish angle, like the proverbial lampshade, spotted by a mix of the visceral, curious, lusty feelings. The disordered angles cause discomfort, bordering on pain.

Twenty years ago, sitting at a table in a tiny Middle Eastern restaurant in Brooklyn Heights, I watched a woman perform one of the most strangely intimate acts I have ever seen. There might have been no more than half a dozen people in the restaurant when the woman, a belly dancer, approached a nearby table. She lifted her pelvis, and one after another, sucked coins off the tabletop and into her vagina. It was not an erotic act exactly. Unprepared, I felt embarrassed, and yet the dancer was clearly someone who understood her body, the history of her art. For twenty centuries, at least, this dance had moved between temple and marketplace.

Novelist Nicholson Baker says he hesitates to reveal odd and personal observations. On one hand he feels everyone must share them, and on the other hand, they seem so much the adhesive of his private life. As soon as I wrote the woman into the poem, I felt as though I had betrayed a female intimacy; perhaps to balance that betrayal, or perhaps because once I had located the point on the map, the stories simply waited their turn, another scene followed immediately. I am standing in the lobby of a elegant, renovated hotel in San Francisco speaking with an elder poet near dawn. We are both dressed rather formally. We met at a banquet that evening. As he speaks I consider the airplane I must catch in a few hours. He is talking in an entertaining and oblique way about passion and paradise. I ask him what his idea of paradise might be, and then he tells me the story of a neighbor on an island in Greece who invited him to her apartment to milk her breasts. I do not think I know a woman who would ask a man to perform this act. If I worked beside him for years, I would never guess that he harbored this vision of paradise, and so I cannot determine whether what he says is more true than sexist, more mythic than manic. Though it makes me extremely uncomfortable, the story, once heard, is indelible. As I haul buckets of water to trees and flowers that summer, I think of the rocky dryness of the Greek islands. I tell myself his story over and over, juxtapose it against my own less colorful life, and each time the curiosity of human sexuality makes me laugh.

By foregrounding the human dramas in "By the Nape," the mediation between animal and human became more comprehensible. The poem itself became less formal. Hélène Cixous writes in the *Ou l'art de l'innocence*: *Life and writing cannot be separated; aesthetics and ethics are closely bound. . . . I think that the truth of literature turns on the struggle between the value of life and the value of writing. . . . Innocence is when, after a work of indescribable mathematicity, by dint of living life at extremely close quarters, and of weighing—querying every scruple living, and of weighing every result of thinking and rethinking and sublimating and replunging into the struggle, and shuffling and sifting, and dis and entangling every step of life, a sincerity hatches to a single white dreamy petal. It is the simplicity at the end of all chemistries.*

I once believed, in the manner of Cixous and Yeats, that a poem was that *single white dreamy petal.* I once believed there was one perfect version of a poem and the writer would know when s/he had reached that draft, and still, in going back to the earlier drafts of poems, I find there is often another truth I have had to leave behind. Part of me will always prefer the blank verse draft in five-line stanzas, in which only the woman and the bird exist.

We map our way through the process poem's constellation and yet, like memory and pain, part of it smokes the body, and, like smoke, escapes. "By the Nape" started as a sensate experience, the pleasure of being swallowed by the texture and tincture of the unnamable. The senses demanded something from memory—and by chance, it became the ducks. The reader found the language and description of the natural world poeticized and asked for a human corollary. So began the poem's journey.

In the gap between what one wants to say (or what one perceives there is to say) and what one can say (what is sayable) words provide for a collaboration and a desertion. We delight in our sensuous involvement with the materials of language, we long to join words to the world—to close the gap between ourselves and things, and we suffer from doubt and anxiety as to our capacity to do so because of the limits of language. While failing in an attempt to match the world, we discover structure, distinction, the integrity and separateness of things. So writes Lyn Hejinian in "The Rejection of Closure."

There was a fifth observation that did indeed float through, but free of the constellation. Occasionally I wake in the dark and do not know what a human being is, cannot remember my name, my home, the room. A body warms next to mine, my husband's, and I do not know him, though we have been together for twenty years. There is something both discomforting and liberating about this discarnate state. The fifth observation, though only smoke in the body, begins to articulate and extend itself. *Sometimes I don't know who I am— / my age, my sex, my species— / only that I am an animal who will love / and die . . .* The brittle grasses, the glossy bridal plumage of the drake, the curious sexuality of human exchange all invoked one small truth. Not even four lines. Poetry enlightens the maker in its making; by the way it takes over, offering words, forms, rhetorical variations, it lives in the palace of the brain, and the conference of the world, and always it escapes.

JULIA ALVAREZ

Dusting

Each morning I wrote my name
on the dusty cabinet, then crossed
the dining table in script, scrawled
in capitals on the backs of chairs,
practising signatures like scales
while Mother followed, squirting
linseed from a burping can
into a crumpled-up flannel.

She erased my fingerprints
from the bookshelf and rocker,
polished mirrors on the desk
scribbled with my alphabets.
My name was swallowed in the towel
with which she jeweled the table tops.
The grain surfaced in the oak
and the pine grew luminous.
But I refused with every mark
to be like her, anonymous.

A First Step with "Dusting"

For a long time as a young writer I had some wrong-headed ideas about what I was supposed to be doing in a poem. The biggest misconception was that I should be writing about something Important and Deep that would impress my readers. My voice in a poem should carry authority and weight as I spoke about the big matters that Milton, Yeats, Homer had tackled. Upon graduation, I felt as if I'd been immersed in the canon and now it was my turn to be blasted out from that tradition into the literary world to make a sensation.

Such wrong-headed thinking! Where did it come from? I don't know. Doesn't every young writer need a spare tank of ego to get him far enough down the road of self-doubt that he can't turn back anymore? I suppose I was also still feeling my immigrant status. English was my second language. I was a newcomer into this literature, tradition, way of making meaning. A few times, I was reminded of that status in a way that inspired radical self-doubt. Once, for instance, a "famous" poet came to my undergraduate campus and pronounced that no one could write good poetry unless he (that was the pronoun) was writing in the language in which he had first said Mama. Sitting in that workshop, a native Spanish speaker, I felt as if I had just been turned back at the border, deported by a would-be mentor from the literary high ground. And so I think I overcompensated for my feelings of literary and linguistic insecurity by making myself learn and master everything I could about the tradition. There is a saying in the old country that the traitor always wears the best patriot uniform.

Of course, there were other voices in my head, other instincts. When I closed my eyes and listened, these voices reminded me, "You call that a blind stitch, I see it!" "You put that much salt on the salad, you'll wilt the lettuce!" "This is the way you make a hospital corner, turn up the edge, tuck in the bottom, fold back the edge, and tuck." As a young woman learning the craft of poetry, I was forgetting that I had already served an apprenticeship as a young girl. Growing up with my Mami and tías and sisters and maids in the Dominican Republic, I had been instructed in the fine points of all the household arts: sewing, making beds, seasoning a salad, embroidering my initials on a hand towel. What these first crafts of housekeeping had taught me was that the focus of a craft is always in the details, that practicing it is a way to serve and touch and nurture other people, that I had to pay attention to the things around me.

But I had forgotten these lessons of my first apprenticeship. They came back to me dramatically one summer. After graduating from a creative writing master's program and knocking around for a few years I had enough publications in small journals to earn a short-term residency at Yaddo, a well-known writer's colony. I remember I had the tower room at the top of the stairs in the big mansion. The rules were clear: we artists and writers were to stick to our studios and studies during the day and come out at night for supper and socializing. For lunch, we ate from lunchboxes that had been prepared for us that morning and put on a shelf for us to pick up. Nothing was to come between us and our work.

I sat up in that tower room and sweated bullets. All around me I could hear the typewriters going (those were the precomputer days) and all I had before me was a blank sheet of paper ready for the important work I had come here to write. People now had faith in me. They had given me this residency, this fine tower room. In fact, my fellow artists had all been impressed that I had gotten "the best room," with 360 degree views of the elegant grounds. But I didn't deserve this faith. I had nothing Important to say. I was a sham. Before me floated the face of the famous writer. "See," he crooned, "I told you so!" I was ready to pack my bags and leave Yaddo, at the very least leave my room and visit with another blocked writer. Together we could gripe about how our major oeuvre was going to come later in our lives when we were seasoned and interesting. But from the sounds of those typewriters clicking away in all the downstairs rooms, I realized those other writers were creating their major oeuvres *now*.

And then, hallelujah—I heard the vacuum going right outside my door. Of course, the Yaddo mansion and grounds were cared for by a crew of men and women. There were maids that cleaned the big house, a gardener who tended the grounds, and a wonderful old cook down in the kitchen who packed our lunches and made our sit-down dinner meal. Immersed in our own work and world, we writers and artists had assumed that our parnassus ran on automatic.

And so, during that first week at Yaddo, this became my routine: Along with the other artists and writers, I woke early, had my breakfast, picked up my lunchbox, headed for my studio, looking inspired and ready for work. I read for a few hours, and then mid-morning, when the typewriters began their maddening clicking, I tiptoed downstairs to the kitchen and talked to the cook or helped the maid cart her heavy industrial vacuum cleaner up to the second floor or yakked with the gardener about what was doing well this year out in his vegetable garden. One day, while gossiping with the cook about the eating habits of some of my favorite writers who had been to Yaddo, I paged through her cookbook. It was one of those old, falling-apart cookbooks with mother's day cards and holy cards for bookmarks, with corrections and deletions and additions to recipes written in the margins, the whole held together with one of those thick, rust-red, post-office rubber bands. As I read through recipes, I was struck by the musicality of cooking terms. I began writing down the names of cooking procedures: knead, poach, stew, whip, skirr, score, julienne, whisk, sauté, sift. Then the names of implements: cup, spoon, ladle, pot, kettle, grater, peeler, colander, corer, waffle iron. Hmm. I began hearing a music in these words. The names of spices: dill, fennel, loveage, angelica, anise, hyssop, paprika.

"You working on a poem there?" the cook asked me.

I shook my head. At that point, I didn't know I was.

A little later, I went upstairs to the tower room and jotted down in my journal this beautiful vocabulary of my girlhood. As I wrote, I tapped my foot on the floor to a rhythm of the words. I could see my mother and my aunts in the kitchen bending their heads over a pot of habichuelas, arguing about what flavor was missing—what could it be they had missed putting in it? And then, the thought of those aunts and my mother led me through the house, the big furniture that needed dusting, the beds that needed making, the big bin of laundry that needed washing.

What had happened was that I had been reminded by my talks with the caretakers of Yaddo of where my own material lay. Not on the shores of ancient Greece, and certainly not on the nearest coast of lightness bordering on light, and not up in the tower with Yeats, but down in the kitchen with my mothers and aunts and sisters. That very day, I began working on a poem about dusting. Then another followed on sewing; then came a sweeping poem, an ironing poem. Later I would collect these into a series I called the housekeeping poems, poems using the metaphors, details, language of that first apprenticeship.

Perhaps because it was the first one of these housekeeping poems I wrote, the poem that broke the silence, a modest little poem that doesn't try to say something Important, but a poem that gave me back my voice, perhaps because of all this, I've always favored the little poem, "Dusting."

The lowly dusting. Any little girl with a rag can do it. But the true master is the mother, who disappears into her craft, and is trying to teach the young girl in the poem that artistry is not about being known or being famous; artistry is about attention to detail, self-eclipse in the service of making the world around her a more luminous place. But still, the young girl must rebel against this very tradition she is learning if she is to become another kind of artist her more tradition-bound mother would not approve of.

Sitting at Yaddo, that first full day of writing, I realized my time had come. I had followed my mother and aunts through the house and learned a certain tradition of anonymity and service as a woman, but it was time to break that mold, trust myself, and take on my role as a writer. I had also been following Shakespeare, Yeats, Dante, Homer through the house of literary tradition, but it was time to trust my own voice. I had learned what I could about craft from all these masters — from Mami to Milton — and now it was time to make my own way.

"Dusting" was a first step.

A. R. AMMONS

Coming Round

The oar squeaks,
a dash sound like
moon-hustle on the river:

reeds
trap and ease the
boat slow

to ripple-tilting sanddown:
the night, a
bubble,

hangs two hundred
thousand miles by
a moon-filament:

I tie up, head for the single
windowlight:
I cut the moon free.

One More Poem

I don't know what guilt I would have to try to excuse myself of if I were a purposeful poet—I've written so many poems. Thank goodness, I can't say I ever have an idea for a poem and then go out walking looking for "close observations of nature." Nor do I ever consider going to the library for "material." Nor do I ever, I think, write about given subjects, such as other works of art. I am afflicted with a constant need to feel imaginative energy, the energy that arises from thinking something new, realizing a connection, seeing a releasing image or configuration. But I don't set out purposefully to find these. I hope to be taken by surprise by them.

When one morning at Cornell a graduate student, Robert Harrison—now a professor at Stanford—stopped by my office, the subject of writing a poem to order came up, and I said I couldn't do that. He bet me that I could, so when he left, I compelled my way, with a lot of scribbling in and out, through "Coming Round."

The derivations are given and obvious, but I had the surprise, at least, that it worked as well as it did. No doubt there are a great many kinds of surprise that spring from doggedness and preparedness, and no doubt some "easy" surprises can be too easy. But this poem is alone of its kind, for me.

DAVID BAKER

Still-Hildreth Sanatorium, 1936

When she wasn't on rounds she was counting
the silver and bedpans, the pills in white cups,
heads in their beds, or she was scrubbing down

walls streaked with feces and food on a white-
wash of hours past midnight and morning, down
corridors quickened with shadows, with screaming,

the laminate of cheap disinfectant . . .
and what madness to seal them together, infirm
and insane, whom the state had deemed mad.

The first time I saw them strapped in those beds,
caked with sores, some of them crying
or coughing up coal, some held in place

with cast-iron weights . . . I would waken again.
Her hands fluttered blue by my digital clock,
and I lay shaking, exhausted, soaked cold

in soiled bedclothes or draft. I choked on my pulse.
I ached from the weight of her stairstep quilt.
Each night was a door slipping open in the dark.

Imagine, a white suit for gimlets at noon.
This was my Hollywood star, come to be lost
among dirt farmers and tubercular poor.

He'd been forgotten when the talkies took hold.
He saw toads in webs drooping over his bed.
O noiseless, patient, *his voice would quake.*

He took to sawing his cuticles with butter knives
down to the bone and raw blood in the dark.
Then, he would lie back and wait for more drug.

And this was my illness, constant, insomnolent,
a burning of nerve-hairs just under the eyelids,
corneal, limbic, under the skin, arterial,

osteal, scrotal, until each node of the 400
was a pin-point of lymphic fire and anguish
as she rocked beside me in the family dark.

In another year she would unspool fabrics
and match threads at Penney's, handling finery
among friends just a few blocks from the mansion-

turned-sickhouse. She would sing through the war
a nickel back   a greenback   a sawbuck   a penny
and, forty years later, die with only her daughter,

my mother, to hold her, who washed her face,
who changed her bedgowns and suffers to this day
over the dementia of the old woman weeping

mama mama, curled like cut hair from the pain
of her own cells birthing in splinters of glass.
What madness to be driven so deep into self . . .

I would waken and find her there, waiting
with me through the bad nights when my heart
trembled clear through my skin, when my fat gut

shivered and wouldn't stop, when my liver swelled,
when piss burned through me like rope against rock.
She never knew it was me, my mother still says.

Yet what did I know in the chronic room where I died
each night and didn't die, where the evening news
and simple sitcoms set me weeping and broken?

*I never got used to it. I think of it often,
down on my knees in the dark, cleaning up blood
or trying to feed them—who lost 8 children to the Flu,*

*who murdered her sisters, who was broken in two
by a rogue tractor, who cast off his name . . .
Sometimes there was nothing the doctor could do.*

What more can we know in our madness than this?
Someone slipped through my door to be there
—though I knew she was a decade gone—

whispering stories and cooling my forehead,
and all I could do in the heritable darkness was
lift like a good child my face to be kissed.

Critical Disobedience:

Nine Ways of Looking at a Poem

T
I.

his really happened. The poet had just completed the evening's reading and eased shut his notebook with tangible relief, glancing first at the reception area, then at the host.

But the host had swiveled to face the audience of about fifty. With eagerness, a solicitous smile, she said, "Does anyone have a question for our guest?"

A young student shot his hand into the air. It was still straight in the air when he asked, "Can you explain what your last poem was about? Why did you write it? I know what it says, but what is it supposed to mean?"

The jug wine and crackers and boxed cookies beckoned.

But the poet opened his book, and took a long breath, and read the poem once more, a little slower.

II.

This really happened. He woke up on his sleeper sofa again, at half past four in the morning, and realized he'd been sick for nearly three months.

He woke up abruptly, as if to an explosion, his heartbeat pounding in his ears, fever running down his arms like fire. His testicles were so swollen that the bedcovers hurt. Snow was falling in the frozen back woods and a hard north wind whipped sleet through the tall pines like rocks. He lay there. He had not written anything for more than a year. He could hardly read. Magazines were too much. The usual shows on the television upset him, set him grieving or shaking with anxiety. Nick at Night was salvation in the early evenings—Lucy, Dick Van Dyke—as was the local paper's easy crossword in the morning.

He went back to sleep, and woke, and went back to sleep.

III.

I want to write poems where the narrative line is bent, subverted, altered, multiplied, its ends splayed out like a broken rope. Or, another metaphor: I want to write something like a photographer's error, a double exposure of story. Or triple. An overlay of times, actions, images, impulses.

In this way I hope to infuse a kind of speculative dis-ease into the simple linear imagination. I want to trouble our thinking, to make it self-aware, at odds with our more typical analytic paradigms. Too often we read—if we read at all—with laziness, inattention, satisfied by the cliched and familiar, soothed by the conventional, the facile: the sloth of the typical newspaper, the despicable formula of the popular novel, the mere condescension of most daily discourse. We want answers without understanding the questions; we want clarity, pure and simple, without dealing with the more natural disorders.

I want a poem that resists the tyranny of order, of easy clarity, of single-mindedness. Consider the possible rhetorical paradigms of the hallucination, the dream, and all the circular, associative workings of memory. These are the mind's most accurate and natural methods in its search for meaning. To give voice and appropriate form to these less orderly, these messier, conditions is to attempt to depict the mind in its fundamental environs.

The real creative question is: How can I best create or recreate the reality of my poetic occasion and subject—by pursuing an answer or by establishing the questions? By solving the problem or by representing the depths of its mystery?

IV.

The doctors refused to name his illness for many months. This was partly because the tests kept coming back normal: for HIV/AIDS, Hodgkin's disease, lupus, a variety of heart disorders, lung ailments, Lyme disease, liver failure, multiple sclerosis, and more. It turned out, in fact, that they couldn't call it Chronic Fatigue Syndrome until after six months of symptoms.

To call this disease Chronic Fatigue Syndrome is like calling blindness "chronic running into walls" or polio "chronic can't walk syndrome." It is an insulting name that merely nominates one rather trivial-sounding symptom of a disease whose characteristics are bizarre and devastating, and whose fuller symptoms are cruel, long-lasting, evolving, and slightly different for each victim.

Here is what happened to him first. He caught a cold. It lingered, and turned into a bronchial infection that wouldn't relent, even with antibiotics. Indeed, antibiotics weakened his immune system by substituting for it. The bronchitis grew acute. He coughed constantly, his throat swelled, burned, the headaches became long nails driven in. He got sicker, run down, stopped sleeping, gradually became depressed. The original infection gave way to a battery of other infectious "opportunistic viruses," which were latent in his blood: the Epstein–Barr virus (the mono virus), cytomegalovirus, others. This took about four months.

Then, all hell broke loose.

He lay on the foldout sofa, because his sleep disturbances were so radical that his wife couldn't sleep. Besides, it hurt every time she slightly shifted. He ran a savage fever of 102 to 104 for weeks. It began to abate, and hovered for another month or two at 100 to 102, then finally gave way, plunging to 97 for several more weeks. Months of burning, months of freezing. Days and nights of being not quite asleep, never quite awake.

He had nightmares in the afternoons, violent hallucinations at night, shaking of the hands so bad he couldn't hold a cup, vision and hearing failures, drenching night sweats, a blazingly painful lymph system (especially under the arms, in the groin, running down the leg, under the jaw), tachycardia, an inflamed heart lining, blue fingernails, swollen testicles, frightening memory loss, liver swelling and pain, recurring anxiety attacks, chronic diarrhea, worsening insomnia, arthritis-like symptoms that moved from bone to bone, tissue inflammations, allergies (to milk, most weeds and grasses—therefore corn, peanuts, wheat—most meats, shellfish, some fruits and vegetables, pesticides, carbonated drinks). He could not read. He could talk clearly but not always sensibly. He might say to his young daughter, "Bling me some cover that bangs tooly." He forgot his phone number. He was often unable to sit up without drooping back down. He suffered from persistent stupidity. Brushing his teeth took planning, a mustering of strength. He might waken at night to find his heart racing, slamming in his ears, or his whole gut convulsing, shaking up and down in spastic rhythm. He couldn't make it stop.

There is no actual treatment for Chronic Fatigue/Immune Deficiency Syndrome. Or there are many treatments—meditation, herbal therapy, blood transfusions, radical vitamin infusion, psychoanalysis, dietary adjustments—none of which is particularly effective. Doctors don't treat viral imbalances with medicines; there's no treatment for the flu or mono, for instance, other than symptomatic relief. But sometimes, after months or many years, CFS just begins to go away. Sometimes it fades, with infrequent or milder recurrences. Sometimes it simply stays, worsening perhaps, or merely always the same.

In the later stages of this disease, after months or years of illness, victims may exhibit lesions on the brain, radical memory loss, liver, pancreas, and/or spleen failure, violent nightmares (if sleep comes at all), chronic depression, debilitating bone calcification, as well as all the earlier abiding symptoms. Many must quit or change jobs. Many divorce. The effects of long-term immune deficiency are perilous regarding the potential onset of cancers and other diseases.

Some still don't believe this is a real disease. Doctors may tell patients to get more rest or not to take things so hard. More than a few old hacks still assert it's "all in your head." Brent Wenegrat, a psychiatrist, in his book *Illness and Power* (New York University Press, 1995): "Insofar as chronic fatigue serves some of the same functions as somatization disorder, it is likely that it too will appeal to persons who believe, often rightly, that they lack social power to meet their needs more directly."

He really wrote that.

"Of course," he mews in his initial acknowledgments, "I am solely responsible for any errors, whether in fact or in reasoning, found in the following pages."

v.

Dr. Jack Kevorkian assisted just last week, mid-August 1996, in his first CF/IDS-related suicide.

vi.

The poet's purpose is to establish, represent, and articulate mystery. The critic's job is to analyze and interpret such mysteries. This is their fundamental difference and the locus of their mutually dependent natures.

There are qualifications to make regarding the critical act. The deconstructive critic, for instance, has presumed to continue and extend the mystery of the creative act, rarely resolving but "playfully" deferring the explanative urge. This makes most poets very nervous, who feel their status usurped. There are three good reasons why poets have a point here. First, most critics fail to exhibit an ounce of imaginative or creative talent, and merely shovel on tons of overbearing "discourse." Second, much contemporary literary criticism seems uninterested in actual literature. This perhaps explains the overfondness many poets demonstrate for trying to enact a critical project within their own poems, creating as well as self-explicating their work, since critics are no longer interested or able to do so. Third, the hypocrisy of deconstruction seems obvious: that this critical stance, which purports to represent victimization, marginalization, the decentered, is the result of a highly advantaged education, speaks in a radically rarified, codified language, and remains aloof as the discourse of privilege.

Another failure of criticism is when it seeks to explain a poem's mystery by attempting to trace the details of the poet's life. As if biography is exegesis. As if the imaginative is reducible to mere fact.

Even analytic criticism can be dulling or pointless when it is satisfied to be a plodding "explication" like a fancy book report.

In "Still-Hildreth Sanatorium, 1936" I have wanted, variously, to fuse and diffuse the elements of story, location, emotion, and thought. The details of any one part become the details of any other. Some of it is true to the facts of my life, and some is imagined. I hope you can't tell which is which. I want this poem to be a real experience rather than a true account.

VII.

This really happened. My mother came to see me when I was at my most sick. This poem is really for her. Or, rather, it is for the abiding figure of the women I remember for months saving my life. I remember my two-year-old daughter touching my face with one finger, soft as a breath, mornings as I tried to sleep on the foldout couch, her leaning face like warmth, part of the early light in our wide window. And as befuddled as I was, I knew even then my wife was doing virtually everything to keep me alive, protected, safe, as comfortable as possible. Unhesitating support, selfless care. She became and remains my life's real hero. My wife did everything for months and months.

I remember one early evening, as I drifted in and out, listening to my mother tell a story. She sat in the soft chair next to my bed on the couch, unworried, attentive. Was I six again? Was I already dead? I listened.

When I was about fifteen, my mother's mother came to live with us after she retired from J. C. Penney's in Macon, Missouri, and stayed for the remaining fifteen years of her life. I think now the arrangement must have been hard at times for her, and for my parents, but it seemed entirely natural and wonderful to my brother and me.

When she died, she died at home, and my mother took care of her to the end. I knew little about it then, living far away.

That evening eight years later, my mother leaned toward me and explained the death, its weeks-long marathon of great pain, dementia, the body's relinquishment of all its habits. My mother was an only child, doted over as much as a poor single mother could dote on her daughter, and perhaps this is part of my mother's great sadness, her disbelief, when my grandmother died. The old woman moaned, she curled like an infant, and she kept asking, or crying, for her mother. Not for my mother. For *her* mother. And so my mother took on the role. It is, it seems to me, entirely natural in a state of near-infancy to cry out for the maternal.

My grandmother worked for a while, in the '30s and '40s, at a sanatorium in Macon run by a nearby osteopathic hospital. It must have been a zoo, for they treated the mentally unbalanced as well as the physically disabled, addicts from Hollywood alongside the poorest of farmers and miners in northern Missouri. The building still stands, huge, institutional, relic.

One night I woke up, pitch dark, and spoke a long and lovely while with my grandmother, who sat beside me in my high fever. It was a late spring night. I was very happy.

To this day I swear it was her.

To this day I have no words to describe clearly my gratitude and love and amazement for the figure of the woman waiting with me while I tried to live.

If I can tell you anything useful, and critical, and explanatory about this poem, I can tell you that it takes place in several locations and in a single place, at several times but in just one instant, that it is about memory as well as the imagined. It is about strength and sheer helplessness, the support of others but the isolation, the absolute loneliness, of us all.

It is a love poem.

VIII.

Disease: an illness; a chronic health disorder. *Disease:* lack of comfort; a disturbance of the familiar.

IX.

The student's question after the reading was good enough. It was earnest, honest, and curious. We aspire to capture or contain mystery by means of rational explanation.

But whose job is it to explain?

Deconstruction and its murderous pretense that "the author is dead" notwithstanding, I wrote this poem. I planned it, constructed it, changed it, loved it, fought it, thought and thought about it. I am its author. But who holds the responsibility for this poem's interpretation and meaning? I am the author, but who is the authority? Not me. I gave that to you.

PETER BALAKIAN

The Oriental Rug

I

I napped in the pile
of the brushed and bruised
Kashan on our living room floor

an eight year old sleeping

in vegetable dyes —
roots and berries,
tubers, shafts, dry leaves

the prongy soil
of my grandparents' world:
eastern Turkey, once Armenia.

The wine-red palmettes
puckered with apricot buds
and fine threads of green
curling stem-like over my cheek

leaving a shadow like filigree
on my eye as I closed it.

The splintering green wool
bled from juniper berries
seemed to seep, even then,

into the wasp-nest cells
breathing in their tubular ways
inside my ear and further back.

*

On certain nights
when the rain thrummed
against the clapboard

and my father's snoring issued
down the hall
I slept on the rug
curled and uncovered

and the sea of ivory
between the flowers
undulated as if the backs
of heavy sheep were breathing
in my mouth.

The prickly cypress
down by the friezed border
spiraled in my night gazing.
Armenian green:

dwarf cabbage, shaded cedar,
poppy stem, the mossy pillow
where my grandfather
sat in the morning dark

staring at the few goats
that walked around the carnage.
Outside my house the grass
never had such color.

II

Now I undo the loops
of yarn I rested my head on.
Under each flower
a tufted pile loosens.

I feel the wool give way
as if six centuries of feet
had worn it back to the hard
earth floor it was made to cover.

Six centuries of Turkish heels
on my spine-dyed back:
madder, genista, sumac—
one skin color in the soil.

I lose myself
in a flawed henna plant
jutting toward the scroll.
Its rose-pink eyes burst

off the stems.
The auburn dust
which reddens the women
returns with a sharp wind.

The vine of lily-blossoms winding
by the fringe once shined
like fur when a spray of sun
flushed through a curtain—

that gracious shape hardens now
like a waxy twig at summer's end.

I hear wind running
through heart strings.

I hear an untuned zither
plucked by a peacock's accidental strut.

Warp and weft come undone;
sludge spills back to the earth

(my liver's bitter
as the pomegranate's acid seed).

III

The heavy mallet a Parsee boy
once used to beat the knots
beneath the pile so
the weft would disappear

vibrates in me
as the knelling bells
over the Sea of Marmara
once rang toward the civilized West.

I pitch myself,
as into a waterfall,
into the spinning corolla
of an unnamed flower

coral, red, terra-cotta,
and tangle in its lattice of leaves
and follow lines

from my palms
to the dark balm
of the marshy hillsides

of my far away land—
the poppied acres
of Adoian's hands.

IV

I pry my way
into a rose—
undoing its blighted cliché.

I strain for the symmetry
of its inflorescence,

slide along the smooth
cup of a petal
till I rush head-first
down the pistil

feeling the tuby walls
muscle me to the ovary
where a bee is swooning
on some pollen.

Wrapped this tight
I suck my way into the nectaries;
feel a hummingbird's tongue
and the chalky wing of a moth.

That wet, I wash
to the cool leaflets,

rim their toothed edges,
then back-rub

the remains of sepals
which kept the rose alive
in blighted April
when Adana and Van were lopped
off the map.

I come apart in the thorn—
(the spiky side that kept the jackal out)
and disperse whatever is left
of me to the downward pull
of cells sobbing in the earth.

v

I walk with a rug on my back.
Become to myself a barren land.
Dust from the knots
fills my arms

which in the peaceful new world sun
becomes fine spume.

A sick herbalist
wandering in a century
mapped by nations wandering.

The dyes come through the wool,
break the grid of threads
holding the shapes to form:

safflower, my Dyer's Thistle,
carry me on your burr
so I may always feel
dry gusts on my neck.

Kermes, dried like a scab,
crush me to your womanly scarlet chest.
I feel your scales
flutter in my eyes.

Madder root—
which makes the red of Karabagh
bleed along one long hallway.

Tyrian purple, from a mollusk shell
lodged in Phoenician sand—
gurgle all your passion in my ear.

for my daughter, Sophia

Kashan: floral Persian rug.
madder: herb yielding red dye.
genista: spiny shrub yielding yellow dye.
Marmara: sea between Asiatic and European Turkey.
Adoian: family name of painter Arshile Gorky, who was born in the Armenian
province of Van.
Van: Armenian province in eastern Turkey.
Karabagh: mountainous region of Armenia famous for its long rugs.

Falling Into a Rug: Some Notes on "The Oriental Rug"

I believe in the animating power of things. Not only the things of the natural world, but of the human-made world. Certain artifacts have significance for us. Certain artifacts have evocative powers. Certain artifacts have psychic presences. One of my tasks as a poet is to discover the artifact, to find out what the artifact might mean. What buried life lies in it.

Before I explore how a particular oriental rug, that is, a Persian rug known as a Kashan, came to have a particular meaning for me, I need to say something about my sense of the context for the rug. Both artifact and poet come with a history. The rug comes with a context, and the poet comes to the artifact with some sense of that context and his own context. For no literature is made out of a void, or a simple self. In this poem, I bring to my Persian rug the history of the Armenian Genocide.

The genocide of the Armenians by the Turks is a watershed event in twentieth century history. The Armenians, who had been conquered by the Turks in the fourteenth century, were the largest Christian minority of Ottoman Turkey. Between 1915 and 1917, over a million Armenians were systematically exterminated by the Young Turk regime, and about another million were exiled, resulting in the killing or deportation of the entire Armenian population from its homeland of three thousand years. Hitler's statement to his military advisors only eight days before invading Poland in 1939, "Who today, speaks of the extermination of the Armenians?" says something about the moral necessity of memory.

Because all art happens in memory, because we are creating from recollected instances, we are forever reinventing the things, events, people that have made up our lives. This Kashan rug is inseparable from my memory of childhood, inseparable from growing up. It's that part of life that's packed in us, and that comes alive again, when at a certain age, or for a certain reason, we begin to dream back on the significance of things that have made up our lives and our world. The Kashan was a central artifact of my domestic landscape. It was an object I walked on, lay on, slept on, rolled around on with my brother and sisters and, later, girlfriends. It was the assumed ground of my domestic life at 57 Crabtree Lane, in the affluent suburban town of Tenafly, New Jersey.

My parents bought the rug in 1951, the year of my birth, with wedding-gift money from my father's uncle Edward Benlian, the big-wheel rug merchant of the British Isles in his day. Although no one ever spoke about it as an epithalamium, the Kashan was an artifact of celebratory value in our house: an object of family significance, of wedding ritual, of beginnings.

What happens in the process of the mind's movement toward the artifact? As I began to think about using the rug for my poem, I began to feel its presence as a place of things stored, and as an embodiment of both its essence and its personal meaning. It's connected to personal feeling, to something evocative. When you first begin to discover the beloved artifact, you begin to sniff it out like a dog taking in old but newly discovered ground. You establish a ground of intimacy with it. For me, the rug was something synonymous with my being, and the length of my life. I've stared at it, gazed on it, daydreamed into it, for longer than I know, for more hours than I can measure by the clock.

But I'm also drawn to the rug because of its historical resonance. It's an artifact with a cultural context. First, in the Near East for example, in Armenia in my case, rugs are complex and unique things. They are, in some sense, the equivalents of oil paintings in Europe—a high mode of visual art. But, unlike the painting, the rug is also a functional piece of furniture, it's used in the domestic space to give warmth, to cover floors, to decorate. Not only is it functional in that way, it is also a part of an individual and family legacy; it's what one passes on to the next generation; it's an object of familial and sentimental value. And to top it off, it's also an object of monetary value. The older it is, the better, and as the auction catalogs make clear, oriental rugs appreciate in value with time. The oriental rug is singular for these reasons, and I bring, whether consciously or unconsciously, my sense of all this to the poem. It's part of the underlying assumption of the poem. It's a universe that, if you unlock it, will give the poem a good deal of life.

So, how can the rug open up for me? How can I fall into it? Well, given the richness and personal and historical meaning of the rug, I'm already on my way. And now, I just need to get my head and body deeper into its thing-ness. The Kashan attracts me too because of its organic nature. It's still alive in some way. It's alive because it's made of wonderful fine wool, and spun by women and men in the villages and towns of Persia. It's made by hand on looms by women and children, knotted with almost hypnotic rhythm, with precision and knowledge of pattern and form. And then there's the color. The fabulous part of the art. The brilliant, resonant, evocative, often variegated tonality of color. The dye-makers, like the weavers, are heroes in this art. They are assigned the task of making beautiful color that will last. If the colors don't last, the rug loses its presence, its art. Color is everything. The older it gets, the richer and deeper and more complex it gets. The dye-makers are alchemizers, they take substance from the material world and they transform it into something permanent. They use roots, herbs, leaves, stones, dirt, berries, the crushed thorax of the kermes insect, the shell membrane of a mollusk. Dye-makers are like poets, using everything they can for their art, and in that they are most thrifty. So, dye-making has a sense of *ars poetica* here. "Safflower, my Dyer's Thistle, carry me on your burr so I may always feel dry gusts at my neck." If the color lasts, the art will last.

Once you sense that the artifact has enough for the poem to be something, you need to push things further, to open up the artifact to see its inner life. I want to move into the inner life of the rug, and hence back into history, and also into my own emotion and memory. The rug becomes a flying carpet in this sense.

> Now I undo the loops
> of yarn I rested my head on.
> Under each flower
> a tufted pile loosens.
>
> I feel the wool give way
> as if six centuries of feet
> had worn it back to the hard
> earth floor it was made to cover.

The poem opens up as the rug opens up. Back, back, back. Down, down, down. Into the stuff inside the stuff. It's important, I think, for the poet to find the connections. To let the mind flow and free associate. To see how the larger culture and history of my exploration can connect to the rug. I want to keep color and form alive as imaginative triggers, so that things like a henna plant, a zither, a peacock, can emerge as sensual and cultural emblems. I want to move by textures and sensory intuition. Texture yields text. Words come out of the sensual threads embedded in the thing, so that at a certain point in the poem, I'm lost in the thingness of the rug. And I want to be lost. I don't want to follow some logical connection, or rational path, I want the rug to take me up, the way a lover takes you up, the way the wave of intense feeling pours over you.

What the rug opened up for me was process—unfolding, ongoing. Again, the sensual image is key. You must know your artifact. The idea of the oriental rug is a garden. A garden framed by beautiful borders. A garden of encoded images for the inside of the house. A dynamic, moving garden. I want to follow the play and mystery of the rug-garden. Its floral images, the movement of motifs in the field of the garden, in this rug a warm ivory field. The scrolling movement in the borders. The color and all its seductive messages. Its come-ons, its caresses. The images in the rug trigger movement, and the movement leads to discovery. The sensuality of the rug beckons for a kind of imaginative wandering. Let yourself wander, let yourself love the textures of the image, colliding and moving, always voyage and discovery. I don't want to think of the poem as trying to solve a problem, but as a way of opening up a problem.

So, the pattern of flowers on that Kashan rug and its colors are necessary for my being able to fall into the images of the rug, so that they become emblems which keep opening up. The rug can lead me into the process of its own making and also to place. To historical place, in this case to the place of tragedy where the genocide of the Armenians happened. Places on the map, places of massacre. Once I'm in the rug, there's more mobility and I can move by leap and surprise. From sense and texture to history and pain. The rug echoing with emblems of the genocidal past.

> The heavy mallet a Parsee boy
> once used to beat the knots
> beneath the pile so
> the weft would disappear
>
> vibrates in me
> as the knelling bells
> over the sea of Marmara
> once rang toward the civilized West.

If the rug is a representation of a garden, a vision of a timeless pastoral world, then I must resist that kind of romanticism. For, as a poet exploring the inheritance of trauma and genocide, innocent nature is no longer a viable reality. After genocide, nature too is spoiled, hence my journey into the beautiful natural images of the rug is also a journey of reckoning. That's why I say, "I pry my way / into a rose / undoing its blighted cliché." I want to subvert the rug's tradition. I want to make it new. I want to come to a dark place where the inheritor of genocide travels into a world of nature's anatomy; there, nature's passageways allow me to confront my sense of the tragic past. Thus, the anatomy of flowers becomes a mode of consciousness, a passageway to the pain of inheriting loss, the loss of a culture, the loss of a land. When I move into the inner world of the rose, I need to stay alert to the opportunities of engaging history. In the last section of the poem, the colors and their sources become vehicles for moral and commemorative agency. Each dye and its plant is a kind of flower of history. Each flower propels me toward the necessity of remembering; toward the passion of hearing the dead so that one may pass on the meaning.

The Book of the Dead Man (#70)

1. About the Dead Man and the Picket Fence

Ten to one, the one in question made it home safely.
Everyone was glad the party was over, and the seance had ceased that was
　　　　seeking the lost art of conversation.
The three metaphysicians left early.
The seven alchemists did not come out of the kitchen all evening.
No one brought up the red leaves of sunset, there was not a hangnail to be
　　　　seen, nor were shoes mentioned, nor saw blades nor
　　　　　　carburetors, nor
　　　　a pencil with an eraser nor the shell of a crab nor the
　　　　　　imaginary
　　　　eyebrow of a hummingbird.
It was as if a world without turtles hastened time, and it took a
　　universe free of
　　　　glue, spittle and the secretions of bees to tour space.
A world without means or ends, a world of process without a project.

2. More About the Dead Man and the Picket Fence

Always to be the swirl blown into the bottom of the glass bowl, the
　　finger marks
　　　　on the stoneware, the ember that went upwards as the
　　　　　　kiln fire
　　　　reached cone ten.
The dead man reconstitutes the story of the blind man who could see,
　　the deaf
　　　　man who could hear, the mute who could speak.
Nor scuttlebutt, nor buzz, nor yarn—reports of a dead man who lives
　　have been
　　　　documented.
The dead man was seen scraping gum from the sole of his shoe.
His wool cap and thick trousers were glimpsed going down an alley.
He was seen from a distance placing a white egg on a picket fence
　　where no
　　　　one would see it.

His presence was detected in a darkened movie house.
He was observed without his knowing making snowmen and mud
   pies, sand
         castles and leaf piles.
His fingerprints appeared in the clay.
He was seen trying not to be seen the day the sky fell.
Everyone loves the shine of the ordinary, the dead man too.
All may study the rainbow, the dead man also.
Not a man or woman does not envy the owl its privacy, the dead man
   besides.

About the Dead Man Poems

Reading poem number 70 from volume 2 of *The Book of the Dead Man* refreshes the feeling I had when I wrote the Dead Man poems. I can't now put it into words—the poems did that—but I can enumerate some of the symptoms: a rage for inclusion, a reconciliation with the human condition, a demand that words go beyond words, a metabolic rush akin to dance. Poetry is only poetry, but where else can one accommodate opposites or spot the compass points that describe a place in the mind beyond merely this or merely that?

I come from a long line of people who had to make a living. Therefore, I write late at night and only when the pot boils over from long simmering. Of course I have learned how to turn up the heat. After that, it's a matter of how long I can put off the dark. My usual way is to write from midnight on, sometimes until dawn—or until I succeed in stamping out my brain.

I sometimes barely had the stamina to last through the writing of the Dead Man poem underway. In this way I understood early that it might take as much stamina to read *The Book of the Dead Man* as it took to write it. I thought of the poems being read over time, parts of the book quickly, the whole of it as an extended meditation. In the end, *The Book of the Dead Man* is a commentary that invites more commentary.

I wrote the first of what would be the Dead Man poems in the winter of 1986–87 in Port Townsend, Washington. It bore certain insistent characteristics: a two-part structure with overlapping titles, a poetic line determined by an elastic sentence, a long view, parallels of phrasing and thought, and the conviction that ideas should have a little dirt on their shoes—in that sense, be embedded. Writing had never been so physical for me, such an act of stirred metabolism. When finished, the poem seemed a part of something else, as if it were a new chapter of an old text: perhaps one lost to antiquity, perhaps one never written down. If it was not of the *Tibetan* (or *Egyptian*) *Book of the Dead*, it was conceivably of something proximate in purpose.

I titled it "from: *The Book of the Dead Man*," though there was no such book, and I had no intention of writing it. In fact, I did not write another Dead Man poem until four years later. Those years prepared me internally. Returning to the first Dead Man poem, which I had written in a fit of who-knows-what and immediately turned from, I was again engulfed by the sound, the metabolics, the stance, the reach, and the outlook of it. For the next several years, I could not imagine writing poetry in any format but that of the Dead Man, with the Dead Man's reach and the Dead Man's outlook.

The Book of the Dead Man appeared in 1994. The last line of the last poem ("About the Dead Man and a Parallel Universe") declared, "The dead man is over the top." To me that was not a reference to a surplus but to the Dead Man having risen from a trench, gone beyond, transcended, or just plain moved on. But the Dead Man was not out of sight, and I could not yet cap the dead man poems. Volume 2, subtitled *Ardor*, contains another thirty-seven and completes, for now, *The Book of the Dead Man*.

After seventy-odd Dead Man poems (some would be abandoned), I saw that I would have to write my way out of the structure. I liked it too much, I understood it too well, to continue. Thus, calling *The Book of the Dead Man* finished would be a matter of choice. For the form and idea of the Dead Man poems had proved to be—like the mind itself, like our picture of the universe, like a Möbius strip or a Klein bottle—endless. Therefore, I set about writing number 69 ("In Which the Dead Man Speaks for Himself"), intending it to be my way out, and indeed, with one more, it was.

To a friend, the poet Laure-Anne Bosselaar, I communicated the fact that I had written the last Dead Man poem and added, "Goodbye to the man of my dreams." The next morning I received this remarkable message from Laure-Anne:

Bonjour Marvin,

I truly must tell you about a vivid, strange dream I had early this morning. I know other people's dreams are boring, but listen to this:

You were sitting in a café I used to go to in Brussels. You had a pile of paper in front of you and were drinking something red—like grenadine, or cranberry juice, or campari. You were wearing a thick, gray wool scarf. You had a red ball point pen in your shirt-pocket. I greeted you, embarrassed and awkward, for I felt you needed to be alone, and yet felt I had to disturb/distract/greet you. When you looked up at me, you seemed troubled, perplexed, sad. You handed me a pile of pages. When I asked you what they were, you said: "I wrote all these poems entitled 'The Sound of the Resurrected Dead Man's Footsteps' and I can't put them in my book because I wrote the last poem last week." When I woke up, it took me a while to figure out that it had been a dream—it all felt so very vivid and real.

I was deeply grateful for Laure-Anne's dream because it spoke permission to continue as I am.

The lyric tradition carries most of the poetry I admire: the poem that deserves a frame; the poem that, like a spider web, trembles everywhere when touched anywhere; the poem so well sewn that it might never be unraveled. The very sanity of the polished lyric is its own reward. Nor need it be otherwise.

Nevertheless, though I came to writing through the lyric tradition, I am not wholly of it. For I came to understand that I was crazier than that. I could not help it if I saw things otherwise for myself. For one thing, I prized the spontaneity and new connections at the heart of poetic composition. I had come to believe that only a certain spontaneity of mind could call forth the *poetry* in poems, even for the slowest and most methodical writers. However detailed one's plan, however comprehensive one's intention, for the mind to spark requires that at some point one must touch naked wires together.

Also, behind everything else was my belief that it is disabling, if not vain, to take death personally.

These two convictions—that ideas need to be embedded in the physical world, and that death should not be taken personally—took away from me much that is inherently poetic. I could not enjoy beautiful fictions as much as many others do, and I had little interest in poems that juggle other writers' ideas for effect. My heart is most moved by those works whose affirmations can stand up to physical and social circumstance.

I don't want to get technical about the Dead Man poems, except to say that long thought and practice lay behind my decision to let the sentence determine the poetic line. "Free verse" is not a form, nor an absence of form, but a method for inventing new forms. In the Dead Man poems, I redefined the free verse line by discarding many of its material particulars: the common emphasis on enjambment, for example. Others have done it in works I thought not totally dissimilar: poems by Christopher Smart and Walt Whitman are examples, as are "wisdom books." I have always felt that the key to free verse is the sentence. That is, syntax provides the opportunities to enjamb or not, and syntax determines the character of the line. The free verse line without reference to syntax is like a train without reference to tracks.

Likewise, there were motives for establishing the convention of seeming to write each poem twice (the two-part architecture of each Dead Man poem may make it appear that I write it and then I write it again), the use of baldly overlapping section titles, and other techniques —some of them not illustrated by poem number 70. I took pleasure in going against the grain: using extravagant similes, linking prepositional phrases, disdaining enjambments, sewing each poem together with strange needles and new stitches. How far could a stitch reach and still hold? That was one of the questions that possessed me in writing the Dead Man poems.

And always the pretense (the fact!) that the Dead Man is alive and dead at the same time. Microscopics and macroscopics. Oddly transported.

Volume 2 bears the subtitle *Ardor*. Dead Man poems are observably in love with life and with love itself and are resistant to religious and political stupidity. They honor the Zen admonition, "Live as if you were already dead." In being alive and dead at the same time, the Dead Man is like everyone, with this proviso—that he knows it. He doesn't just say it, he knows it. He participates that much more . . . because he knows it. Everything in life is intensified . . . because he knows it. He longs to affirm life without blinking before the fate of mankind.

Dead Man poem number 70 was my goodbye-for-now to the Dead Man and is the Dead Man's cautionary goodbye to the reader. It proffers enough for us to know that the Dead Man's absence is not the Dead Man's death. It takes back his privacy; mine, as well.

What drew me to poetry is that it can say in words more than words can say. Sometimes this requires a circuitry, a circularity, a tautological character, lest the fullness of the expression be stopped short by the finality of things in the foreground.

It will be the absolute precision of the thing that undoes the thing. Likewise, our minds traveling any distance to the unseen rub up a fog and a static. It is therefore with no-mind, with perfected fallibility, with the fullest participation, and with no strings attached that the Dead Man inhales the beginning and the end.

Readers have asked, "Who is the Dead Man?" I never thought to ask the question of myself. To me, the Dead Man has been more of an overarching consciousness than that of one person. Yet Dead Man consciousness contains my life and is free to use it, as the following example may illustrate. In poem number 14 ("About the Dead Man and Government"), there appears the line, "The dead man is the anarchist whose eyes look up through the bottom of the glass raised in toast." The line stands in a context, but one might ask from where it came to be so formed, and in this case I know and can say.

In 1983, I traveled for a month in Yugoslavia, during which I attended the Sarajevo Arts Festival. On the final night, the festival writers, our translators, civic officials, and others gathered for a banquet. Toward the end, I left with my translator for a tavern frequented by writers. She introduced me to a table of young poets. They spoke little English, and I spoke no Serbo-Croatian. She explained that I was a visiting American poet. Immediately one of them lifted his glass high and said, in English, "Fuck Reagan!" Then he asked my translator to find out if I was a Democrat or a Republican. "Neither," I said, "Independent." When my translator relayed this, he again raised his glass in toast and said, "Ah, Anarchista!" Hence, "The dead man is the anarchist whose eyes look up through the bottom of the glass raised in toast."

All that may be known or supposed, sensed or imagined, here or there, now or then, visible or invisible, awaits its moment to make the fullest sense, beyond the limited term of a biography. The source of a line (a tavern in Sarajevo) is a hole in time long sealed.

Of course, what could I do after Laure-Anne's dream but write "Sounds of the Resurrected Dead Man's Footsteps no. 1?" I knew that I would someday have to exit the Dead Man poems. Laure-Anne's dream lit up a path. In the autumn of 1996, I continue along that path, still within earshot of his footsteps.

As to the half-hidden references and humor in some of the poems— Kierkegaard is said to have philosophized that laughter is a kind of prayer. It is a most mysterious aspect of aesthetics that there can be pleasure in assembling the truth even when the facts are harsh.

PHILIP BOOTH

Hot 5th of July

A housepainter ladder'd up
on a white clapboard house.
Out on the street, across
the lawn from its Toro rider,
a T-shirt kid, scrawny, maybe
thirteen or eleven, parked
in the rusted-out box
of an old Dodge Ram. Must
be his boy, maybe serving
a sentence. Or not all there.
Hard to know. Hunched up on
the wheelwell, his body slumps,
his eyes scan nothing. He
sits there, hot hot hot, all
morning, diddling a piece
of trash from the box, then
sticking his mid-finger up
his nose. Head bent, no cap,
waterjar empty or never
filled, he slumps there, beyond
choice or prospect. Only
wishing, one of these times,
his old man might get down,
let him out, let go,
let him scream the Toro
around the scorched lawn.

Speaking for the Speechless Kid

"If it be true that good wine needs no bush," as Rosalind tentatively says in the epilogue of *As You Like It*, " 'tis true that a good play needs no epilogue." Good wine or no, I'd like to think that "Hot 5th of July" is a poem that needs no authorial bush, that it implicitly speaks for itself even as my lines speak for the speechless kid who's sweating something out—God knows what—in the box of his old man's old pickup.

I like the poem. I liked seeing it in print this spring in *North Dakota Quarterly*. I liked it last year when (amazingly, for me) it took only three days of drafts to make it whole, whole not least in its pacings and fictions. What engages me now, as this anthology asks for some kind of essay, is that this recent poem returns me to recall how my early poems have evolved toward such poems as "Hot 5th of July."

Forty-some years ago, my predominantly pastoral first book, *Letter from a Distant Land*, contained only one explicitly political poem. By 1961, I now rediscover, my second book, *The Islanders*, included four demonstrably political poems ("Mores," "Spit," "The Tower," and "Nebraska, U.S.A."), each of which engaged various political vectors. *Weathers and Edges* (1966), mostly written in Syracuse and Manhattan as well as Maine, immediately began with poems as overtly political as "Choosing a Homesite" and "Incident in Santo Domingo" before it modulated into such poems as "After the *Thresher*" and "Under the West Side Highway." Whether the most obviously angry of these earlier poems were specifically catalyzed by the Hiss trial, the McCarthy hearings, Korea, the Cuban missile crisis, the anguish of the Civil Rights movement, Vietnam, or the assassination of JFK, I can't now sort out. I do know that "After the *Thresher*" and "Under the West Side Highway" are, like "The Man on the Wharf" and "The Ship," precursors of comparable poems in *Margins* (1970): "Crosstrees," for instance, or lesser poems like "The Misery of Mechanics," "Labrador River," and "Bolt." Differently charged as these six poems are, each refuses (as lines in "The Ship" make clear) to be "self-exiled by anger" or "prided . . . with outrage."

After my foolish reordering of the selected poems in *Margins*, the new clarities of *Available Light* (1976) owed much to its first epigraph from Karl Jaspers, which begins, "Being comes out of all origins to meet me," and is reinforced by the photographer Paul Strand's famous aphorism, "All light is available light." Even now, I'm not sure I know what aspects of my work I seemed to be giving up in order to *give in* to what I felt I was writing. I only know that I was moving beyond whatever sentimentality blurred some of my early poems, and that I was becoming increasingly engaged by the *process* of creating, by the integrity of boatbuilding, of woodwork, mechanical work, dreamwork, photographic work, the working through of one's lifetime. I was opening to the passionate acuity of such photographers as Strand and Walker Evans; I was focusing on further artists as disparate as Cezanne and Steinberg, writers from Chekhov to Arendt. As I delved into their worlds, my own work, as if by osmosis, gained new authority. Even as I was increasingly fictionalizing the "I" of many poems, I was multiplying perspectives available to an author-omniscient. Just as earlier books had brought me to slants of March or November light, so did *Available Light* allow me to enter the darker depths of *Before Sleep* (1980).

Poems beget poems, books beget books. *Relations*, the intentionally inclusive title of *Selected Poems 1950–1985*, means what it says. *Selves* (1990) and *Pairs* (1994) continue to relate how lives *necessarily* relate to each other in what I recently heard Robert Hass call "the given world." Given the world we have made and come to, I feel more than ever that poetry must speak for, as well as to, humankind, kindred as we are, whether or not we know who hears or reads us. Minority as both poets and their audience are, both know how poems can move our lives from despair to resilience. I think of Emily Dickinson's embracing "the Common Day" as a "Vitallest Expression"; I hear Hopkins' "Not, I'll not, carrion comfort, Despair, not feast on thee," even as I hear Frost listen to "A Servant to Servants" who needs her listener; I feel with Dr. Williams for Elsie, and for ". . . A Poor Old Woman" whose "solace of ripe plums" gives him solace as well as a poem. All yearn, as we each yearn, for a meaningful life, even as fewer and fewer of us have language to express—and thus ease, or achieve—that yearning.

I yearn for poems beyond my own, I yearn for all levels of peace; I yearn for joy. I am not immune to good wine, but in my own house I want home-brew poems. Until that boy in the back of his father's truck

can be freed or free himself into a life that is other than mean, I can-
not—in whatever weathers—*not* hear Blake:

> Can I see another's woe,
> And not be in sorrow too?
> Can I see another's grief
> And not seek for kind relief?

ROSELLEN BROWN

from Cora Fry's Pillow Book

They need a sign: *No mothers in the body shop!*
I call out "Chip!" and my voice is a dropped wrench, loud
as I can make it. In the dead light, motes swirling, standing still,
caught in its oil, black rags, sour iron smell, the hissing and clanging,
through it all I can barely make out his features. And he turns away in
     a rage.
I call out to him again but he is so ashamed of my softness here—
as if they are his fault, my breasts, I know it. My hips
in worn blue cotton. My hair that fuzzes at my neck inviting breakage.
Broken already.
Everything in here is harder than I am, the tools' thick surfaces, the
     machines, chuffing,
that eat the bolts off tires, the dangle
of fan belts cluttered on the wall behind him, and nozzles like parts of
     his body
I mustn't see anymore—he is embarrassed for himself, so reduced. Not
for me, this is:
for himself and the others. For Jimmy
back in the office and Horace out front pumping gas, gabbing. For
     baby Fitz
who just last week married his pregnant sweetheart and she's already
guilty as I am, swelling up in secret, scaring the boy half to
     death. When
     I talk to my son
he hits a button and a silver car rises
and rises between us on a hard oiled stalk.
He keeps to the other side of it, poking
its underparts. He is the only man in the shop, of course,
who came out of such a delicate darkness as mine. The only one
who cried when they lifted him up from his bloody nest, lunging and
     gasping. As if
he was born cold as a wrench or a hammer, slicked shiny with motor
     grease.
As if I was ever
as fragile as he things I am today.

About Cora Fry

The more I have thought about which of my poems I like best (not at all the same as which I think *is* best), the more complex the task has become. I've already raised one question inside that parenthesis. Others follow: Which poem gave me the greatest pleasure in the writing or the revising? Which, that is, in its particular time? Have some poems worn well, and others become exhausted, given away their barrenness and limitation? Which crystalized the most compelling, complex, difficult, or intractable emotions or ideas (a subjective judgment, really, not necessarily to be appreciated by readers)? And, of course, which readers *are* those anyway, intimates or strangers?

The questions proliferate. It has been interesting simply to prize them apart and list them out, and I've only just begun. Add to the fact that there is no correct response the reality that there is no lasting choice because an author's response to her or his work should be a live, fresh thing, fed like an embryo by the ebb and flow of the poet's bloodstream.

So I am left with this morning's opinion, caught on the fly, this morning's only—I am not stalling—which today is affected by the memory of a reading I gave last night. I was presenting to a New Hampshire audience my collection of New Hampshire poems, *Cora Fly's Pillow Book*, which is to say, though not poems inacessible to other readers, still a special pleasure to read on home ground where a lot of nuances strike a special chord. And so, there's another factor to add to the mix: What passes between poet and live audience introduces a whole new set of possibilities.

The poem I will write about at this moment gives me great satisfaction—that's all I will say about it. When I read it aloud, there is always deep, silent concentration and attentiveness to its detail, and a surprised exhalation of breath at the end.

The poems in my two Cora Fry books (the first, *Cora Fry*, published in 1977; that and a sequel were published together in 1994 as *Cora Fry's Pillow Book*) were not meant to be free-standing; the books are conceived almost—almost—like a novel. Some of the poems cannot stand alone, some can; others can be read as single poems but lose considerable resonance because, like the moments in a long fiction, they exist in time and they represent aspects of characterization, an accretion, a succession of responses not only to states of mind but to an entire imagined life and to an ongoing situation called, loosely, a plot.

Thus, by the time readers or listeners arrive at this poem (which, like the others, has no title) they have already seen Cora Fry through the eighty-four poems of the first book, in which she speaks of country pleasures, country pains: a moose glimpsed by the side of the road, tomato canning, her husband, her children, her parents, friendships, town, city, waitressing, snow, and gardens. Not to mention a lot of sex, repressed, denied, balked, denigrated, even once in a while enjoyed or at least anticipated: sex as ground bass. Or perhaps it's background noise. One way or another, it plays a larger part in Cora's world than she would ever admit to.

When I read the poem aloud as I did last night, I do a manipulative thing: Since I'm the one picking and choosing out of the many poems here (*Cora Fry's Pillow Book* has 179 pages) I give myself permission to turn my audience's attention to what I admit to them is an egregiously sentimental poem in the first book. Cora's little son Chip, riding a merry-go-round on the town green and thinking the white horse is going to take him away, hangs on and shouts a terrified goodbye to his mother. The poem ends: "When you saw me come / round the second time, / I got to see your face."

Then—admitting to the manipulation, which seems useful to me because a live reading is a drama and only a partial representation of a book—I read this poem, which takes place eighteen years later when Chip's innocence and sweetness are a distant memory:

"No mothers in the body shop" tries to bring us closer to Cora as (1) a woman (2) at a certain time in her life (3) expressing what some might call her "feminist consciousness" but which she wouldn't name but only perceive as a complicated ongoing pain (4) to which she responds with greater self-awareness and a more amused and superior bitterness than she has felt in the first book (5) amidst a series of physical descriptions of the body shop rendered with precision and even gusto and (6) a very sexualized (but, again, quite unacknowledged) vision of her relationship to her grown son (7) in an overwhelmingly masculine domain which she sees as an expression of a helpless, almost pathetic, frightened, defensive and therefore hostile attitude toward women in general and mothers in particular. In "baby Fitz's" pregnant sweetheart, we can see the transformation from woman to mother (she is barely a wife) already taking place, "scaring the boy half to death."

The poem, in other words, does a lot of work, and it does it both as object providing (I hope) its own independent pleasures, but also as one tile in the mosaic of Cora's life. There is a delicate balance between such a poem's existence as itself, with its echoes and cadences and syntax sufficiently interesting minute to minute, and as a scene within an ongoing dramatic context. Cora asks for, but does not beg for, sympathy for herself and for other women and mothers. Her vision of the hostility between the sexes began, after all, way back on page 7 of the first book when she not so innocently tells us, " 'Fry,' I said / when he touched me on / my breast. / Do you think / of women, / other women, when / you're touching me there?' " and Fry reassures her, telling her not to worry. "No one you know." It doesn't end here in the body shop either. And there are also a good many other poems that are sympathetic to men and grown-up boys; this one must be seen within the web of the whole of Cora's life. She is growing, even as we watch, into a sad, savvy woman who knows she is speaking to listeners who understand what she's talking about.

One last element, like so much of the whole, not visible here. The poems in the original *Cora Fry* were syllabic; each poem worked with a slightly different count and pattern but all were tightly controlled, pared to a minimum in order to keep Cora's speech laconic, spare, as it tends to be in parsimonious New England. But in the second book, I have abandoned the syllable count for a more expansive, looser line; many of the poems (as well as their lines and stanzas) are long and rangy—Cora is, in many ways, far more relaxed and eager to tell stories and paint characters at leisure, and she revels in the details. Thus the far more clotted, almost lush quality of this poem, the satisfaction Cora clearly takes in exercising her verbal muscle. (In the earlier book, if she spent many syllables on anything it might be the names of squashes and other inanimate objects less prickly than people.)

But this, too, is a feature that, like the grown-up Chip seen against the child on the merry-go-round, gains a dimension by contrast: Not only the sound but the look of the poem on the page is utterly different from the visual quality of the first *Cora*, some of whose poems are tiny—four lines as frail as bird tracks on snow.

But ask me tomorrow and I might choose another poem to dare to enjoy publicly. I promise myself that the day my judgments become static is the day I'll cap my Rolling Writer and close my notebook for good.

TERESA CADER

Wind, Horse, Snow

I.

The Eskimo children balance their blackboards
on their knees and write with soft fat chalk.

A storm skitters across the frozen sea.
Smidgens of ice have swirled into pinwheels.

2.

The painter Magritte is dabbing black paint
on his canvas. Beneath the clock he writes
'wind,' beneath the door 'horse.'

3.

The Eskimo children have a new teacher,
from Connecticut, who wants them to learn
a poem about stopping by the woods
on a snowy evening with an intelligent horse.

4.

It is summer in the ragweed field.
Magritte says there is no picture without a frame.
When he stares from his attic window, does he see
the field, or a composition of the field?
Is it possible for me to love you
without inventing you?

5.

The Eskimo children admire the horse most.

6.

The children must pick a word to describe
the snow that batters their windows.
If it is too wet, their fathers might freeze

as they paddle home. If it is dry and powdery,
the dogs can make the run to town for food.

7.

"The word dog does not bite,"
observed William James,
who admired Magritte's horse.

8.

If my language has no future tense,
am I the same person I was as a child?

About "Wind, Horse, Snow"

The large arched window in my third-floor study was once narrow and cracked, with limited visibility through its black-ribbed panes. I had taken an old table and placed it squarely in front of the window and had rigged up a standing lamp beneath the sagging insulation. I wanted to know if I could think and write in this space: I wanted to know if I could convert this barnlike attic into a studio.

On the table lay books about the painter Magritte and books about the invention of writing in ancient Sumeria. I had recently given up a studio, where I had been the only writer in a building filled largely with visual artists. An artist I admired immensely worked in pastels in a style I will call realism. Her representation of a bowl of peaches was mouth-watering. Yet the hunger for realism seemed to me peculiar: Had writing not moved in the opposite direction, from pictorial representation in cave paintings to a system of abstract symbols signifying sounds? This movement from eye to ear, from drawing to writing, made me understand how pivotal the invention of the alphabet was in history. I marveled about it for weeks. I could picture the black sails of those Phoenician boats as they pulled into a sleepy Greek fishing village and the clever boys who copied the new alphabet. I could picture it all, but I could not write about it. What did this *mean* to me? Why was I obsessed with this image?

As I thought about this, I stared out the window. Soon I noticed that if I moved my chair to the right, I could see a turreted red brick building that reminded me of the splendid buildings in Prague. It was dimly associated in my mind with the Hradčany Castle, with its historical opulence and grace and with its somber sterility in Communist Czechoslovakia. And I noticed that if I moved my chair to the left, the building disappeared and instead I was looking out on a field and a steep hill lined with towering evergreens and maples. By establishing a point on the horizon with my eyes I could skew the perspective so as to be gazing into a forest whose depths I could not fathom (never mind that I knew a house to be located behind those trees). By moving back from the window I could make the telephone wires disappear. My attic window had become a frame for a multitude of compositions I chose to invent.

And what did this have to do with the invention of writing, I asked myself? As I looked through my books on Magritte, a painter quite different in style from the pastel artist, I saw for the first time Magritte's understanding of *language as invention*. A green wooden bowl could be called a boat, or a cat, or a book. A clock could be labeled 'wind,' a door 'horse.' (As I understand the idea now, there is no bowl, there is only 'bowl.') The distinction between an object and the name we give it was not something I had thought about deeply before, although I had known those paintings by Magritte.

I remained obsessed with these ideas, which had for me the allure, the thrill of discovery. I read more about the invention of writing and about the implements and materials used for it throughout history, including clay, rocks, wood, bamboo, and paper. While I experienced that tightening in the gut that tells me a poem is pressing to be written, I had no anchoring for a poem. I had not reached the place where intellect and emotion meet, where a rigorous mental passion ignites the gut, and vice versa. One day, however, as I stumbled through a treatise in modern linguistics, I found myself thinking about snow. In boredom I stared from my window onto the hill. Children were sledding and tubing in deep snow. A pasty sky suggested fresh snow might be on the way. I was bemused by how sentimental this scene appeared. I also thought about the numerous words Eskimos have for snow, most of which are used to communicate critical information about conditions that affect the food supply, the movement of dog sleds, the stability of igloos, etc. Suddenly I had a hilarious image of Eskimo children confronting the word snow in Frost's famous poem, a word *cum* metaphor touted to be so universal even his horse understands it. Those Phoenician sails became blackboards.

CARL DENNIS

Sarit Narai

Now that the light holds on after supper,
Why not walk west to the end of Ferry Street
And linger where the ferries used to dock
Before the bridge spanned the Niagara.
Why not enlarge the thin verge of the moment
With the Sunday crowd on deck fifty years ago
Riding to Fort Erie and back just for the fun of it.
The wind from the lake ruffles their hair
As the low sun glances along the water.
Just as they left their rooms to join the flow
So you can go back to them for a moment
And lead them forward into the present
Where the gulls are gliding, swinging beneath the bridge
In figures that blur as you watch, and disappear.
And why not call up the boys you used to see here
Playing on the boulders in the bridge's shadow
Before the fence was put up to stop them.
If one of them lost his footing, his chances were slim,
The push in the channel too hard and heavy,
The water of Erie beginning its headlong, brainless rush
To join the Ontario, as if an extra minute mattered.
Remember the evening you found a crowd here
Waiting beside an ambulance with its motor running
And a squad car where a woman sat in back
Head in her hands? Dark-haired. Next morning
Leafing through the local news, you found the story—
Woman from Thailand, three years in the States,
Loses her son, eleven, to the Niagara.
Let yourself go, if you want to enlarge the moment,
And imagine what might have happened if the boy
Sarit Narai, had been fished from the river in time.
Try to think of him as your son's best friend
At Niagara school, where friends were scarce,
Quieting a wildness you could never manage,
The mild manners of Asia persuasive by mere example.
And what if your daughter admires him even more
And comes to choose him for her life's companion,

Not the drab complainer she ended up with.
The world turned left that day on the forking path
But the path on the right still runs beside it
Though never touching. A bountiful Buddha smile
As he explains to your granddaughters and grandsons
How to climb the eight-fold path to freedom
As gulls like these swoop over the gray stones
And the ferries steam back and forth if you let them.
Freely the crowd on deck empties its mind of thought
And welcomes sensation, the sun and wind.
And then the riders waken to see the skyline of home
Beckoning from a distance as if it missed them,
So they're ready to take up their lives again
As the ship pulls in where now a line of cars
Waits in the twilight to pay the bridge toll
Not thirty yards from the spot where the ambulance waited
And the woman cried in the back seat of the car.
After an hour the crowd moved off, dissolving to families,
To couples musing on twilight pastimes.
For a moment, though, each may have hesitated
To change the subject and appear small-souled.
The mist of sorrow already thinning and fading
That would have remained if they'd lived in Eden,
The one kingdom where the sorrows of others
Feel like our own. When Buddha neared Nirvana,
One story goes, he looked back on us as we drowned
In the sea of endless craving, and was filled with pity,
And chose to postpone his bliss till all were saved.
But how can a climb from the world be managed here
When the crowd on the ferry wants the sunset to linger,
And the mother would sell her soul to get her son back,
And the boy still struggles to grab the slippery rock
And pull himself up, his friends all helping
So he can grow old among them. An old man
Looking back on his deeds of kindness. Now the few
Who met him and the many who never did but might have
Feel the phantom gap he would have filled
But are ignorant of its cause and blame their wives,
Their husbands, their children, their towns and jobs,
And hunt around for new gospels, new philosophies.
If you see them this evening pacing along the bank
Where once the ferries docked and the Sunday riders

Lost themselves awhile in the sway and shimmer,
Pity their restlessness. There must be a way
To step forward and name the one they miss,
Sarit Narai, in a tone so resonant
It holds them a moment beyond loss and longing.

Poetry and History

Though this poem implies a protest against the brute fact that we live in time, that the present is always sliding away from us into a past no future will ever be able to restore, it also suggests some power to resist time by enlarging the present, and so it allies itself with traditional notions of the difference between poetry and history: namely, the greater place poetry gives to individual human agency. Rather than comment on my particular treatment of this theme, I want to dwell here on the common refusal of all poetry to let time have the last word. This refusal is implied in Aristotle's observation that the actions of poetry are not only more universal than the narratives of history, excluding the idiosyncratic and accidental, but also more beautiful, satisfying a basic human need for unity and completeness, possessing a clear beginning, middle, and end, with all extraneous elements excluded. The emphasis on beauty is related to Aristotle's assumption that poetry has a moral component that history need not have, that it focuses its attention on moments when individuals make significant choices or judgments, and so indirectly always affirms human freedom. The freedom that the speaker in my poem presumes in advising "you" about enlarging the present is kin to a freedom that all poetry presumes in its subjects to make their history as well as suffer it.

To say that poetry features individual human agency is not to say that the figures in literature, as opposed to history, are presented as being in complete control of their own lives, only that what happens to them is presented as a function not only of situation but of character. Achilles' choices in the *Iliad*, to use an example familiar to Aristotle, are sharply restricted. He can choose a life of honor only by choosing an early death, and his nobility is partly a function of his understanding how beleaguered he is by forces he cannot alter. But the poem constructs its massive account of the Trojan War around the hero's limited choice, to fight or not to fight, and to this extent the action of the poem is not only typical in its account of what war is, and unitary in its plot, but also affirmative as a testimony to the power of the individual. In the case of tragedy, especially Greek tragedy, the power of the agent is even more strictly limited, the action often flowing less from character than from situation. But however much the hero is hemmed in, he or she is not merely a victim. His fall to some extent results from his own actions. The fall of a blameless man, as Aristotle says, is not a fit subject for art. The story may possess universality, for blameless men do fall in fortune. And it may possess unity, for one can imagine an organic plot in which the trust of a good man is betrayed by people who prove unworthy. But the result would be, as Aristotle says, "disgusting." The problem is not that we expect art to press for the triumph of strict justice, for Aristotle specifically excludes from tragedy the kind of plot where a fault-ridden protagonist receives the punishment he deserves. Rather the problem is the more basic one of emotional engagement. We cannot be moved by a tragedy, cannot feel pity and fear, unless we can identify with its protagonist, and we cannot identify with someone who has no significant control of his own life. A figure like Oedipus may seem to test this generalization in that he has inadvertently committed the crimes exposed in the action of the play; but the effect of the play is not "disgusting" despite its unblinking revelation of human ignorance. In the process of seeking out the source of the plague Oedipus reveals the kind of rashness and willfulness that led him to flee his homeland and kill his father. And in conducting the investigation with scrupulous thoroughness he stands as the central force for truth in the play, refusing to back down when he is advised to do so by others, pushing on even at the end when he guesses the painful truth, and finally blinding and banishing himself as his own judge and punisher. To appreciate the modicum of freedom that the play allows Oedipus one might try to imagine a play in which Oedipus never discovers what he has done, where he remains until his death the happily ignorant king of Thebes, avoiding in scene after scene by a hair's breadth the kind of questions that might bring the truth to light. It's hard not to see such a play as doomed to failure, the distance between what we know and what the hero knows being too great for us to become engaged in his fate. And yet it isn't hard to imagine a historical account of such a character that maintains our interest though the ironic distance is never closed. History does not require us to identify with the people it investigates and hence does not require its characters to be free. In a similar way we might imagine an interesting historical account of an Oedipus who knows what he has done but systematically destroys every piece of evidence and every witness necessary for his exposure. But if such a character never deliberates a moment about alternatives to his deceit, never feels any wish that might be in conflict with his wish to maintain his power, we would be likely not to regard him as a sufficiently large subject to occupy the center of a play. He would be free in name only, too limited to understand the moral significance of his own career and hence too distant from us to win the kind of investment in his fate that poetry requires.

In poetry that is not narrative or dramatic, where the action takes the form of a sequence of thoughts, not a sequence of deeds, the assertion of freedom is found in the poet's ability to define his situation precisely and completely. When the act of definition entails a deliberate widening of context, the assertion of freedom is obvious, as it is in my "Sarit Narai," which invites the "you" to include in the present not only the past but also what has never happened. But even in gloomier poems the plot always entails a movement toward clarity, not a movement away from it; and this movement entails a choice among perspectives. However stymied the poet may feel, if his poem is to move us it must present us with a moment in which some important judgment is being made and defended. In this sense the poet is always an active agent, never a passive victim. As a test case here I offer Emily Dickinson's unequivocally gloomy little poem, "The Heart Asks Pleasure First":

> The Heart asks Pleasure—first—
> And then—Excuse from Pain—
> And then—those little Anodynes
> That deaden suffering—
>
> And then—to go to sleep—
> And then—if it should be
> The will of its Inquisitor
> The privilege to die.

It's hard to think of a more restrictive assessment of the progress of human life, life as an inevitable movement from hope to hopelessness in the face of constant disappointment. And yet the poem indirectly makes a counteraffirmation of human freedom through its power of compression, through its success in distilling the essence of life into eight lines of careful discriminations. A long period of silent selection seems to have preceded the poem in which all irrelevancies and distractions have been cast aside, including even the distraction of lamentation and complaint. Though we might have expected the theme of disappointment to be handled with first-person testimony, the speaker has chosen to make a statement not about herself but about the human condition in general. Whatever feelings of personal distress may have precipitated the poem, the poet speaks now from a point of view of sibyl-like calm whose only purpose is to announce the truth, not apply it or explain it. How the speaker has been able to reach the distant viewing place from which she observes the drama of life spread out before her is not made known to us, but her having reached it gives her a dignity that her list of narrowing possibilities cannot undermine. She proves herself a fitting judge of any "inquisitor" who has ultimate power over life and death.

The assertion of freedom made by poetry implies a resistance to an historical perspective to the extent that this perspective diminishes the importance of individual decisions. Poetry resists most obviously any form of historical determinism that regards historical process as unrelated to human intention, the result of impersonal forces like class or race or natural environment. Less obviously it resists what may be considered the occupational hazard inevitable in an approach that gives a primary place to the context of an action, to the matrix of contingencies that encompass it, and not to the logic of the agent. Poets may be willing to concede that we are all to some extent products of our times, shaped by the particular historical context into which we are born. They may grant that no poet can hope to stand wholly removed from his world, free of the taint of provinciality. But to admit this absolute is not to disallow the importance of degree. The difference between bad writing and good, they would argue, is in good part the difference between a lazy acceptance of the clichés of the moment and the willingness to hold up one's values to critical scrutiny. That scrutiny will always be incomplete, but the poet who makes the effort to achieve some distance is likely to attain a larger perspective than one who doesn't. And the possibility of success is enhanced, most poets would contend, if they enter into dialogue with writers outside their own immediate society, inhabiting a second society of poets from a variety of times and places who were able to distance themselves enough from their own times so that they are still read long after the society that helped produce them and audiences they were written for have ceased to exist.

The kind of freedom embodied in claims of poetic truth would likely be recognized by some historians as kin to the freedom they hope to embody in their own work by achieving a critical distance from their own times. But they might find their sympathies strained by poems that refuse to accept the essentials of the world as it is, that oppose the world as given to the world they would like to find. For the historian concerned with why things have happened as they have, the world as found tends to comprise the real world, while to poets concerned with what should be as much as with what is, the world as found is only one of many possibilities. Beside any path actually taken from one point in time to another runs a myriad of ghostly paths of the might-have-been, all at one time equally possible; and this perspective, which is chosen overtly in "Sarit Narai," means that poetry has to find an important place for regret, for the exploring of lost possibility, as well for the accepting of what one is given. This different attitude toward possibility is even more obvious with regard to the future. To the extent that historians are interested in writing about the future at all, they tend to concentrate on predictions based on extrapolating from those forces they have identified as salient in the past. But for the poet the future tends to be an alternative to the past, not an extension of it, the home of unembodied possibilities that need to be kept alive in order to give purpose and value to the present. Poetry, in other words, makes a significant place for wishing, from a grand public wish like that of Blake's prophet, to build "Jerusalem in England's green and pleasant land," to a grand private wish like that of Marvell's lover for a world rich enough in space and time to allow him to court his lady with the leisure and lavishness she deserves. Circumstances may force the wishers to compromise, as they do in Marvell's poem, but the recognition of how much is lost in that compromise is just as important as the recognition of what is salvaged. And many poems fulfill themselves simply in expressing wishes that have no chance at all of ever being embodied.

Because I began with Dickinson's poem that systematically destroys the hope of satisfied wishes, it seems only fair to end with a poem of hers that gives wishing the highest status:

> Wild Nights—Wild Nights!
> Were I with thee
> Wild Nights should be
> Our luxury!
>
> Futile—the Winds—
> To a Heart in port—
> Done with the Compass—
> Done with the Chart!
>
> Rowing in Eden—
> Ah, the Sea!
> Might I but moor—Tonight—
> In Thee!

It's hard to think of a poem where greater claims are made for the value of love, where the joining of lovers creates a realm of such complete safety that it turns a night of violent storm into a luxurious entertainment. This is a poem of wishing in that the union it presents can't be enacted, but it focuses less on frustration than on the joy that would be experienced if the union were possible, devoting itself to an emphatic assertion of the joined lovers' self-sufficiency. Indirectly the poem affirms the strength of the speaker's commitment to her beloved, which is not weakened by separation. In its confident tone and emphatic rhythms, it makes clear that longing here is not a sign of weakness but a sign of strength, of the lovers' power to create a counter world that can turn the threats of the ordinary world into pleasures. That the lovers are not weary with life, but are rather enlarging and completing it, is made clear in the last stanza when, having reached the safe harbor of their union, they set out to sea once more. Eden is not a refuge from adventure. It provides its own sea that the lovers take pleasure in exploring together. This paradise is, to be sure, a private one. It contains only two people. But the Biblical name suggests indirectly the bold claim that the power ascribed in Genesis to the Creator has been transferred to the lovers themselves, who do not merely inhabit the garden, like the original Adam and Eve, but actually bring it into being by the completeness and intensity of their love, or at least would bring it into being were they able to join. No history book will ever mention this unrealized Eden, no history of public life or even of private. To find it one has to visit the Bureau of What Hasn't Happened. But unless one makes this visit, the meaning of what has in fact happened is not fully revealed.

MARK DOTY

A Display of Mackerel

They lie in parallel rows,
on ice, head to tail,
each a foot of luminosity

barred with black bands,
which divide the scales'
radiant sections

like seams of lead
in a Tiffany window.
Iridescent, watery

prismatics: think abalone,
the wildly rainbowed
mirror of a soapbubble sphere,

think sun on gasoline.
Splendor, and splendor,
and not a one in any way

distinguished from the other
—nothing about them
of individuality. Instead

they're *all* exact expressions
of the one soul,
each a perfect fulfilment

of heaven's template,
mackerel essence. As if,
after a lifetime arriving

at this enameling, the jeweler's
made uncountable examples,
each as intricate

in its oily fabulation
as the one before
Suppose we could iridesce,

like these, and lose ourselves
entirely in the universe
of shimmer—would you want

to be yourself only,
unduplicatable, doomed
to be lost? They'd prefer,

plainly, to be flashing participants,
multitudinous. Even now
they seem to be bolting

forward, heedless of stasis.
They don't care they're dead
and nearly frozen,

just as, presumably,
they didn't care that they were living:
all, all for all,

the rainbowed school
and its acres of brilliant classrooms,
in which no verb is singular,

or every one is. How happy they seem,
even on ice, to be together, selfless,
which is the price of gleaming.

Souls on Ice

In the Stop 'n Shop in Orleans, Massachusetts, I was struck by the elegance of the mackerel in the fresh-fish display. They were rowed and stacked, brilliant against the white of the crushed ice; I loved how black and glistening the bands of dark scales were, and the prismed sheen of the patches between, and their shining flat eyes. I stood and looked at them for a while, just paying attention while I leaned on my cart— before I remembered where I was and realized that I was standing in someone's way.

Our metaphors go on ahead of us; they know before we do. And thank goodness for that, for if I were dependent on other ways of coming to knowledge I think I'd be a very slow study. I need something to serve as a container for emotion and idea, a vessel that can hold what's too slippery or charged or difficult to touch. Will doesn't have much to do with this; I can't *choose* what's going to serve as a compelling image for me. But I've learned to trust that part of my imagination that gropes forward, feeling its way toward what it needs; to watch for the signs of fascination, the sense of compelled attention (*Look at me*, something seems to say, *closely*) that indicates that there's something I need to attend to. Sometimes it seems to me as if metaphor were the advance guard of the mind; something in us reaches out, into the landscape in front of us, looking for the right vessel, the right vehicle, for whatever will serve.

Driving home from the grocery, I found myself thinking again about the fish, and even scribbled some phrases on an envelope in the car, something about stained glass, soapbubbles, while I was driving. It wasn't long—that same day? the next?—before I was at my desk, trying simply to describe what I had seen. I almost always begin with description, as a way of focusing on that compelling image, the poem's "given." I know that what I can see is just the proverbial tip of the iceberg; if I do my work of study and examination, and if I am lucky, the image which I've been intrigued by will become a metaphor, will yield depth and meaning, will lead me to insight. The goal here is inquiry, the attempt to get at what it is that's so interesting about what's struck me. Because it isn't just beauty; the world is full of lovely things and that in itself wouldn't compel me to write. There's something else, some gravity or charge to this image that makes me need to investigate it.

Exploratory description, then; I'm a scientist trying to measure and record what's seen. The first two sentences of the poem attempt sheer observation, but by the second's list of tropes (abalone, soapbubble skin, oil on a puddle) it's clear to me that these descriptive terms aren't merely there to chronicle the physical reality of the object. Like all descriptions, they reflect the psychic state of the observer; they aren't "neutral," though they might pretend to be, but instead suggest a point of view, a stance toward what is being seen. In this case one of the things suggested by these tropes is interchangeability; if you've seen one abalone shell or prismy soapbubble or psychedelic puddle, you've seen them all.

And thus my image began to unfold for me, in the evidence these terms provided, and I had a clue toward the focus my poem would take. Another day, another time in my life, the mackerel might have been metaphor for something else; they might have served as the crux for an entirely different examination. But now I began to see why they mattered for *this* poem, and the sentence that follows commences the poem's investigative process:

> Splendor, and splendor,
> and not a one in any way
>
> distinguished from the other
> —nothing about them
> of individuality.

There's a terrific kind of exhilaration for me at this point in the unfolding of a poem, when a line of questioning has been launched, and the work has moved from evocation to meditation. A direction is coming clear, and it bears within it the energy that the image contained for me in the first pace. Now, I think, we're getting down to it. This élan carried me along through two more sentences, one that considers the fish as replications of the ideal, Platonic Mackerel, and one that likewise imagines them as the intricate creations of an obsessively repetitive jeweler.

Of course my process of unfolding the poem wasn't quite this neat. There were false starts, wrong turnings that I wound up throwing out when they didn't seem to lead anywhere. I can't remember now, because the poem has worked the charm of its craft on my memory; it convinces me that it is an artifact of a process of inquiry. The drama of the poem is its action of thinking through a question. Mimicking a sequence of perceptions and meditation, it tries to make us think that this feeling and thinking and knowing is taking place even as the poem is being written. Which, in a way, it *is*—just not this neatly or seamlessly! A poem is always a *made* version of experience.

Also, needless to say, my poem was full of repetitions, weak lines, unfinished phrases and extra descriptions, later trimmed; I like to work on a computer, because I can type quickly, put everything in, and still read the results later on, which isn't always true of my handwriting. I *did* feel early on that the poem seemed to want to be a short-lined one; I liked breaking the movement of these extended sentences over the clipped line, and the spotlight-bright focus the short line puts on individual terms felt right. "Iridescent, watery," for instance, pleased me as a line-unit, as did this stanza:

> prismatics: think abálone,
> the wildly rainbowed
> miror of a soapbubble sphere,

Short lines underline sonic textures, heightening tension. The short a's of *prismatics* and *abalone* ring more firmly, as do the o's of *abalone*, *rainbowed* and *soapbubble*. The rhyme of mirror and sphere at beginning and end of line engages me, and I'm also pleased by the way in which these short lines slow the poem down, parceling it out as it were to the reader, with the frequent pauses introduced by the stanza breaks between tercets adding lots of white space, a meditative pacing.

And there, on the jeweler's bench, my poem seemed to come to rest, though it was clear there was more to be done. Some further pressure needed to be placed on the poem's material to force it to yield its depths. I waited a while, I read it over. Again, in what I had already written, the clues contained in image pushed the poem forward.

Soul, heaven . . . The poem had already moved into the realm of theology, but the question that arose ("Suppose we could iridesce . . .") startled me nonetheless, because the notion of losing oneself "entirely in the universe/ of shimmer" referred both to these fish and to something quite other, something overwhelmingly close to home. The poem was written some six months after my partner of a dozen years had died of AIDS, and of course everything I wrote—everything I *saw*—was informed by that loss, by the overpowering emotional force of it. Epidemic was the central fact of the community in which I lived. Naively, I hadn't realized that my mackerel were already of a piece with the work I'd been writing for the previous couple of years—poems that wrestled, in one way or another, with the notion of limit, with the line between being someone and no one. What did it mean to be a self, when that self

would be lost? To praise the collectivity of the fish, their common iden-
tity as "flashing participants," is to make a sort of anti-elegy, to suggest
that what matters is perhaps not our individual selves but our brief sol-
diering in the broad streaming school of humanity — which is composed
of us, yes, but also goes on without us.

The one of a kind, the singular, like my dear lover, cannot last.

And yet the collective life, which is also us, shimmers on.

Once I realized the poem's subject-beneath-the-subject, the final
stanzas of the poem opened swifly out from there. The collective mo-
mentum of the fish is such that even death doesn't seem to still rob
its forward movement; the singularity of each fish more or less doesn't
really exist, it's "all for all," like the Three Musketeers. I could not
have considered these ideas "nakedly," without the vehicle of mackerel
to help me think about human identity. Nor, I think, could I have ad-
dressed these things without a certain playfulness of tone, which ap-
peared first in the archness of "oily fabulation" and the neologism of
"iridesce." It's the blessed permission distance gives that allows me to
speak of such things at all; a little comedy can also help to hold terrific
anxiety at bay. Thus the "rainbowed school/ and its acres of brilliant
classrooms" is a joke, but one that's already collapsing on itself, since
what is taught there — the limits of "me" — is our hardest lesson. No verb
is singular because it is the school that acts, or the tribe, the gruop, the
species; or every verb is singular because the only I there *is* is a we.

The poem held one more surprise for me, which was the final state-
ment — it came as a bit of a shock, actually, and when I'd written it I
knew I was done. It's a formulation of the theory that the poem has
been moving toward all along: that our glory is not our individuality
(much as we long for the Romantic self and its private golden heights)
but our commonness. I do not like this idea. I would rather be one fish,
sparkling in my own pond, but experience does not bear this out. And
so I have tried to convince myself, here, that beauty lies in the whole
and that therefore death, the loss of the part, is not so bad — is in, fact,
almost nothing. What does our individual disappearance mean — or our
love, or our desire — when, as the Marvelettes put it, "There's too many
fish in the sea . . . ?"

I find this consoling, strangely, and maybe that's the best way to
think of this poem — an attempt at cheering oneself up about the mys-
tery of being both an individual and part of a group, an attempt on the
part of the speaker in the poem (me) to convince himself that losing
individuality, slipping into the life of the world, could be a good thing.
All attempts to console ourselves, I believe, are doomed, because the
world is more complicated than we are. Our explanations will fail, but
it is our human work to make them. And my beautiful fish, limited

though they may be as parable, do help me; they are an image I return to in order to remember, in the face of individual erasures, the burgeoning, good, common life. Even after my work of inquiry, my metaphor may still know more than I do; the bright eyes of those fish gleam on, in memory, brighter than what I've made of them.

RITA DOVE

Parsley

1. The Cane Fields

There is a parrot imitating spring
in the palace, its feathers parsley green.
Out of the swamp the cane appears

to haunt us, and we cut it down. El General
searches for a word; he is all the world
there is. Like a parrot imitating spring,

we lie down screaming as rain punches through
and we come up green. We cannot speak an R—
out of the swamp, the cane appears

and then the mountain we call in whispers *Katalina*.
The children gnaw their teeth to arrowheads.
There is a parrot imitating spring.

El General has found his word: *perejil*.
Who says it, lives. He laughs, teeth shining
out of the swamp. The cane appears

in our dreams, lashed by wind and streaming.
and we lie down. For every drop of blood
there is a parrot imitating spring.
Out of the swamp the cane appears.

2. The Palace

The word the general's chosen is parsley.
It is fall, when thoughts turn
to love and death; the general thinks
of his mother, how she died in the fall
and he planted her walking cane at the grave
and it flowered, each spring stolidly forming
four-star blossoms. The general

pulls on his boots, he stomps to
her room in the palace, the one without

curtains, the one with a parrot
in a brass ring. As he paces he wonders
Who can I kill today. And for a moment
the little knot of screams
is still. The parrot, who has traveled

all the way from Australia in an ivory
cage, is, coy as a widow, practicing
spring. Ever since the morning
his mother collapsed in the kitchen
while baking skull-shaped candies
for the Day of the Dead, the general
has hated sweets. He orders pastries
brought up for the bird; they arrive

dusted with sugar on a bed of lace.
The knot in his throat starts to twitch;
he sees his boots the first day in battle
splashed with mud and urine
as a soldier falls at his feet amazed—
how stupid he looked!—at the sound
of artillery. *I never thought it would sing*
the soldier said, and died. Now

the general sees the fields of sugar
cane, lashed by rain and streaming.
He sees his mother's smile, the teeth
gnawed to arrowheads. He hears
the Haitians sing without R's
as they swing the great machetes:
Katalina, they sing, *Katalina*,

mi madle, mi amol en muelte. God knows
his mother was no stupid woman; she
could roll an R like a queen. Even
a parrot can roll an R! In the bare room
the bright feathers arch in a parody
of greenery, as the last pale crumbs
disappear under the blackened tongue. Someone

calls out his name in a voice
so like his mother's, a startled tear
splashes the tip of his right boot.

My mother, my love in death.
The general remembers the tiny green sprigs
men of his village wore in their capes
to honor the birth of a son. He will
order many, this time, to be killed

for a single, beautiful word.

Writing "Parsley"

For me, part of the trick to writing poems often is to pretend that poetry is the last thing on my mind. The faintest whiff of self-consciousness, the slightest touch of Portent—and the poem scampers away like a spooked deer. And so the task of describing how one such poem came to be snared on the page is a mission charged with equivocation and doomed to partial failure; I can proceed allegorically at most, tacking the course of the creative journey through insinuation and anecdote.

One Saturday in 1980, I was sitting with other writers in a bookshop in West Berlin, when a book on the opposite side of the room caught my eye. I might not have noticed this book if I hadn't been slightly bored by the literary gossip of our group, many of whom had been meeting for brunch every Saturday for years—actually, a brunch consisting of nothing more than champagne and strong coffee, laced with the pungent strains of chain-smoked unfiltered cigarettes. Gasping for fresh air, I got up and crossed the room.

The book was oversized, displayed at hip level on a shelf of art books. I was intrigued not only by its striking coloration—brilliant green on white—but by its peculiar title as well: PETERSILIE—which, in English, means parsley. What could a book with such a title possibly be about?

Hubert Fichte, a respected German novelist, was the author. The book was studded with photographs of palm trees and tanks; the accompanying text chronicled the atrocities committed during the reign of General Raphael Trujillo, longtime dictator of the Dominican Republic. And the title? On the frontispiece, finally, I found Fichte's laconic explanation: On October 2, 1937, Trujillo had ordered 20,000 Haitian cane workers executed because they could not roll the "R" in *perejil*, the Spanish word for parsley.

That was it; no further explanation of why the general chose this particular word, or what the Haitians were doing in the Dominican Republic in the first place. No mention of the French Creole spoken by the Haitians that rendered their "R's" softly guttural, incapable of fluttering at the tip of the tongue. No description of the kind of execution, what instruments were used and how quickly the terror proceeded, no clue to the General's state of mind at the time. Just the bald facts: 20,000 dead, over a word.

I jotted this into my notebook. I had no intention of writing a poem on the subject—the magnitude of the horror, coupled with a graduate school-acquired dislike of "political poetry," frightened me off. But I have one rule concerning my notebook entries, and it is this: No matter how arcane or silly or scary or unsuitable an event or thought might be . . . if it can stop me in my tracks, it goes in, no questions asked.

Each time I stumbled onto this entry during the next few months, I was troubled anew. I simply could not skip over this story and forget about it; the sheer inventiveness of cruelty, the supple brilliance of the deed, stunned me. I had always felt that Evil was some monstrous but essentially alien power; I had not counted on Evil being . . . interesting. And since I could not reconcile these ideas with my perception of the world, I needed first to double-check Mr. Fichte's scholarship.

It took me a while, but I finally found corroboration of the parsley massacre in an American historical text. Now that the incident was undeniable, I realized I had to confront it poetically in order to put it to rest. But how? For once, I had the facts; I was not imagining a dramatic situation, or recasting a personal memory into imagery; this was as real as it got. How could I grasp something this big, this monstrous?

By going back to the beginning, and by starting small. I remembered what first attracted me about Fichte's book: its colors, white and green. Not Kelly or pea or Nile or lime green, but that elemental vegetal hue, cut with a bit of sunlight. What else was parsley green?—not grass, not leaves. I found myself looking everywhere for that color; more than a year after my first notebook entry, I finally found it.

It was now 1981 and I was living in Arizona, a month or so into my first full-time university position. Friends had invited us to a picnic on the Pima Indian Reservation, just south of Phoenix, and it was while sitting in Betty Perez's trailer, waiting for the ice chests to be loaded into the back of the pickup, that I looked at their pet parrot and found, along the red-tipped wings, that precise green. Betty's parrot was amazing: It could imitate anyone and anything—other birds, water dripping, the slam of a screen door. Suddenly a line floated into my head: *The parrot imitated spring.* I went to the bathroom and wrote it down. I also wrote down the equation: *parrot = parsley green.* Then I shut the notebook, joined the picnic, and waited.

Waited for Fate to call. Now, I don't believe in divine intervention or anything like that—I merely hoped that, if I kept my eyes and ears open, details would gradually accrue that would help me find my way into the poem. Whether I was up to the challenge of writing that poem remained to be seen; first, though, I had to discover the hinge that would swing open onto its psychic landscape.

I entered the world of the poem through color, and then through the image of a parrot recreating spring for itself. Later that weekend, a flurry of free-association exercises produced a few more possibilities, which I shaped into a silhouette:

> The parrot imitated spring.
>
> It was as green as parsley.
> El General rehearsed it all morning
> until; he even heard the swish
> of eucalyptus. He'd been once
>
> to Italy . . .
>   he was an average man
> in average shoes (no boots no whip)
> —in fact he even bit his thumb
> when he wasn't thinking (unthinkingly).
> He favored inspiration, pale starred petals
> shattered on a rough pine box . . .
> grit and scintillance.

Except for a halfhearted attempt to humanize the dictator, this version delivered *nada*—nothing but a few ill-conceived images of coffins and military boots, a predictable mix of beauty and gore; I was looking over my own shoulder while I was writing. In the margins I scribbled notes to myself like "Ignore the facts," "too pretty," and the curt reprimand: "verbs!" Then I paper-clipped my drafts together (written with ball-point on college-ruled notebook paper) and put them in the desk drawer for a while.

About once a week I leafed through the poem fragments in my drawer, each time trying to continue but failing. I began to obsess on another question of fact. My opening line had developed into: *There is a parrot imitating spring in the palace*—but then I was stumped again: Were there totally green parrots? I could not continue until I knew for sure. I scoured the library stacks and skimmed enough ornithological texts to satisfy a lifetime of birdwatching, but no green parrot could I find. There were blue-black mynahs and blue gold macaws; there were yellow-fronted Amazons and even the green and violet Imperial parrots, native to Dominica—but no pure green parrot, far and wide.

Then came one of the moments you cannot dare dream of. One afternoon before class, a student rang my office; she was downtown, stuck at the pet shop where she worked because the store owner was late and the new parrot could not be left alone in the shop—could she bring the bird to class? "He's very well behaved," she assured me.

"Of course you can bring him," I replied, "but there's a catch."

The parrot was a perfect gentlebird; he paraded up and down the length of the conference table, occasionally picking up a stray pencil and depositing it before my student; the class was enchanted. A couple of days later, the trainer-student called to report that she had checked into the existence of green parrots and there was indeed such a species in Australia, which was entirely—deliciously—green.

"Great! Thank you," I exclaimed, then immediately sunk into despair. Australia! How in the world was I going to get an Australian parrot to the Dominican Republic? What an extravagance that would have been, what a mad display of power! Most likely the parrot would have been shipped in an equally extravagant container, a cage of gold or even . . . ivory:

> The parrot, who has traveled
> all the way from Australia in an ivory
> cage is, coy as a widow, practising
> spring.

At this point I dove into the soothing waters of further research, studying the geographical and climatic conditions of the lesser Antilles, learning more than I hope I'll ever need to know about the growing and harvesting of sugarcane. Some of that newfound knowledge, such as the fact that gnawing sugarcane can erode your teeth to sharp points, made it into the final version of the poem; most of it merely stoked the embers. In order not to be overwhelmed by the abomination of the historical event I latched onto the reassuring scaffolding of form, employing the interlocking refrains of the villanelle to echo the repetitive horror of the execution (*Step up, speak up, die: Next!*); in order to work out the totemic power of certain images, I took key words (parrot, spring, general, green) to build the skeleton of a sestina.

The villanelle practically wrote itself. I already had its opening 1½ lines. Since I was missing the conclusion of the middle line, I simply skipped to the third line, which sprang full blown from my pen without a bit of help from me—

> There is a parrot imitating spring
> in the palace, _____
> Out of the swamp, the cane appears

—and then the Haitians began to speak for themselves, their terrifyingly gentle and patient whispers rising from the rain-soaked fields.

After five or six drafts, the villanelle was pretty much ready to be shown. The sestina, on the other hand, was rapidly turning into a disaster. (I've never been able to write a decent sestina, but I keep trying.) Here, for the sake of humility, is an early draft:

Who is singing in the palace?
What is it that stands so green
among the curtains? Out in the cane-
fields, the Haitians pause their knives. Spring
is (still) half a world away. El General
must be in love! Or it is a parrot

that imitates the voice of a woman, a parrot
who sings of love in the palace,
whose world is a large brass ring. El General
paces, furious and bored. The green
ribbon he wears in his lapel is a reminder of the spring
his mother died, a simple soul with a cane

who never learned Spanish, who gnawed on sugarcane
in secret, who wept when he went out in crowds. The parrot
was her; it reminds him of spring
and yet he cannot bear to throw it out of the palace
window and watch it float, a squawking green
bouquet, out over the swamp. Furious, el General

paces.

And so on, ad nauseam. But imbedded in this convoluted narrative, this self-conscious array of semiprecious images, are several essential elements that were not there before: the general's mother and her cane, and the green ribbon in the General's lapel.

So I abandoned the sestina, reread the villanelle aloud to convince myself that it was enough, then typed up a pristine copy and put it on my husband's desk for his no-nonsense prose-writer's eye. When he emerged from his study, head cocked slightly to one side, I could tell something was wrong. He handed back the page; I caught myself clenching my fists and tried, unsuccessfully, to fight down the belligerence rising to cover my frustration. "It's beautiful." He paused. "But that's not all, is there?"

"What do you mean, that's not all?" I blurted. "How can there be more? They're all dead!"

"Yeah, I know." Another pause. "Don't tell me that's *everything*."

I stomped back to my room, but I knew he was right. (And he, dear man, let me go. Years before we had made a pact concerning the critiquing of each other's work: All tantrums and protests were not to be taken personally; the tantrum-thrower, for his or her part, was never to resort to personally tinted retorts such as "What do you know, you're just a poet/fiction writer!" If either of these rules were ever violated, all mutual critiquing would be abandoned.)

Time passed. I was back to my weekly review of the poem, whose drafts were now numerous enough to warrant their own red plastic folder. I will never be so arrogant as to pretend that I know how a poem finally comes into being, but I'd just about resigned myself to failure when one evening, while alphabetizing the books in my study, I muttered "to hell with poetry," took out my notebook, and began to write in prose. I was hunkered down next to the bookshelf, scribbling madly away, until my aching knees forced me to continue at the desk:

The word the general's chosen is Parsley—*perejil*. How he found it is ———; it is spring, when thoughts turn to love and death, and in the General thoughts of his mother & death, how she died in spring and her cane planted above the grave which flowered each spring, its stolid 4-piece (doggy) blossoms. So the general pulled on his boots to make his thighs strong, he stomped to her room in the palace, the one with no curtains and a parrot in a brass ring (brought by boat all the way from Australia) & he paced as he wondered/thought who can I kill today. And the little knot of screams in his throat is still, for a moment.

After that evening, as my father used to say, "it was all over but the shouting." Oh, there were still revisions ahead, but I had cracked the code: Even though I had no idea how this poem was going to end, how I was going to explain the General's choice of that particular word, I wrote confidently toward the ending I knew would be there—heartbreaking, inevitable—when I'd be strong enough to meet it. And nearly two years after that first sighting in the bookstore, I returned to Hubert Fichte's title, which first pulled me from the circle of writers that spring day in Berlin: *Petersilie*. Petersilie, perejil, parsley: "a single, beautiful, word."

STEPHEN DUNN

The Guardian Angel

Afloat between lives and stale truths,
    he realizes
he's never truly protected one soul,

they all die anyway, and what good
    is solace,
solace is cheap. The signs are clear:

the drooping wings, the shameless thinking
    about utility
and self. It's time to stop.

The guardian angel lives for a month
    with other angels,
sings the angelic songs, is reminded

that he doesn't have a human choice.
    The angel of love
lies down with him, and loving

restores to him his pure heart.
    Yet how hard it is
to descend into sadness once more.

When the poor are evicted, he stands
    between them
and the bank, but the bank sees nothing

in its way. When the meek are overpowered
    he's there, the thin air
through which they fall. Without effect

he keeps getting in the way of insults.
    He keeps wrapping
his wings around those in the cold.

Even his lamentations are unheard,
    though now,
in for the long haul, trying to live

beyond despair, he believes, he needs
    to believe
everything he does takes root, hums

beneath the surfaces of the world.

"The Guardian Angel"

Whan I consented to write about one of my own poems, I was sure I couldn't say that it was brilliant, or even good, as I might in an essay about someone else's poem. But I wasn't at all sure of what I could, or, more to the point, should say. D. H. Lawrence's admonition about trusting the tale and not the teller came to mind, as well as the well-known eviscerations of paraphrase. After all, doesn't the poem itself say what it says in its chosen, most considered langauge? What could I say about it that wouldn't violate its integrity? Reduce it? In fact, falsify it? On the other hand, in a critical climate such as ours, might it not be refreshing to hear about an author's intentionality, perhaps even make a case for its importance? Yet that felt too defensive. I had no doubt that author's intentionality *did* matter, but also that Lawrence was probably still right.

I think I've always known that to speak after the fact about my work was to create a fiction about it. But I love fictions; they constitute one of the ways in which truth gets approximated. They're among my favorite ways to get the news. "The Guardian Angel" is a fiction itself, and probably can't be harmed by what now will openly be another fiction. If I can write it plausibly, the poem might have a companion. That is, something like itself, but not itself. Maybe as close as a brother, albeit one of those brothers famous in the family for the mischief he brings to the telling of the truth. What follows then is an attempt to recreate how "The Guardian Angel" was composed. Even though it was written over ten years ago, I remember some things about its composition and, in fact, recently, when asked about it, found myself saying something I didn't know I knew. I'll save what that was for the end.

I like to talk about the composition of poems as involving a series of allegiances that we keep as long as we can, but that we're likely to modify and refine as the poem starts to insist upon itself. My initial allegiance was to creating a secular angel, which soon thereafter became a disaffected Guardian Angel. That was the poem's first discovery. I vaguely remember discarding all the language and claims (two or three stanza's worth of warm-up) that had gotten me to that discovery, and beginning right away with his disaffectedness. At this point, it became a *what if* poem. What if there was a disaffected angel? How would he act? What would he be thinking? I had two allegiances now, to serious play with his disaffection and to the imaginative logic that would be its grease. And a drama was unfolding. He was, by definition, a do-gooder, and now was thinking only of self. Worse, he was thinking of results, as if he could be the arbiter of what a result was. Wasn't that for Someone else to decide? I was starting to become interested in him. But only in him. I had no idea yet of what else might be driving the poem.

I suppose the next lines became available to me because I was at a writer's colony. The angel seeks out his own kind, is restored by them, especially by the angel of love who, by example, is able to remind him of generosity and its worth. Prior to these moments, my compositional possibilities were wide open. Now I had narrowed them by choosing to have him healed. He might have been an interesting renegade, confrontational and subversive, disruptive of the established order. He might have wanted a new identity, an angel's job that required less of him. I'm sure I could have written in either of those directions and others. We learn, as Roethke says, by going where we go.

I can't remember if, around this time, I half knew that I was taking him on a rather classical religious journey; that he would lose his way before he found his way, that a passage was involved. Certainly it was apparent to me later. Play will only get us so far. If it hadn't gotten me to some locus of concern, I might very well have been in a purely fanciful poem, perhaps one full of the pleasures of invention, but which essentially is an exercise, whose destiny at best is the tour de force. But I had arrived at some principle of selection, something that could help me find the poem's next moment. And I suspect that I only half knew this principle, and therefore—without becoming too purposeful—could ride its uncodified energy. I had, though, these allegiances to keep: to the poem's adjusted original impulse, to the texture and rhythm of the language used so far, *and* to this new governing drift.

I wasn't conscious (or was I?) of coming up with a series of tests for his new-found resolve, but that's what I did. I was still very much in a *what if* mode. Okay, he comes back to earth. What's likely to be his experience? I was as much committed to a series of interesting failures as I was to a recurrence of his ineffectuality per se. And I was certainly as much committed to rhythm as I was to being interesting, and may have known there couldn't be the latter without the former. Which is to say that content decisions were inseparable from decisions about syntax and rhythm. Earlier perhaps I could have let content alone drive the poem. But no longer. I had promises to keep. Of course there were still various content options available to me. I could have allowed him, say, one success. That would have set the poem on a slightly different course. In this case, what I ended up *not* selecting was instructive. It, too, pointed the way.

By now, perhaps, the poem was leaning into its structure, though in a more localized sense of arrangement it had already found its form. (For a few years, around this time, that step-down three-line stanza had been a way for me to harness and discipline my discursive inclinations.) Structurally, so far, the poem had three movements: the introduction of the disaffected angel, his resurrection into new resolve, and his return to duty, which proved to be no more successful than before. Whatever mixture of intellection and obsession was driving the poem was now calling for a fourth movement. That it would turn out to be the poem's last has to do with that sense of sufficiency and arrival, which are among the mysteries of closure. The poet's temperament and compositional tics are always involved in that mystery, not to mention his ambitiousness, and all of that is mixed with the overt promptings and inner weather of his poem. I was aware of less than half of these.

It would be inaccurate for me to say I *chose* to have him live with his ineffectuality. I don't think I ever considered having him quit again, which now seems like a reasonable option. It just felt right to have him find a way to continue in spite of repeated failure. I didn't know why. I was in fact following dictates that were subterranean. I knew I had moved him from disaffection, but to what? Acceptance? Resignation? A desperate hopefulness? Maybe all of those. It seemed a place to stop.

That's one fiction. Another, which will be even less coherent and therefore, I think, closer to the truth, is that the poem was composed during many sittings, had many false starts, much extraneous language, and had its stanzas in various orders. Parts of it, as I vaguely remember, were cargoed in from other poems, the failed poems that most of us save and steal from. I revised it over a period of months, and many of the revisions were arrived at because of the exigencies of rhythm and the seeking of cooperative sounds, what weight of language a stanza could bear, and other considerations that had more to do with problem solving than with genesis. At some point I was seeking that recognizable and followable thread, famously invisible when the poem isn't right, which if found gives you a chance of creating that illusion of orderliness and authority without which there is no poem. I think it starts to become visible the more the poem's surface felicities and the pulse of its undercurrents get in some concordance with one another. I found it at some point, and, as Stafford said we should, pulled it through. Composition by excavation and lifeline. I take credit for recognizing it in among the rubble and loose ends. The digging was simply my job.

Now, having said this, I recognize that from the start I was the god of this universe, and had considerable time before book publication—cool, considered time—to assay and evaluate all of my choices, conscious and unconscious. I am responsible for everything in it, and could, had I been foolishly or even perhaps wisely willful, have changed its direction, pulled the thread through to a different conclusion, made it happier, sadder, etc. My overriding allegiance was to the poem as a whole (what Larry Levis calls "its rings of flesh") and to none of its individual rings unles they contributed to that whole, to the poem therefore as fiction—something distilled and framed and held vibrantly still for others to bring themselves to. Finally, we leave or abandon our poems because no more aesthetic decisions seem available to us that will help enact or explore our subject. At least I could think of none before "The Guardian Angel" found its way into *Between Angels*.

But "finally" is premature. Several years after the poem was written, I was visiting a colleague's classroom where some of my poems were under discussion. She was, in fact, teaching *Between Angels*. One of the students asked if I would read then comment on "The Guardian Angel." I might have told him something like what I've just said, but I hadn't read the poem in quite a while, and as I read it it seemed clear to me what my hidden subject had been, though I didn't know I had a hidden subject. I smiled as I told the class that the poem is an analogue of the poet's condition in America, a smile of recognition and of the absurdities of self-knowledge. The poet does his job, I said, and hardly anybody listens. All his life he lives with his ineffectuality, his invisible presence, the reality that poetry makes nothing happen. But

> . . . trying to live
>
> beyond despair, he believes, he needs
>   to believe,
> everything he does take root, hums
>
> beneath the surfaces of the world.

There it was, my dogged optimism, my little anthem for continuing on. This "what if" poem, this verbal construct that had found enough about itself to sustain the angel's journey from disaffection to endurance was a personal poem after all. This hidden subject, I was sure, was what had been the poem's driving force, its secret glue.

But wait. If what I just said is convincing, there's one more wrinkle. If the poem's hidden subject and the thread I pulled through are similar, as they now seem to have been, then how can what I said about locating the invisible thread be plausible? How can I have pulled through a thread that I didn't become conscious of until years later? There seem to be two possibilities, neither of which excludes the other. That the thread itself is no more than a metaphor for what happens when a poem reaches a satisfactory conclusion. Or that in fact I did it, I pulled it through while thinking only of an angel's problems, and that such things happen and take their not unfamiliar places among the mysteries of composition.

Trust the tale.

JOHN ENGELS

The Silence

The one child having in manner of speaking fled,
his brother ran out to the porch to call him back;
Philip! he cried out, *Philip!* I caught him up,
thinking if ever the dead were to be recalled

it would be in a similar voice flung confident
into that raving light. Since then
each fall when the woods have darkened with color
the horror has been absurdly to wonder

if I in my sternest father's voice
had commanded into the bloodied gullet of the day
Come back! Come back! he might have heard.
But up on the hill

the pines had strained to a power of wind.
Come back! I might have cried, but I did not,
and silence stormed. Meanwhile
he is speechless, dark, of no intent.

"The Silence": Life Through the

Lens of Structure

The Silence" was written some fifteen years after the death of our infant son, whom the night before he died I had heard crying in his bed, and who in the morning, while I was on the phone, was discovered by his mother, who came to me and said, "The baby is dead." I dropped the phone, and she said, "The baby is dead." My seven-year-old daughter, whose room was directly above the telephone, and open to the downstairs through a heat register, heard this, and the other children, six and four years old, hearing the strangeness of our voices, came running in, wanting to know what was wrong.

And being American, I resorted to euphemism. "Philip's *gone*," I blurted out, whereupon the four-year-old, my son John, ran to the front porch and shouted into the woods (where to his mind little children became lost), "*Philip, come back!*" It overcame me. My wife stood, still unmoving, by the dangling telephone, and I ran out on the porch and caught him up and carried him into the house — which by then, having undergone some weird contraction of time, was filling with neighbors, friends, a priest from the college where I taught . . . the colleague to whom I had been speaking on the phone had heard everything, and had undertaken to save us. But we could not be saved, though I tried my best in the only way I knew how, which was to find a name for what had happened to us.

I've written many poems about this child's death over the years, the first in 1967, and the last in 1986. They have addressed in one way or another my sense of responsibility for what is right or wrong in the world of my family — in this case, somehow or other, clearly I had not responded properly, should have done something — not mistaken the child's night cries for something ordinary, a damp diaper, a little dream — done something, anything, perhaps asserted my paternal authority.

In between the first and last poems came several others, one, a long poem of direct address, which concluded, ". . . look back from the white field / on the place you used to live," another that said, "what color we remember, burns inward from the eye," one that cried out "Oh, our children die beyond our seeing, always . . ." and an anniversary poem that ended in self-rebuke:

> . . . *how could I not have known*? Even
> in the dark as I lay in my bed about to sleep, and the child's cry
> came and when it came
> was nothing, nothing, only
> the ordinary voice in its unexceptionable lament
> from some darkness of this old
> and powerfully retentive house . . .

and more, many more that I have never been able to resolve, and have long since abandoned.

Like any poet, I've always given much thought to the ways in which forms are revivifications of life, in their peculiar ways participating in the lives they reimagine, actual human lives, in all their patterns of thought and feeling—the poem in its being changing the world, and, being part of the changing world, itself perpetually changing. Thus it is, perhaps, that these poems about this child's death have been poems of more than usually strong endings, and, furthermore, endings that have seemed to me *given*, whether centering on allusion or on what may be allusion or actual quotation in the final line of "The Silence."

Something happened when I was finally able to address the issue. I—who had always gloried in the big noise, the hyperbolic, the alogical and adjunct, in what Henry Rago once called (speaking of one of my poems) the "overwrought and over-wrought," in what I now consider to have been an affected elegance—I could not work that way with this subject, and have not been able to work in the old way since. The death poems came out, with one exception, quite strictly formed. In fact in 1968 I was accused by a reviewer of "trivializing" the subject matter by framing it conventionally.

Of all of the poems I've written about my son's death, this one has sustained itself best for me for over twenty years now, in fact remains capable of moving me so that I find it at times positively dangerous to read aloud. I suppose that if I were able to regard this poem from any kind of distance, I might concentrate on some of the technical elements.

But I approach the assignment to talk about this poem from a somewhat different necessity. I like this poem for its simplicity, by which I do not deny its complexity. I simply mean that it is true, that is, alive to me, with nothing in the way of demonstration, show, or spectacle. But by this I don't mean that I was not consciously *crafting* a poem.

And that deeply troubled me. "Art in the light of conscience," Marina Svetaeva said, and my conscience told me that I was, in *making* something of this terrible event, *exploiting* it.

Robert Lowell, commenting on "Skunk Hour," declares that "The author of a poem is not necessarily the ideal person to explain its meaning . . . [which] varies in importance from poem to poem . . ." but is always "only a strand and an element in the brute flow of composition." He goes on, "For all this the author is an opportunist, throwing whatever comes to hand into his feeling for start, continuity, contrast, climax, and completion," concluding "It is imbecile for him not to know his intentions, and unsophisticated for him to know too explicitly and fully."

I suppose what Lowell meant by the poet's *knowing* his or her intentions ought to be fought out here, though there is not space for it. I take some comfort in his disclaimer that it is inappropriate to know them too well. But certainly in writing these poems I did not "know" my intentions at all, never mind "too well."

At the time I saw a poem as no more than an artifact, an *illusion* of reality, a thing derived from the love of things that resembled other things, and were capable of being organized so as to extend themselves somehow to the community. So that in writing this poem I was demonstrating myself to the world. I was playing with words, making analogies, when the great truth, the only truth, was that a child, my child, was dead. How could a poem pretend to the occasion?

There I was concerning myself with sound locks, line breaks, watching tempo, deciding between this word and that, this typography and that, this strophe and that. It seemed impious, blasphemous, a terrible inversion of values.

Perhaps, as my friend Jim Laughlin has suggested, after reading an early draft of this essay, "It may be that your deep misgiving, even loathing, may have arisen less from the idea of the artist exploiting and playing and more from the particular circumstance out of which you wrote. You say more than once that you were dealing with guilt, with a sense of responsibility. In that state it would be hard to avoid wondering whether the writing were being generated to cast some of that off, appeasing the self.

"Another factor may be that your son was so young that it denied you the route of most elegizers/eulogizers—in some way honoring and celebrating the individual life by recounting or at least gesturing to that person's tangible and spiritual contributions to the community. How to speak of one who has barely begun that process? Isn't the speaker left focusing on the self, on his reaction to the loss versus the person lost?" Perhaps.

But I went on with it, and finished the poem, the last line coming to me so wholly and immediately that I have always suspected it of being either given or recollected.

This is, of course, an old story, the notion of the artist as selfish and exploitative, who defeats the monster by naming it, by fixing it against the restlessness of the general background. With these poems about my son's death, I came close to losing faith in poetry. It is not too much to say that I despised myself for what I was doing.

But sometimes friends can save you, as did Jack Beal and Sondra Freckelton, who pointed out to me what in paintings is called the "sacred center," that point in the painting, in the direct center, where what is most important is made manifest by its placement. It is almost a matter of geometry, a way of containing the uncontainable, of confining its energy almost, but not quite, to the point of the intolerable.

Jack speaks of Caravaggio's painting of the death of the Virgin, which was criticized by its patrons as presenting the Virgin as resembling a drowned whore . . . she lies on the bed, unassumed, her arm dangling over the edge, "reduced," they felt, to the "merely" human.

Perhaps. Perhaps I approached my subject in the same spirit as the painter—to reimagine the form and energy of event, to directly access the preverbal sensibility. Perhaps "The Silence" is not history, but a bypassing of circumstance to the dark center of its origin, an assertion of individuality in community, an act of faith against all the evidence of our experience that can be understood by, and understand, others. Perhaps "The Silence" is life focused at its dark center through the lens of structure—not my child's death, though certainly that; not my son's attempt to call him back, though that too; and not my assumption of guilt, though perhaps that above all.

The obligation was necessarily sacramental—some operative principle was inherent in the death of my infant son, and my aim, though I did not realize it, was to clarify that presence, not define or analyze it. Perhaps the making mind that contemplates two simultaneous truths is excused from its customary tasks, and need not abstract from what it views.

In fact in writing "The Silence," my obligation was to see clearly and represent truthfully the configurations of that experience, and to try never to forget the equal necessity to see both ways at the same time, to see the extension of reality to its coincidence with the unseen and contingent, at which point, together with the emergent life of the reader, a new reality would burst into existence. "I wanted to write a poem / ," says Williams, "that you would understand. / For what good is it to me / if you can't understand it?"

"The Silence" is an effort at understanding and providing understanding, of grasping the essence of this particular reality thing by discovering in me its communal name. This poem is what I present to you in the hope that you will bring to meet it your suffering and helplessness, so that between us will coalesce a new reality, an icon of suffering, grief, helplessness, guilt.

"The Silence," like any good poem, ends properly in mystery and, I think, in what Mahler referred to as that dead silence that follows on the stroke of the muffled drum, a silence that extends itself gradually beyond the possibility of the world, but that we in perfect faith recognize as extending itself in infinite diminuendo, much as a flashlight pointed into the sky propels its beam beyond visibility into an interminable voyage through space.

This life-making struggle between the personal and the general plenitudes manifests itself throughout the whole fabric of "The Silence," the whole fabric of any poem—line against sentence, strophe against syntactical continuity, rhyme against expectation, the obliquities of figurative language against "plain seeing" and "straight thought." And, most of all, the simultaneous exclusiveness of the poem and its passionate and incontrovertible longings to inform, monumentalize, fix for all time, affirm, become its pure potency.

The ultimate life of the poem lies here, in its organization of life according to the necessities of our conscious being. The life of the poem arises from our various and perpetual struggles to maintain form against the apparent formlessness of the natural plenitudes, which we so easily allow to confound, even render inoperative, that which is whole, harmonious and intelligible—to assume, absorb, subsume.

Scorn

She thought of no wilder delicacy than the starling eggs she fed him
    for breakfast,
and if he sat and ate like a farmhand and she hated him sometimes,
she knew it didn't matter: that whatever in the din of argument
was harshly spoken, something else was done, soothed and patted
    away.
When they were young the towering fierceness
of their differences had frightened her even as she longed for physical
    release.
Out of their mouths such curses; their hands huge, pointing, stabbing
    the air.
How had they *not* been wounded? And wounded they'd convalesced in
    the same rooms
and bed. When at last they knew everything without confiding—fears,
    stinks,
boiling hearts—they gave up themselves a little so that they might
    both love and scorn
each other, and they ate from each other's hands.

Starling Eggs

I know some people whose pets have too much personality—more, perhaps than the people have. And I've heard introductions at readings that have made the poems seem pale by comparison. I hope to avoid this sort of problem by revealing nothing especially remarkable about the composition of "Scorn," nothing more complicated, or simple, than what the poem already suggests.

The early resistance to expression I felt in the composition of the eleven-line poems I began to write in 1991 seemed to give way by the time I wrote "Scorn," three years later. I must have sorted through the difficulties inherent in keeping to a set of rules and aesthetic principles because the kind of lyric I was trying to write began to feel familiar. I'm not sure what I felt I knew, though, beyond the sense that I could afford to expose the art of the poem to the contradictions and complexities of experience, where earlier I felt hard-pressed to meet the, more or less, formal requirements of length (eleven lines) and lineation (long) in ways that could sustain my and the audience's interest. What I mean by this is that I could play with the shape, creating the room—in each poem a different sort of room—for the dramatic process to unfold, and at the same time I knew how to work through the various tensions set up in the eleven lines. When the poem ended, the logic wasn't concluded so much as a variety of dramatic forces and of attitudes was brought into equilibrium, often tipped toward irony. Naturally, I'm talking about the nine or ten out of nineteen that succeeded that late spring. I tear up or otherwise rid myself of the failures, failures I *finish* so I can figure out what went wrong in the poem before I destroy it.

She thought of no wilder delicacy than the starling eggs
she fed him for breakfast, / & she was sorry she'd broken
        & if   & ate   the yolks,

~~she told him so.~~ H̶ he sat like a farmhand, ~~& ate~~
~~whole~~   & she hated him   ~~not looking~~
                    sometimes,   ~~up from the~~
                                          ~~plate~~
                                       ~~with a clatter~~
she knew it didn't matter: that ~~there was a sense in which~~
                              ~~whatever~~ in the din of argument
~~& desecration of~~   whatever   ~~& desecrations~~
                             ~~smoothed~~ soothed & patted away.
                        done
~~there were moments~~   something else ~~reversed~~
        spoken
was harshly ~~said~~   ~~there were moments whose~~   ~~to~~
                      ~~unmoved~~   ~~which~~
                    towering
When they were young the fierceness / of their differences had frightened her
                                Out of their
even as she longed for an almost physical release/ ~~How she cursed~~
                                       mouths
        their   ~~pointing,~~   stabbing
such curses~~, and~~ hands, huge, ~~pointing, gripping~~ the air: /
                                       ~~doors slammed.~~
8   ~~Then one day~~   been   And wounded they'd convalesced
How had they *not* wounded? ~~Yet~~   ~~they~~   ~~together~~
                                      in the same rooms & bed.
9   they
And when at last, ~~she~~ knew everything without confiding—fears
              ~~& could remain~~   stinks,
10 ~~scorn &~~ boiling hearts— ~~they became as two~~
                             ~~loving and scornful~~
                they gave up themselves, so that they might both love &
                    ~~(a little)~~   scorn
11   each other
and they ate from each other's hands. ~~& they were rarely~~

In the yellow paper tablet from June 1994, "Scorn" appears on a single page in nearly completed form. Two pages later "Joy" appears, also on a single page. The difference between the two is that for "Joy" I had decided upon the basic metaphoric equivalence before I wrote the poem. At the top of the page I'd written "joy-ark." For "Scorn" I'd had no initiating idea or emotion, and no metaphor to focus my concerns. The day before, though, my husband had removed a nest from the cone of our satellite dish and retrieved three small, speckled eggs. I don't remember whose idea it was that we cook them. What was one to do with eggs from the discarded nest? It takes as long to boil a starling egg as a chicken egg. Fried, the tiny starling eggs taste neither more nor less intense than farmer's eggs. Well, my husband ate them, and that became the beginning of a poem the next day.

The few changes in the poem seem chiefly to concern my sense that much of a narrative can be suppressed. "Not looking up from the plate" gives us more of the tangible scene but is unnecessary and even, perhaps, a distraction from the lyric impulse. Where, though, might the detail "she was sorry she'd broken the yolks, / she told him so" have led? At the time it seemed to be too bland, as if a potential dramatic tension had been drained away at the moment of its introduction. I suppose that the line, however, may well have given me an idea for the discrete tension for this poem. It has always seemed to me that a poem's tensions must be significant enough so that their reconciliation matters. For it isn't enough only to unify a poem; in poetry harmony and discord exist together. "Scorn" starts in one dramatic position, the speaker giving the man something, and quickly introduces a change, even contradiction, in "she hated him sometimes." If the poem works, it works, I think, in paradox, in the struggle of opposites all through the poem—"wilder delicacy," "was harshly spoken[,] something else [was] done[,] soothed and patted away," "frightened her / even as she longed for physical release," "How had they *not* been wounded? And wounded they'd convalesced," "they knew everything without confiding—fears, stinks, boiling hearts—they gave up themselves," and "so that they might both love and scorn each other."

The release from the tension that the poem hopefully produces comes twice, first in the form of a memory of sexual pleasure, and then more powerfully in the last line, where the violence of the hands in line seven has turned to tenderness—"they ate from each other's hands." One hopes that the gesture is saved from sentimentality by the phrase right before, which links love and *scorn*, scorn, I think, being the stronger, if slightly, of the two abstractions here because of its echo to the title.

Essentially I had no idea what I was going to write about that June morning when I began "Scorn." I knew the poem would be eleven lines long, that it would be a lyric, and that it would in some sense "define" an abstraction. I didn't know what the abstraction was until after I finished the poem, as this draft shows. My search for early hard copies of the poem has proved fruitless, so I can't tell you when I titled it or even for certain if "Scorn" was the original title. I think it was, having a vague memory of a *frisson* when I wrote that word, realizing at the moment it scratched from my pen that this was what the poem had worked toward from the start without my awareness. And if the phrasing that could measure scorn's precise emotional importance (not "scorn and boiling hearts" or "they became loving and scornful," but "they might both love and scorn each other") and its connection with love in the poem evaded me, just as the subject of the poem had evaded me, the *writing* (and the wrong turns) became the way to know what it was I felt or knew and ultimately meant to say.

Partial awareness is the state of mind I court when I write. I distrust, in myself nearly always, and often in others, full awareness. I even distrust logic, which may be why I am more susceptible to the lyric impulse than to the narrative impulse. Oh, I want things to make sense; but sense for most people, even artists, often underscores a certain banality of thought and feeling. Nonsense isn't the only alternative. A certain dreaminess *can* create space for something new, for change, and make the small gods of homogeneity fear for their well-being. Once what I have come to think of as the form of my eleven-line poems became strong enough so that I felt I could play with it (its shape, motion and tempo in the shape, the play of imagery, the ratio of narrative to lyric factors, the aura of words, the short or long sequences of phrases and clauses, the abiding rhythms, and rhythmic shifts), it began to support my natural disinclination toward knowing beforehand what the composition was to be about. Then I could *improvise*, writing in real time, quickly, and making quick changes, almost taking them out of the thin air. —As memory, or something purely invented? I simply don't know.

ALICE FULTON

Echo Location

Stop quivering
while I insert straws in your nostrils
and wrap your head in cloth
I have immersed in plaster.
        For a life mask, the subject
must be rubbed with gelatin.
And you must be the love du jour.
        I have studied the duct-taped mullions
of monarch wings for inspiration.
I've learned the paramedic's rip.
            Don't squirm.
(But I ran my finger down its spine
        when its back was turned.)

A perfect containment invites trespass,
            the wish to shave below the skin
        and write in seed ink, *mine.*

        I can testify
the tic of prayer persists in nonbelievers.
        Under my distressed surface, under duct tape,
the Hail Mary has a will of its own.
        The spirit uses me. It holds me up
                to the light like a slide.
It claims a little give, a quiver,
        can prevent a quake.
Says copy the vibrato inside trees—
                the star shakes, heart shakes—
        that ruin the wood commercially.
Says you must be ready

        to freeze your extremities
anytime for a better glimpse of the blur.
        Not the blur made firm, mind.
        The blur itself
and not a clearer version of the blur.

Will you hold it up to the light like a slide?
Will you pledge your troth
            and tear this edge off first?

The Norman name for quiver-grass
was *langue de femme*. As in gossip, as in meadows,
      one ripple leads to the next, as in cascade
experiments: one touch and worlds take place.

That's why a little quiver can inscribe a night
            into your left breast,
a day into your right. Can shave below the skin,
            and write in seed ink, *thine*.

But when I think I've ripped the surface
            to the pith, queen substance,
      when I've diagrammed the cry, I

      remember a quiver is a fist
of arrows and the arrows' case, their clothes.
                  Is the weapon and the tremor,
      the cause and the effect.
Once the arrow leaves the bow—
                  will-of-its-own-will-of-its-own—
there is no turning back.
      You must be the visceral river.
You must think a little give
      leads to affinities: the arrow
                  resembles the bird it will fly into.

A Descant on "Echo Location"

Poetry is a form of extrasexual procreation. Rather than trying to duplicate reality, it emerges from the amniotic of what-is with its own solidity. It grows out of experience without recounting experience. It isn't mimetic, but it isn't fashioned from whole cloth either. Out of the chronic wilderness it comes.

As I remember, "Echo Location" retained its mystery while I was writing it. I didn't understand it while it was unfolding as well as I do in retrospect. Even with hindsight, the poem's residual quirks and weird lyricism are slightly beyond my grasp, which is why I wanted to think about it here. To my mind, "Echo Location" considers the grounds between lover and beloved, artist and art object, religion and aspirant. It's interested in reciprocity—by which I mean a relationship between self and universe that shows cause and effect without showing equity. Reciprocity, as I know it, isn't quite kosher or karmic. However, even without underpinnings of justice, the give and take of things seems significant—perhaps sublime.

The poem's title severs "echolocation": the sonic waves used by bats and dolphins to orient themselves and avoid obstacles in darkness. The animals' high-frequency emissions, when reflected back from environing surfaces, tell them the distance and direction of surrounding objects. This means of navigation suggested human interconnectedness: thoughts and glances that extend and rebound from what they touch, the self strummed by an otherness that flinches under scrutiny in its turn.

At the start, the poem's speaker is making a life mask of a model. There's an element of sadism in the dominion of maker over creation, in saying to a pet theme, "Be still, so I can have my way with you." Artists want to—have to—impose stasis on what-gives. Rather than letting the world thrash through them, they whip up their own versions of things.

While artists have the power to expose and express, their objects are shuttered in the hush of various covers, unable to ward off attentions, however unwanted. When I delve into the external, ripping the surface, unfolding wings sticky with mucilage, prying those wings right off, if need be, to reach the pith and mechanism, am I motivated by a wish to comprehend or a wish to control? In reimagining others, I demolish some volatile aspect of their beings. I freeze-frame the breathing object, selecting form from the infinite strands of flux.

I didn't want to assign dominant or subordinate roles to a woman or a man in "Echo Location." Consequently, neither the speaker nor the spoken-to has an identifiable sex or gender. In the first stanza, the model is referred to as "it," a pronoun usually viewed as dehumanizing. But "it" is uncategorical, and, to my mind, potentially liberating. Plural bodies, such as the senate, are called "it." A work of art or an animal can be "it." The lowly can be, and omnipotence must be. Later in the poem, the spirit is an "it" because, of all pronouns, "it" is the most uncanny.

Tonally, "Echo Location" passes through sadism on its way to helplessness and recognition. I like to mix tonal colors by stealing words and phrases from disparate areas of diction. Sometimes the phrases are at odds with the context in which they appear, as when a monarch's wing is said to be "duct-taped." Duct tape, the adhesive of choice for abhorrent scenes of bondage, envenoms the pretty butterfly image with sadism. By such inclusions, I try to broaden the emotional range without resorting to anecdote or exposition. Thus, "love du jour" lends a flavor-of-the-month fickleness to the voice. And, while "the paramedic's rip" evokes scenes of medical trauma, it also might suggest sex of a seriously violating or benignly kinky sort. "To shave below the skin," taken from a razor advertisement, lets the language of commerce into the poem, implying the merchandising of the art object. Heard literally, the slogan sounds anguishing. Heard metaphorically, it describes the artist's wish to peel back the skin of things and excavate the hidden. The artist, while telling the world to hold still, nonetheless harbors a perverse wish to disturb its perfect repose: to toss a pebble and watch the water twitch. By "artist," I also mean writer. Writers want their "seed ink" to leaf out in the reader's head.

Religious diction flickers through stanza three's opening line, "I can testify." Here the grounds of power shift, as the artist, overtaken by the radiant spirit, feels like a slide colonized by the light that dives through it. The speaker is seized by vestigial traces of belief—the habit of prayer that just won't quit. Despite my agnosticism, in a crisis I'm likely to send the high frequency of prayer toward some affirmative surface, some god, from which I imagine my plea rebounding in the form of favors. Of course, not everyone resorts to prayer in times of need. While talking casually with a friend, I asked her if she ever found herself praying, despite her professed disbelief. She said that since she hadn't had a religious upbringing, she'd never prayed in her life. I wondered what she — and others like her—did with their minds in moments of extremity. What does the mind do, if it can't implore the universe? My own prayers come unbidden. Rather than subjecting faith to my will, I'm subject to the hopefulness sown in me as a child. Under sealed layers of logic, religion lingers, wiggling in the depths of skepticism. Just so, the poem's speaker is ruffled by the knee-jerk reflex of belief.

"Echo Location," like many of my newer poems, is polyphonic: various voices weave through it. Stanza three has some presumptuous lines in the voice of the universe (or multiverse), figured as "the spirit." To hear me tell it, the universe values flexibility as a means of avoiding fracture. The spirit claims, as in *possesses*, the speaker's elasticity. But it also claims, as in *posits an opinion*. "Copy the vibrato inside trees — " it advises: go quiver. Vibrato, in singing, refers to a slight wavering of the voice that increases the emotional quality of the tone without a noticeable change of pitch. In like fashion, I wanted the poem's voice to fluctuate without any clearly delineated change of persona.

The spirit also directs the speaker to copy "the star shakes, heart shakes — / that ruin the wood commercially." Shakes are natural defects in wood formation. A star shake is comprised of a number of splits radiating from the pith. I learned this while rewriting the legend of Daphne and Apollo. Daphne's metamorphosis into a laurel led me to a highly technical book on the inner life of trees. The book (*Spiral Grain and Wave Phenomena in Wood Formation*, J. M. Harris) gave advice on how to grow trees for harvest and profit. To wit: "Northcott (1959) described the combination of star shake and spiral grain as one of the most serious defects for the manufacturer of sawn timber or plywood." These "serious defects" are flaws to those who view trees as lumber. From the trees' point of view, shakes are no hindrance to well-being. In theory, such "defects" might prolong the tree's life by lessening its commercial value. Hence, the spirit's advice to cultivate warps and tears.

At the end of this third stanza, the universe recommends a posture of readiness. Picture yourself in a blizzard, fingers exposed, succumbing to numbness as you wait for revelation. It's your figurative extremities that will get you into trouble. Still, the universe says expose them. Don't retract when endangered. What if the sublime appeared while you were hiding? The old tales—of angels seeking succor in strangers' houses, Christ seeking a manger—advise a ready welcome. As I hear it, the universe says prepare to be chilled—by solitude and singularity—for a glimpse of, not a good look at, God: a form too fast to see, too nebulous to know. Seekers want a clear configuration of the divine: icons, slides.

It's easier to adore fixed objects than to worship the blur. But clarity can falsify complexity. Objects undermine the mess.

"Will you pledge your troth / and tear this edge off first?" In these lines, the redemptive passion of courtly love downshifts to the dry instruction printed on mass mailings. So packaged structures—of romance, religion, commerce, incorporation—must be torn in order to know. Courtly love led me to Norman English, where "quiver-grass" was called "woman tongue." Imagine a meadow in motion, each blade chattering in the wind: a meadow as a gossipy thing. Historically, women's experiences—of childbirth and valor—have been handed down as gossip, while men's experiences—of combat and valor—have been written down as epic. The more private the experience, the more likely it is to arrive as gossip. When the infinite becomes familiar, we'll hear the gossip, rather than the music, of the spheres. With gossip, "one ripple leads to the next, as in cascade / experiments. . . ." A cascade experiment is a domino effect, in which a single catalyst triggers a waterfall of events. Such effects can occur naturally. To wit: "a spiral angle of 1 degree will induce a change of 46 degrees in the angle of a heart shake at opposite ends of a 5-m log. . . ." A small perturbation in a chaotic system will amplify into vast differentials of result.

Now maybe it was the arrows of medieval epics. Maybe it was the necessity of trembling. Somehow "quiver" became an entrancing word for me. In stanza six, a "quiver" inscribes the other with "*thine*," rather than the possessive "*mine*" of stanza two. "*Thine*," a willing concession of self, bespeaks reciprocity. In the sixth grade, we learned to diagram sentences. The prepositional phrases plunged like roots from the flat of syntax, and I understood a little of how English works. But where is the subject, where is the object, in the shrieks of mating cats or a dying rabbit's cry? Working the external into words, I'd like to honor those emotive languages beyond grammar, outpourings so pure and heartfelt they would be lyrical were they not unlovely. As a verb, "quiver" signals crisis in the body. As a noun, it's a vibrato, an arrow, and a case for arrows. From a small action, pulling and releasing the bowstring, come tremendous effects: death, mutilation. Like most poets, I've tried to grasp some fundamentals of excruciation, but unless I'm sundered myself, I won't understand. I must be the echo of what I dissect. So *quiver*, oscillating between weapon and tremor, tells me.

Woman with Gardenia

for Barry Schactmann, his "life class"

I.

Breda strikes another classic tricky pose
part dance part factious sway, a grace she's hired
to hold for half an hour, to dare us to
approximate with strokes of conté crayon
on cheap blank newsprint. The tilt of her torso's
third dimension (toward me) is hard to fake, as is
her elbow's angle from my eye-level, just below
the contrapostal jut of her hip. I get the bone
    logic of the stance, but not her ease.

Her head is a halo of backlit red-gray hair
against framed daylight. I'm trying to be good,
and get the planes of her skull, her face, her
neck in line with what I imagine "Mabel,"
the skeleton in our life class closet, would
allow supportable. Despite the glare,
my eye keeps catching on one forbidden
detail: her body's naked, but there's a flower
    tucked above Breda's right ear.

Novice that I am, I do know better
than start my drawing by drawing this
one uninherent outré item out
from curls of shadows equally flimsy, light-
weight, irrelevant to the discipline
of volumes in space, her deep-embodied
gesture, balance, basic planes, her body's
undecorated complexity. Her form is all that,
    for the life of us, we need get right.

Scars, ankle chains, nipples, birthmarks—all that
crude frosting, will never make your lousy cake
taste better. Don't draw the belly button before

the pelvic slant is set. And yet, by the light
that sneaks through Breda's dazzled frizz of hair,
I can see how her gardenia must be put
above mere distraction in the scheme of her
appearance today. I'll ask her, during our break,
            how she . . . why . . . the gardenia?

Tick tock. Tick tock tick. No one would ever say
our Breda's easy, however willing she is
to lend her body's dignity to our haste
of scribbles, freak miscalculations, waste
and slack of effort. Breda shows no surprise
when, taking five, she sees all the boundlessly
plump, footless, headless, tipsy, versions of
the self she must have dreamed she was up there,
her gesture composed of greed and pride and love.
            She shrugs. One could have done better.

III.

She strolls in a flowered robe toward the water fountain.
I follow her to say how much I like her gardenia.
She knew I'd noticed, and she is glad to tell how
this bloom was the first from a plant she managed to make
grow up from this tiny dead-looking slip tossed out
in the alley back of where she lives. Just look,
she says, at what comes of . . . And to leave it in the dark
alone all day. . . . She thought she might wear it to work.
            Her next pose tips toward me.

"Every mark you make," he shouts again,
"had better aspire to be specific. Don't
you dare go looking down expecting your own
mistaken mess to tell you if something goes
or not. Don't make a line that doesn't stress
your eyes' commitment to her *body*. How often
have I said this?: '*Sorta' ain't good enough!!*" And then,
I have nothing but time to lose, and "sorta" want
            this last pose, with that first one. . . .

As always, too few minutes left. But I begin,
despite—God damn it!—to draw what I want, Breda's
whole human body invisibly raising it.

No need to go below her neck for this.
The nose of my conte crayon turns on minute
sweet details—eyelash, wrinkle, mole, gardenia. . . .
How easy one grows—the breast-thick petal, a thigh-
solid leaf, well-turned; her crown, deep garden.
    Time! I hand my drawing to Breda.
    She hands me her gardenia.

Dressing Up Naked:
A Life Class in Revision

Friends who have it I do wrong
Whenever I remake a song,
Should know what issue is at stake:
It is myself that I remake.
—W. B. Yeats

T *1. Will the Proper Subject Please Stand Up?*
he subject, properly, is revision: any such as a poem, or person, is eager to solicit, to resist. I have consulted a number of poems that I myself have committed and sentenced to life. How do they like being subject to "critiques" (in workshop parlance)? The answers of some of the most persistently unfinished are hardly surprising, yet difficult to explain exactly. To illustrate: I have elected "Woman with Gardenia," a nag of nearly twenty-five years standing, and a subject of mine born with a terrible mind of her own.

My specific subject/collaborator is a life class model, and I call her verbal presentation "Woman with Gardenia." I would like you to imagine her framed for hanging, guilty or not, in a visual field merely appropriated, with scarcely an excuse of substantial likeness, by poetry. My life class model is all for criticism, *entre nous*. But as far as the "others" go, she'd not consider me worth a haunt. Whatever revisions we do are essential, and essentially dialogic, untheoretical, and disciplined to the very brink of anarchy.

As one subject invariably leads to another, the life class student enters as a necessary corollary to the subject of the "drawing" here. "I" am the student. "Breda" is the model. What goes on between us is both ultimately and intimately critical, as I try to translate her posed three-dimensional body into two-dimensional scratchings on a flimsy newsprint surface. Her solid body, silently holding its pose, implicitly calls my attention to the differences between my actual attempts at drawing the subject and the eventual proper subject of my poem.

The subject, ultimately and intimately, is revision. Its occasion, whether literary, graphic, musical, or academic, is the *desire to translate* one form of being into another, such that they comprehend each other as truly as can be.

2. *"Woman with Gardenia,"* 1972–1996

In the summer of 1972, waiting for my doctoral dissertation to be typed, I signed up for Professor Barry Schactmann's basic figure drawing course at Washington University's School of Fine Arts. I knew a bit about drawing, and I had loved Comparative Anatomy à la the Biology Department; but I was not prepared for the particular ecstasy of "life class." I choose the word "ecstasy" here with care—I mean by it the serious happiness of "standing outside," a place both heavenly and "beyond the pale" of ordinary eagerness with regard to understanding the form and the mystery of *having* a body and *investigating* the relation between *this* body and *that, it* and *hers, its* and *mine.* (Training and skill in draftsmanship, which I had not, I'm sure would blunt the anxious excitement of this "ecstasy," part of which is plain unfamiliarity.)

Her name is Breda. She is ready for us, sitting at a corner desk under the windows, not noticeable. At the dot of nine, she stands, disrobes, and steps up onto the model stand. Professor Schactmann announces a series of ten one-minute poses, and Breda assumes one after another, timing herself and each time reconfiguring herself as well as the air around her and between her and each of us.

Breda is, as they say, "of a certain age," and I'm half that. Her body is lithe but landmarked by gravity, bunched and slacked in ordinary ways by time. I feel strangely, under the thin cover of my summer dress, that I am essentially nakeder than Breda; there are no lines on my body, barely any bulges, creases, moles, or landmarks of any kind. I feel like a blank piece of paper, the blank pad of newsprint in front of me that I hope her figure will be drawn to fill, my hand being willing.

Breda is dressed for work in her body. Poems have "bodies," too, but they seldom come posing naked as subjects, nothing coy or cloaked, articulated by necessity, poised to move, gravity centered, feet grounded. Literary "style" is commonly compared to "clothing," in that different fashions and extents of elegance or silliness, "period" apparel, rags glad or royal or low demotic, all have their linguistic equivalents. Occasionally, when Professor Schactman is a few minutes late for class, Breda will begin, on time, with great authority and her own selection of poses. Poems, on the other hand, despite having bodies in reserve, do not obviously do this. But might they?

Breda has been at this a long time. She *is* the language we want to learn. But then, so are we. All our bones and muscles, their syntax and grammars, tensions and energies and slackings and twistings, are the same. The difference is that Breda is in control of her expression, and we submit ourselves to study the way she presents herself partly in order to know how we might arrange our bodies in just that way, from the inside, without unnecessary fuss and fidget and concealment of necessary outlines and volumes. Breda is a generous teacher, an essentially wordless one. So, too, is a poem that has taken its place and time in the world.

3. Life Class

Life class, technically, is about art, not life; it is mechanical rather than hoop-la creative; is the grammar and syntax of the human body, and is naturally a prelim to all serious advanced art studies. Might there be a "life class" with respect to poetry, fiction, or other kinds of "creative" writing that would feel equally vital to the art's best performance? Language comes in "bodies," after all. The articulations of its sentences are, moreover, not far from describing acts of flesh and blood and bone. Consider the "copula" (to be), possessives, correlative conjunctions, prepositions, genders, and the privacy of those parts of speech we fool with to prove our creative capacities.

But the subject was revision.

In Life Class, there are no original visions. The subject is the same for everyone; the body of the subject, on any given day at any given hour, is the same, the ordinary human body. If Breda takes a day off and is replaced by a male model, our attention, as a student body, has not been given a new subject, but rather a revision of the one ongoing one. Revisions from "her" to "him" or vice versa, as may notably be seen in drafts of Emily Dickinson's as well as Walt Whitman's better known poems, do not significantly obscure their original visions.

The subject of life class is communal and dual, open and intimate. Its discipline is obviously collusive, illusional, formal, and strictly "reality-based." Perhaps the counterpart tuition in poetic art might be called "life sentence." Beyond the elementary aspects—all the finger exercises, memorizations, routine conjugations, and practical solutions—classes introductory to art, unlike the 101's of many "scientific" or scholarly disciplines, provide nearly unlimited access to aspects of "high" performance, including profound (as well as practical) evocations of elegy, amusement, evanescence, disappointment, anger, and exuberance.

"Easy" access to the rewards and true aggravations of advanced practice may account for both realistic and capriciously destructive perceptions of professed interest in "the arts." On one hand, painting or sculpture or creative writing or dance, or whatever, as "major" studies are perceived as fitting for persons of self-convicted genius, great potential, world-class human value. On the other (much larger) hand, these studies are (not entirely wrongly) perceived as offering a kind of pseudo-academic fall back for sissies and nincompoops. Both these perceptions are in need of massive revisionary effort.

Is Life Class any help overall, in the long run, as an example? Is Life Class properly subject to poetic revision? Or vice versa? I wonder why Breda won't let go, why she won't let our portrait be finished and the both of us laid to rest.

4. Getting It Right

I grow fond of Breda. I begin to talk to Breda during our breaks. Breda knows I do not really belong in a rigorous art class (she occasionally strolls around to look at our drawings of her, *sans* comment), but she does not pity me. She tosses me angles, wordless, she thinks I need to practice. I chafe at how my conté crayon keeps violating, against my will and all reason, Breda's body's effortless assumption of form is the timed and graceful termination of each of her poses.

One day Breda turns up with a luscious gardenia pinned behind one ear. I focus on this departure from her everyday intentional lack of adornment. Does it not tease, violate her ideal anonymity and my detachment from her off-dais existence? The gardenia is, to me, intriguing to the point of confusion. I look around. Students who know better how to draw the figure are not bothered by this detail.

I know if I want to get around to drawing the flower in Breda's hair, I have to earn the luxury by first getting the big things right. This is life class, not free verse or improv. In literary terms, Breda's skull's decoration might be seen as a self-indulgent stylistic flourish, which, without a "body" properly arranged on the page to bear it naturally, would reek of sweet amateurish grandiosity, betray (in the context of apprenticeship) an unseemly assumption of mastery. Having not *that* much talent, I kept longing for a right to figure in Breda's highly personal gardenia.

Life class is the opposite of grand, despite its name; it addresses the practices of apprentice-level draftsmanship, producing (in various individual degree) side effects and after-shocks of sudden humilities, wonders, failures, and curiosities. And revision and frustration. Starting again. And revision and frustration. Starting again.

5. Breathing Lessons

Poems come with bodies and minds of their own. They come with critical needs to be met and vital statistics not to be dismissed by the non-assassins of the poetically conceived. As a basically pro-choice person, I allow myself to dismiss on occasion and when convenient; as pro-life, I am no less willfully lethal, but considerably more suspicious of "experts" who would diagnose a case of creation that is not reasonably subject to any "criticism" but that of self and author.

Emily Dickinson asked her favorite "outside" literary critic, Thomas Higginson, of her submitted verses: "Do they breathe?" Imagine! She even brought up the issue of "surgery." As if! And Higginson doubtless thereupon pocketed the sensory scalpels of his editorship, in favor of this odd and unpublishable humor.

In this connection, critically speaking (but only as pertains to the "inner" critical circle of creator and creature), I am bound to ask myself (as undoubtedly Emily D. did): How do "I" feel, from inside my poem's body, about being misunderstood, misrepresented, badly articulated, unnecessarily uglified, apparently caught off balance, physically mocked in any case, exposed to false diagnoses, outrageous treatments or pity— and all from the incompetence of the "critic" who is neither maker nor in my way particularly made? How do I feel, being claimed, as "subject" to revision by an other's hand or others' eyes. Literary critics are not divinely (or strictly, or in any other reasonable way) licensed to operate on the material of living organisms. Nor would I declare a poem's viable status, or speak for its unobvious "feelings," if I were not authorized by a creditable origin in myself.

Any clairvoyance I, or anyone else, has along these lines is limited, not only by self-knowledge, but insofar as any intuitions of mine about the "person" of my mother tongue are no more intrinsically or profoundly rooted than the muscle that fills my mouth.

6. And in Passing

I have only one real conversation with Breda, the one that mediates the vignette of my still unsettled poem, "Woman with Gardenia." She tells me the history of the gardenia, and I can see the alleyway back of her house where she found the dying twig a neighbor had thrown out with the trash. I see this in streetlight, moonlight, perhaps some shining from recent small rain. None of this gets into the poem so you would notice. Nor does my clear picture of Breda's neighborhood, which I have never seen in person, nor of the room where she nursed the ragged twig back to life. What I see, I suppose, are variations on my own back alleys, south-windowed rooms, Victorian thresholds. I even see the slant of light on the morning she harvested this first bloom, the moment she decided to put it in her hair. To give it its world's view, to let it die in company of that, to be given (up), taken (in), played (out) in the spirit of Breda's own wanting to make this dumb thing grow.

Even if I were a master draftsman and not the rudest of mechanicals, I doubt I could come to an end of attempting to portray precisely the moment of "Woman with Gardenia." For to portray this exactly, as distinct from my picture of Breda, the flower in her hair, or myself failing to "get it right," is, to my mind at least, an overextension of my self that is not allowed by the laws of ordinary selfhood. Much as I would like you to know how it felt, how I feel, how I think one might ideally understand this moment between would-be artist and generously proffered subject, I am not all that hopeful.

Considering art's medial limitations, and the fictive complexities of human neurobiology, and the ceaselessly irritating "return of the repressed" that dogs all human efforts to please the gods, a state of interminable revision with regard to some subjects must be acknowledged, honored. Not without gratitude, simply without hope.

The mind is the mortal part. And if it means anything to say that a work of art "has a mind of its own," I'd take it to refer to an essential issue that is not the brainchild of either the artist or the work, but of something between them that is yet to be resolved. I understand neither the original brainchild nor the vengeance of the piece I call "Woman with Gardenia." Why does she re-insist? Why can I not ignore her nagging, her claims of irresolution, her invitations to pointless collusion? Why don't I tell her to go to Hell when she accuses me of stopping short, of not "getting it"? Who does she think she is? Who does she think I am?

DAVID HUDDLE

Basket

Needlepoint for the church
she did back when she could, a strip
of kneeler-facing she pretended
to do after she couldn't anymore:

now she's never out of her room
without the basket of it,
fussing at recreation hour,
teasing out the same old limp piece,

clucking and shaking her head at it.
It's in her lap when they sit,
as they do after meals,
out by the station,

Mrs. Webb, Althea Fromberg, Ella
What'shername, and the others,
the dreadful others
my mother despises.

But who, anyway, can work
in such light? —
this unnatural buzzing
glare that makes these old

fools moan, drool, fall napping
into their trays . . . My mother
rises and begins to walk away.
The light chases her

down corridors . . . all
the same, this is so . . .
and where's her . . . basket?
Someone has taken it

again, God damnit,
she hates . . . just wants
to . . .
        When they
hear her crying and come

to the corner where she
has crumpled to the floor,
the aides know what is wrong,
they know what to do.

"Has anybody seen
Mrs. Huddle's basket?"
they call out to the ladies
by the station, because

they all know this part.
"Here it is!" Althea pipes up.
Another calls out, "Here—
she left it here." One lifts it

with two hands into the light
and gives it over. The aides carry it
to her, my mother on the floor,
who grabs and clutches

the thing to her chest. She cries
a little more, getting up,
letting them guide her
back to her room, her bed.

They set the basket
on the blanket right
beside her—"See, now here
it is, Mrs. Huddle."

At last my mother can sleep.
Under its lid and mere
inches from her hand,
her coiled cobra can rest, too.

About My "Basket":
Looking for Closure

M̲y strongest poems have addressed major traumas of my life— the death of my grandfather, the illness and death of my father, my service in the army in Vietnam, the loss of my youth, and my separation from the land of my birthplace, a small mountain town in Virginia. My poems are autobiographical, they're accessible, their language stays within the boundaries of the spoken, and they're not technically flashy. When I was a graduate student at Hollins and at Columbia, I wrote inscrutable, surrealistic poems—because that was the fashion among us graduate students. But when I settled into my life here in Vermont, I began to try to write poems that meant something to me personally, poems that marked something important about my life.

As I compose, I consciously set forth to "feel" my poem. Writing helps me clarify and resolve the emotional forces with which I struggle. When I am writing a poem, however, I am not thinking so much about examining my life as I am about making it—constructing something with words. Life-examination occurs as a by-product of poem-making. Quite often improving the poem in revision requires further clarification of the emotional issues out of which I'm writing it. To make my poem more understandable to both my reader and myself, I'm required to probe further into the psychological forces out of which I'm writing. Thus, in order to write well, I'm forced to a deeper understanding of myself.

The gradual development of my mother's Alzheimer's disease made it an insidious presence in my emotional life. It evolved in such a way as to encourage me not to confront it emotionally. Some years ago, a doctor gave us a warning about it from a CAT scan carried out on my mother; this was at a time when she was bright in spirit, alert, and witty. She was so much herself—with only occasional slips of memory—that it was easy to disregard the doctor's warning. As her forgetfulness increased, so did her ability to disguise it and to demonstrate ongoing mental competence. She became adept at deception, rising to the occasion of family visits so that my brothers and I and our families all persuaded ourselves that Granny was a little absent-minded but no more so than each of us was on certain occasions. My mother desperately wanted to be able to continue living in her house and maintaining her independence. We children and grandchildren desperately wanted her to continue being the stable, healthy person she had been for all of our lives. She was the matriarch, the "rock." By the time it became evident that she was too ill to continue living by herself, her situation had become extreme. One week she was living in the house where she'd lived for seventy-some years; the next week she was trapped among strangers in a nursing home. She went from being a person to being a patient. Circumstances required my brother and me to empty out the family homeplace, lock it, and board up the windows to protect it from vandals. For her and for us, death might have been kinder.

If emotional turmoil fuels my poetry, then my mother's Alzheimer's disease had me carrying around a full tank for at least a year. A classically emotion-hiding man, I "bottle my feelings up," as they say. On the occasion of visiting my mother in the nursing home for Alzheimer's patients in Warner Robbins, Georgia, I'm sure I did not reveal—even to myself—any of the horror I felt in seeing how my mother actually lived in her new circumstances. I'm not sure I even felt what I felt at the time. Nowadays I'm such a habitual writer that most of my emotional life is located in my writing. My emotional responses to "real life situations" are stunted; for me to fully realize my emotions about something in my life, I have to write about it.

Apparently when I actually go through an emotionally charged experience, I "gather data." When I did finally begin writing these poems about my mother's Alzheimer's disease, I surprised myself with how many details I had stored up ready to use in constructing written evocations of the experience.

In retrospect I see that conjuring up the scene of the group of patients —mostly women—sitting around the nurses' station must have come out of my ambivalent response to what I witnessed in "real life": that my mother was part of a community was comforting; that other members of that community were severely disabled was disturbing. She appeared to be a sane person among lunatics. Her Alzheimer's was in a relatively early stage, whereas the whole gamut of the disease's progression was represented by the home's other patients. The politics of the community was very much informed by that progression: because she still had many of her faculties intact, my mother held a relatively powerful position in the community. Thus, my mother's basket of needlework became (in both "real life" and in my poem) a symbol of her political power. She had to pretend that she was actually doing the needlework, but even her pretending was a higher accomplishment than most of the other patients could manage.

At the home I learned that my mother took her basket wherever she went but that she often forgot it or misplaced it. I learned that "Mrs. Huddle's basket" was famous throughout the nursing home. This information was fascinating to the narrative-writer in me. What I had learned about the basket was enough for me to be able to construct for myself a little story. Running the sentences of that narrative through the discipline of relatively short-lined quatrains helped me condense it and intensify it. As I composed those stanzas, I became aware of a building emotional content to the narrative. Simply by following my own imagined elements, my poem carried my mother back to her bedroom and to being "settled down" by the nurse's aides who had recovered her lost basket for her. I clearly envisioned the aides setting her basket on the bed beside her as she settled into her nap and reassuring her that her valued possession was within easy reach. I won't say "that much was easy," because it took hours of concentration, looking for the words to make the drama visible and crafting the lines to work within the self-imposed discipline I had established with my form of short-line quatrains. But that wasn't the hard part of writing the poem.

I needed an ending. I needed an ending that would release the emotional buildup of the poem's narrative. My early draft of the poem ended with final lines that went something like "that shimmering / power close at hand." After drafting the poem through to its tentative conclusion on the second morning after I'd begun it, I thought about it all day. As I carried out my errands, I conducted a craft discussion with myself about what the poem needed. I was aware that with the word "power" I'd simply named one of the poem's main thematic concerns—a move in composition that I almost always consider a mistake. Naming the theme—which usually occurs in the title or the conclusion of a work—often robs a poem of its natural ambiguity, and that certainly seemed to me what I'd done with my early draft of "Basket." One of my mottoes is, "If possible, end with an image." So in my craft discussion with myself, I had the advantage of knowing what the problem was and knowing, at least theoretically, what the solution would be. I needed a concluding image to bring the poem to release meaning into the text.

My problem was that image-finding is not something I'm good at, except when I do it in the natural "flow" of composition. If I think about it, I freeze up. Or I think of something trite or mechanical or utterly inappropriate. The image of the cobra in the basket entered my mind while I was driving on Williston Road up the hill by the University of Vermont, and I was both thrilled and amused by it when it arrived. I snorted to myself with the outrageousness of the notion—my mother's sewing basket at the nursing home containing a cobra.

The more I thought about it, though, the more the cobra appealed to me—in some part because it *was* so inappropriate. My mother's basket actually contains needlework, something I hadn't mentioned in my early drafts of the poem, and the word *needlework* seemed to me usefully suggestive of cobra fangs. What I wanted was a piece of needlework that would be a "strip," something that might be "snakelike." On my own I couldn't think of such a thing. I knew the piece in the actual basket was the square or rectangular covering for a sofa pillow. I had the good sense to consult with my wife about these matters. I asked her if she could think of a kind of needlework that would be a long strip of something. Lindsey gave me not only a more suggestive word—*needlepoint*—but she also came up with the idea of a needlepointed facing for a kneeler pad, because someone in her church was working on such a project. I was immediately taken with the idea of a piece of "religious work" becoming a cobra.

When I returned to the poem, I composed a new first stanza for the poem, and in the second and third stanza, I devoted a bit of work to establishing elements of the needlepoint project in my mother's basket that might visually suggest "snake charming." My mother's losing her basket and having it returned to her is an oft-repeated performance in which members of the nursing home community participate, a little drama in an otherwise boring day, a ritual slightly similar to the performance of a snake charmer. Power accrues to the performer, but there's also a (poisonous) power and danger that goes with the performance. The scary and evil associations that go with the serpent I associate with the scary and evil associations I have with my mother's Alzheimer's disease.

"Basket" is still new for me. I'm still excited about it, and that's usually a good sign. What a poem means to its maker is an important measure of its value, and I suspect that this poem will continue to matter to me over the years. It's a poem that faces down some of the fear I feel about my mother's illness and what has happened to her and what inevitably will happen to her as her Alzheimer's progresses. I consider the cobra image a gift—something that came to me out of the writing process, something around which my emotional turmoil could coalesce. I'm grateful to the image for its contribution to my psychological well-being. But most of all I'm grateful to it for moving me forward. Though it ended that particular poem, the cobra in my mother's basket has prepared me to receive the poems still coming to me.

RICHARD JACKSON

Do Not Duplicate This Key

It is not commonly understood why my love is so deadly.
At the very least it uproots the trees of your heart.
It interferes with the navigation of airplanes like certain
electronic devices. It leaves a bruise in the shape of a rose.
It kisses the dreamless foreheads of stones.
Sometimes the light is wounded by my dark cliffs.
Around me even the moon must be kept on a leash.
Whenever I turn you will turn like a flower following
the day's light. Sometimes I feel like Ovid's Jove,
hiding behind the clouds and hills, waiting for you
to happen along some pastoral dell thinking
what I might turn you into next. Then I remember
the way he turned himself into a drooling bull to scour
the pastures of Arcadia for Europa. Forget myth, then.
Forget Ovid. According to Parcelus, God left the world
unfinished from a lack of professional interest
and only my love can complete or destroy it.
Sometimes I come home, open a bottle of Chalone
Pinot Blanc and listen to the Spin Doctors'
"How Could You Want Him (When You Could Have Me)?"
My love is so deadly because it holds a gun to every despair.
But this is not the case everywhere. In some places
the heart's shrapnel shreds our only dreams. Even
the trees refuse to believe in one another. Sometimes
it seems we've put a sheet over Love and tagged its toe.
Someone thinks it lives in the mother of the Azeri soldier,
Elkhan Husseinar, because she puts, in a jar on his grave,
the pickled heart of an enemy Armenian soldier.
This is love, she says, *this is devotion.*
Someone else assigns Love a curfew. There's the 25 year
old sniper who targets women in Sarajevo to see
what he calls "their fantastic faces of love"
as they glance towards their scrambling children.
This is when the seeds desert their furrows for rock.
This is when Despair pulls a Saturday Night Special
from its pocket and points it at the cashier in the 7-11 store.
This is when it seems each star is just a chink in our dungeon.

It is at this hour that I think entirely about you.
My love is so deadly because it wants to handcuff
the Death that has put all our lives on parole.
I myself escaped long ago from Love's orphanage.
I invented a world where the moon tips its hat at me.
I have this way of inventing our love by letting
my words rest like a hand on your thigh.
I have this way of gently biting your nipples
just to feel your body curl like the petal of a rose.
Even when I sleep you can detect my love
with the same instruments scientists use to see
the microwave afterglow of the Big Bang that created
the universe. My love is so deadly
the whole world is reinvented just as Parcelus said.
I love even the 90% of the universe that is dark matter
no light will ever embrace. Rilke died from the thorn
of a rose because he thought his love was not deadly.
My love is so deadly it picks the blossoming fruit tree
of the entire night sky. I can feel, in the deepest part
of you, the soft petals stir and fold with the dusk.
So deadly is my love
the call of the owl is thankful
to find a home in my ear. The smoke
from my cigarette thanks me for releasing it.
The tree changes into a flock of birds.
So deadly is my love other loves fall asleep in its throat.
It is a window not attached to any wall.
It is a boat whose sails are made of days and hours.
It rises like Botticelli's Venus from the sea.
This is not some idle myth.
In fact, it has been discovered that all life
probably began on the surface of deep sea bubbles
which came together in Nature's little cocktail party
carrying most of the weird little elements we are made of,
the kind of molecular sex that excites chemists.
My love is so deadly it starts spontaneous combustions.
The whole universe grows frightened for what comes next.
The sky undresses into dawn then shyly covers its stars.
Sometimes I think your love is a compass pointing away.
Sometimes I discover my love like the little chunks of moon
they dig from under the Antarctic ice. My love is
so deadly it will outlast Thomas Edison's last breath
which has been kept alive in a test tube

in Henry Ford's village, Dearborn, Michigan. Even the skeptic,
David Hume, 1711–1776, begins to believe in my love.
My own steps have long since abandoned their tracks.
My own love is not a key that can be duplicated.
It knocks at the door of the speakeasy in Sarajevo
and whispers the right word to a girl named Tatayana.
This, of course, was from before the war,
before everybody's hearts had been amputated from their lives.
Now my love abandons all my theories for it.
This is why my love seems so deadly.
It is scraping its feet on your doormat, about to enter.
Sometimes you have to cut your life down
out of the tree it has been hanging in. My love is
so deadly because it knows the snake that curls inside
each star like one of Van Gogh's brush strokes.
My love is so deadly because it knows the desire of the rain
for the earth, how the astronomer feels watching
the sleeping galaxies drift away from us each night.
I am listening to your own rainy voice.
I am watching the heart's barometer rise and fall.
I am watching like the spider from your easel.
My love is so deadly, birds abandon the sluggish air.
Their hearts fall from trees like last year's nests.
The smoke awakens in the fire. The rose abandons the trellis.
My love is so deadly it picks the locks of your words.
And even tonight, while someone else's love tries
to scavenge a few feelings from a dumpster, while someone
lies across the exhaust grating like a spent lover,
my own love steps out from my favorite bar under
a sky full of thorns, weaving
a little down the sidewalk, daring the cabs
and after-hours kamikazes like someone stumbling
back into a world redeemed by
the heart's pawn tickets, holding a pair of shoes
in one hand, a hope that breathes in the other.

Talking Poetry at the *Cafe Tazza*

O nly the autobiographical parts of this poem are true," I found my-
self teasing a friend over coffee recently. The coffee shop is a small one in
Chattanooga, but the selection induces vertigo: not just the usual trendy
cappucino, mocha, and latte selections, but flavored coffee in styles
ranging across the palate of the globe. "So what isn't autobiographical?"
was the equally ironic answer. Of course we were both thinking of how
Wordsworth in his *Prelude* wrote about the "growth of a poet's mind" in
a way that restructured, added, and subtracted to the point where auto-
biography became fiction, or rather revealed the truth of feeling, the
truth of the mind instead of recounting mere fact. And we thought of
how Whitman's self becomes eventually the world because it extends
so far out along the periphery of the poetic self that the original auto-
biographical self seems finally galactic. Both poets certainly understood
the problem of solipsism: how to write an autobiographical poem with-
out just writing about the self.

The self is elsewhere, wrote Pascal. But where? For him it was con-
stantly emerging from among the fragments and pieces of his *Pensées*
that could be pasted together in a variety of patterns. Gaston Bachelard
writes in *The Poetics of Space*: "the spiraled being who, from outside,
appears to be a well-invested center, will never reach his center. The
being of man is an unsettled being which all expression unsettles. In
the reign of the imagination, an expression is hardly *proposed*, before
being adds another expression, before it must be the being of another
expression." Where is the real self, then? The couple at the next table
were drinking a kind of coffee that had so many toppings it looked like
an ice cream sundae. How does anything hold together if the center, as
Yeats lamented, does not hold? "So you see," my friend says, "in 'Do
Not Duplicate This Key,' the statements, aphorisms, really, are linked

by questions of extremes, wild statements and claims, how extreme love leads to suffocation which is a kind of death, and that's why the references to the Azeri soldier, or the war in Bosnia in what is, after all, a love poem." Yes, we are both thinking, the "fantastic faces of love" are one thing, but to see them on the faces of women who have been shot in Sarajevo only to see their children die is quite another, and another sense of love. There's no easy place to settle here, the poem whispers, there's no place on earth that is safe *for* love or safe *from* it.

It was already time for a second iced cappucino. All those coffees, I was thinking, it's a way of forgetting or repressing that you are just, after all, having a cup of water poured over some crushed beans. "Yes," my friend says, "all those references, all those facts are just ways to disguise the self, to find metaphors for what the self feels, to repress the pain of what the speaker feels will eventually be a failed love." And it's true: a basic strategy was probably to begin with an outrageous statement and then see how it is addressed—the story of that conversation between images being the poem itself as a tracing of the self's struggles. "More than that," my generous friend adds, "it suggests a speaker who sees that love and failure everywhere, who sees death, the end of things in everything from a grain of sand to the cosmos. The only thing he has to combat it is the bravura of the tone, the sense that he can get away with any claims, a sense that anything might be possible, that hope might still exist here." By this time his iced coffee has been abandoned so long it's dripping down the side of the glass and making a spreading pool on the table. "Let's face it," he sighs "there are so many shifts and slides here that it seems impossible to pin down a single self." Perhaps, I am thinking, that is why Rilke says in his third elegy that the self "contains multitudes."

"Where does this take us?" would be the next logical question. And is this talk about the poem any more accurate than what the obfuscated self in the poem reveals. Can we really talk sensibly and honestly about poems? "Where did that come from?" is usually the happiest question the poet can ask when the poem is over. Where indeed. In this case, the lineage certainly traces back to jazz, the improvisations of middle Charlie Parker, say, or the symphonic extensions of later Coltrane. To be able to put one statement next to another that doesn't make as much sense as one wants for at least a few lines when the digressive strain returns for a moment before being again "unsettled" has always been a delight—and more, a portrait of how the mind and heart, the self, work, by placing one parenthesis inside another for as long as possible. It's a way to move toward that periphery Whitman aimed for. It's a way of holding off any final definition of a self and life, and of holding off the consequences of the troubles it faces. Anything can mean anything for a while, we agree, and that allows for a certain Keatsian "negative capability," a certain optimism. And, yes, here we are in the *Cafe Tazza*, which means *cup* in Italian, but *fresh* in Arabic, pretty unrelated notions unless you are talking about coffee, as we are, in which case they become essential, related, one.

Other influences? At some point the Italian *Improvvisiatori*, at least through Byron's understanding of their sense of the "perpetual activity" of the mind, what he called a "jar of atoms," has some influence. Like mixing coffee beans to create your own blend. There's the way the comic, the quirky, the bravura in Byron only hides the tragic, or better, holds off the tragic for a brief time. Thus we can see a love that "interferes with the navigation of airplanes like certain / electronic devices." Powerful perhaps, overstated certainly, but love as an electronic gadget already promises its own death. So one mood then is always undercut or redefined by another. One could also turn back to Blake's "Auguries of Innocence" and Samuel Johnson's satires for their aphoristically quick turns; or Christopher Smart's wild assertions that end up asking only for love; or Sextus Propertius' quirky use of myth and history to the point of ironically undercutting his declarations of love. "The strangeness is always lurking," Ovid says in *Metamorphoses*, "always there but seldom visible."

It's interesting to note, in the context of this poem, that Byron uses the word "mobility" to describe this discontinuous manner of fragmented or aphoristic writing in *Don Juan*, and the word in Italian has a number of rich associations for our self-conscious love poet. After all, as the Duke sings in Verdi's *Rigolletto*—*La Donna e mobile*—the woman is fickle, as fickle, he goes on, as thistledown in the wind. But all of opera is in a sense *mobile*: one aria cuts across another in a series of competing emotions and allegiances, and melodies begin to diverge and come together. How do all these divergent voices come together? How do all these various lines and references start to define each other? How do they pull further and further away from the confessional self and still define it? We're on our third cappucinos now.

This multiple perspective is really the key to escaping the simple solipsistic self, the self prone to confess its pains to all the world. "When you gaze at our motley costumes, don't forget there are hearts underneath," Tonio says in the *Prologue* to Leoncavallo's opera *Pagliacci*. "Laugh at the sorrow that destroys your heart," Canio says later as he must perform the role of a clown having just discovered the unfaithfulness of the younger woman he loves but has, in a sense, smothered. "Vesti la giubba"—on with the motley. So there's the goofing around with Ovid's Jove chasing after a nymph in the guise of a bull—could this be our author? Could this be that true self? And what has he said about his sources, how he understands them, and so understands himself? Remember, he calls upon the discredited Parcelus, and Thomas Edison, to support his case. And he thinks the dead skeptical philosopher, David Hume, actually believes in this love. "Don't worry," my friend says, there is something of Canio's situation in all of us. We are almost ready to try one of those multicolored and multiflavored coffees. But we are going to remain purists. We are going to remain our own selves.

Which brings up the question he's been wanting to ask all along: who is she with her "rainy voice"? She seems almost buried in the poem addressed to her, a few lines here and there—as if the speaker knew he couldn't hold her very long in this poem or she would fall victim to a love that kills. Yet he ends both painfully and hopefully, hailing cabs "under / a sky full of thorns," holding "the heart's pawn tickets." Is she real or a projection made of the speaker's projection of one proposal, one image on top of another as Bachelard suggested? After all, this is a woman whose body has "curled like the petal of a rose" beneath him, inside whom he can feel each movement. Has her reality passed only into imagination. Can we ever, in our own lives, tell the difference? Has the love of the poet killed the love of the poet?

Taken one way we see a series of expansive digressions, but taken another way an obsessive speaker for whom each digression is in fact an intensification, a raising of the stakes, a taking possession of the otherness of the world for the self. No wonder the love is so deadly. And a love that knows itself as deadly, as headed for its own death, but still, with all its digressions and diversions, and yet pleading, as in Ecclesiastes, "Any wound but a wound of the heart." But who can escape it: life fulfills the poem's Jeremiad of fears, squeezing what it loved to death. It was a love poem after all, as my friend said, which means it didn't work, it was doomed from the start. On the wall there's a coffee ad from the thirties or forties: coffee was 17 cents a pound then. La vita e mobile. Vesti la giubba.

ERICA JONG

The Buddha in the Womb

Bobbing in the waters of the womb,
little godhead, ten toes, ten fingers
& infinite hope,
sails upside down through the world.

My bones, I know, are only a cage
for death.
Meditating, I can see my skull,
a death's head,
lit from within
by candles
which are possibly the suns
of other galaxies.

I know that death
is a movement toward light,
a happy dream
from which you are loath to awaken,
a lover left
in a country
to which you have no visa,
& I know that the horses of the spirit
are galloping, galloping, galloping
out of time
& into the moment called NOW.

Why then do I care
for this upside-down Buddha
bobbling through the world,
his toes, his fingers
alive with blood
that will only sing & die?

There is a light in my skull
& a light in his.
We meditate on our bones only

to let them blow away
with fewer regrets.

Flesh is merely a lesson.
We learn it
& pass on.

Gestations

People always ask where poems come from—and the truth is not even the poet knows. Especially not the poet.

A line comes into your head. Or an image. If you are waiting in attentiveness for a poem to knock on your skull, you catch the line and write it down. Or maybe you only catch a fragment of the line and then allow it to suggest another and another and another. Sometimes the line or fragment waits for years in a notebook for you to pick it up again. Sometimes it is lost. But, as with a dream-fragment, it is important to catch whatever you can. By its toes if necessary. The rest of the body may follow.

"The Buddha in the Womb" started like that. "Bobbing in the waters of the womb" came into my head. And then the poem followed. Or I followed the poem. It is hard to tell whether the poet follows the poem or the poem descends like Mary Poppins on a kite string.

What was the occasion for the poem? A headstand. I was practicing yoga. Inverted in the headstand, I thought: What if I were pregnant and the fetus was rightside up because I was upside down. Paradoxes breed poems.

So I am balanced on my head. I love seeing the world upside down and the rush of blood to the brain—a cheap, natural high. And then an imaginary baby appears, glowing behind my solar plexus. His little skull glows with the light, the energy, the *prana* that I have transmitted by imagining him. Any form of creation is an energy exchange. Creation breeds light and heat.

At the time, I was definitely not pregnant. I did not even admit I *wanted* to be pregnant. But I was at that dangerous age in a woman's life —early thirties—when twenty years of clockwork menstruation have made their point: "You were born to breed and die and the heart breaks either way" (as I said in another poem written then).

So I was toying with the *idea* of fecundity if not with fecundation itself. And I imagined a pregnant me, in the headstand posture wondering about the creature within. The poem I pulled out with the first line is really a poem about our spirit's passage *through* flesh to get *beyond* flesh. It asks: why make a baby if we are only spirit? Why make a baby if we are doomed to die? And it answers: because the soul expands through creation even if the created thing is impermanent. Permanence is not our business, but creation is.

And *who* is the creature we create really? The creature is "infinite hope," a "little godhead," the promise of future life. The creation may be a poem, one's own Buddha-nature, the hope of outlasting the fate of ordinary mortals who sing and die. The point is we create because we *must*, because we are creatures whose self-definition implies creation. We are makers, mothers, fabricators, poets. Even if our creation does not endure, our need to create is eternal. This passion to create defines our humanity. It explains why we resonate with a creator-godhead. We share the urgency to replicate ourselves, to make creatures and name them, to set them in the midst of predicaments and tell their stories "Since flesh can't stay, we pass the words along," I said in a poem called "Dear Keats." And I still believe it. Words are our antidote to mortality.

"The Buddha in the Womb" has often been anthologized with poems about motherhood and pregnancy. In fact I was not pregnant when I wrote it—but my imagination was. It is one of many poems I've written that meditates on generativity and creativity: a woman's ability to create with her body and also create with her mind.

Women tend to be obsessed with this duality—at least during our childbearing years. We find it confusing that two forms of creativity are available to us and we tend to think we have to choose between them. Most women poets grew up in a world where womanhood was not honored, nor was motherhood. In fact, poetry did not even *include* motherhood. The women poets we studied and honored were the divine exceptions—the divine Dickinson, Millay the mad flapper, Marianne Moore who lived virginally in Brooklyn with her mother. There *were* women poets who had been mothers—Muriel Rukeyser and Adrienne Rich among others—but the difficulty of their choices was neither honored nor studied. Poetry, we were made to feel, was a male preserve. And women were born to be either muses or mothers.

My generation was destined to change all this. Of course we could not know that in our schooldays. We were destined to breed poets like Eavan Boland, who would later comment on the fact of growing up in a world "where the word *woman* and the word *poet* were almost magnetically opposed." Nor did you have to be Irish to feel the force of those powerful magnets. They were felt in America too, felt strongly enough for a poet like Sylvia Plath to feel she had to kill her mythic "Daddy" to become a poet at all. Felt strongly enough for a poet like Anne Sexton to live in conflict between the poet and the mother and to make that conflict the essence of her work.

The women poets who grappled with these paradoxes sometimes gave their lives for them. Poetry was a dangerous art for a woman. Virginia Woolf asked: "Who shall measure the heat and violence of the poet's heart when caught tangled in a woman's body?" You felt that a woman poet had to renounce her life as a woman or else renounce her art. The woman poet had to cut a deal with the devil. She had to put her heart on the chopping block in the kitchen and watch it drain itself of red blood.

The baby or the book? This fearful symmetry has haunted every woman writer I have known who chose to be a mother. It is not surprising to find that it informs our work. "The Buddha in the Womb" is an early exploration of this dilemma. At the time, there was no actual baby to consider. Later there was. I returned to the theme with more self-knowledge in *Ordinary Miracles*, and I wrote many poems for my daughter, Molly, which are about poetry and motherhood and the similarities and dissimilarities between them. But whether I resolved the conflicts posed in "The Buddha in the Womb" remains to be seen. In "The Birth of the Water Baby," the deep identification between mother and daughter makes moot the paradox of wanting/not wanting to become that dualistic being—a mother:

> Little egg,
> little nub,
> full complement of
> fingers, toes,
> little rose blooming
> in a red universe,
> which once wanted you less
> than emptiness,
> but now holds you
> fast,
> containing your rapid heart
> beat under its
> slower one
> as the earth
> contains the sea. . . .

The mother *is* the child and the child the mother so how can there be any question of choice between them? How can you choose between two creatures which are one?

In "Anti-Conception" the strangeness of one creature bringing forth another is contemplated.

Could I unthink you,
little heart,
what would I do?
Throw you out
with last night's garbage,
undo my own decisions,
my own flesh
& commit you to the void
again?

The mother-poet decides that she must get out of the way and let creation happen. She thinks of herself as publisher, producer, midwife, to the baby's grand spectacle:

you are the star,
& like your humblest fan,
I wonder
(gazing at your image
on the screen)
who you really are.

Though the poems in *Ordinary Miracles* are tender and loving, curiously they are not as strong as the "Buddha in the Womb"—written before there was an actual child to distract me from the paradox.

The child and the poem are forever diverse. One grows and changes. The other remains fixed in words. The two forms of creation forever mock each other. But flesh is the lesson for both. Flesh, however, is perishable. If anything remains, words do. We learn them and pass on. Knowing this, we write as if our lives depended upon it. They do.

X. J. KENNEDY

B Negative

M/60/5FT4/W PROT
You know it's April by the falling-off
In coughdrop boxes—fewer people cough—
    By daisies' first white eyeballs in the grass
And every dawn more underthings cast off.

Though plumtrees stretch recovered boughs to us
And doubledecked in green, the downtown bus,
    Love in one season—so your stab-pole tells—
Beds down, and buds, and is deciduous.

Now set down burlap bag. In pigeon talk
The wobbling pigeon flutes on the sidewalk,
    Struts on the breeze and clicks leisurely wings
As if the corn he ate grew on a stalk.

So plump he topples where he tries to stand,
He pecks my shoelaces, come to demand
    Another sack, another fifteen cents,
And yet—who else will eat out of my hand?

It used to be that when I laid my head
And body with it down by you in bed
    You did not turn from me nor fall to sleep
But turn to fall between my arms instead

And now I lay bifocals down. My feet
Forget the twist that brought me to your street.
    I can't make out your face for steamed-up glass
Nor quite call back your outline on the sheet.

I know how, bent to a movie magazine,
The hobo's head lights up, and from its screen
    Imagined bosoms in slow motion bloom
And no director interrupts the scene:

I used to purchase in the Automat
A cup of soup and fan it with my hat
   Until a stern voice from the changebooth crashed
Like nickels: *Gentlemen do not do that.*

Spring has no household, no abiding heat,
Pokes forth no bud from branches of concrete,
   Nothing to touch you, nothing you can touch—
The snow, at least, keeps track of people's feet.

The springer spaniel and the buoyant hare
Seem half at home reclining in mid-air
   But Lord, the times I've leaped the way they do
And looked round for a foothold—in despair.

The subway a little cheaper than a room,
I browse the *News*—or so the guards assume—
   And there half-waking, tucked in funny sheets,
Hurtle within my mile-a-minute womb.

Down streets that wake up earlier than wheels
The routed spirit flees on dusty heels
   And in the soft fire of a muscatel
Sits up, puts forth its fingertips, and feels—

Down streets so deep the sun can't vault their walls,
Where one-night wives make periodic calls,
   Where cat steals stone where rat makes off with child
And lyre and lute lie down under three balls,

Down blocks in sequence, fact by separate fact,
The human integers add and subtract
   Till in a cubic room in some hotel
You wake one day to find yourself abstract

And turn a knob and hear a voice: *Insist
On Jiffy Blades, they're tender to the wrist*—
   Then static, then a squawk as though your hand
Had shut some human windpipe with a twist.

I know how, lurking under trees by dark,
Poor loony stranglers out to make their mark
   Reach forth shy hands to touch some woman's hair—
I pick up after them in Central Park.

About "B Negative"

B Negative" is an early effort, first printed in *Poetry* during one of the editorial reigns of John Frederick Nims. Slightly revised, it went into *Nude Descending a Staircase* in 1961. Now that the passage of years has pretty well detached me from it, I can talk about it at last without agony.

Back when it first appeared, I was deeply hurt to have it condemned by two critics I respected, John Simon and Randall Jarrell. But today, looking back on their objections, I can see that those astute gentlemen pointed out two of its features that remain most highly questionable.

The first is the theme. Simon, reviewing *Nude* for *The Hudson Review*, accused me of stealing this ingredient from Donald Hall. He added that he could understand someone's imitating a great poet, but to imitate Donald Hall—well, that was beneath contempt. It now seems clear from the career of Donald Hall that he is a poet well worth imitating. Even at that time, I respected him and his work, and I had read and remembered his early poem "The Lone Ranger," which dismisses that celebrated horseman as a nonentity: "He was abstract." Simon rightly found an echo of that line in "B Negative." It occurs when my narrator (and only character) remarks,

> Down blocks in sequence, fact by separate fact,
> The human integers add and subtract
>   Till in a cubic room in some hotel
> You wake one day to find yourself abstract

—and he goes on to consider suicide. That was, to my mind, the best way to state the central notion of the poem: that to be alone in a city reduces a human being to a cipher. I hadn't realized that I was indebted to Hall's poem until Simon noticed the resemblance. "The Lone Ranger" had become part of me, and unconsciously, I had echoed it.

That, by the way, is always a danger for a poet, especially a poet who reads other poets: to steal unconsciously. I worry about that, nowadays. Sometimes when I'm working on a poem, lines occur that make me think, "Damn! that's good." Right away, I start doubting that those lines could possibly be mine, and try to recall where I stole them from.

The title of the poem tries to indicate what it is driving at. The phrase "B Negative" is the speaker's blood type, encoded on a medical bracelet or a military dogtag. As an enlisted man in the Navy, I had worn such a metal plate on a chain around my neck, stamped with my blood type in case I ever needed an emergency transfusion and with the kind of religion to be asked to bury me. The epigraph, the line beneath the title, has puzzled some readers, but it too is statistical: M/60/5FT4/W PROT— the description, "Male, age 60, five feet four inches, white Protestant." I guessed that those might be abbreviations used by a social worker to identify cases. I might have added the protagonist's social security number. Actually, the reader need not pay any attention to the title or the epigraph; the rest of the poem should make the theme clear. I was thinking of a tendency that has only gone on and intensified in recent years, when most people have telephone area codes and nine-figure zip codes and, the more affluent, e-mail addresses.

In its closing lines, the poem attacks our cipher-promoting society. At the time, I was living like a monk, committed to poverty, chastity, and obedience. A teaching fellow carrying a heavy load of freshman comp, I was also assisting as a paper grader and taking graduate courses such as medieval literature from a demanding old Prussian. Most of the time when off duty I was alone. Working on "B Negative," I felt drawn toward the speaker of the poem, who works in New York's Central Park, impaling litter on a stick with a pin at the end of it.

New York was familiar territory. Having grown up in a town 34 miles from Times Square, I had hung out in the Village as a teenager, and later, in 1950–51, had gone to Columbia. In that whole year, while earning an M.A., I had made only one friend. And I knew that curious feeling that the city can incite, the sense of being absolutely alone in its cavernous streets, even though surrounded by a crowd. I could see how a man living alone in a flophouse and working at a meaningless job could turn into a strangler for sure.

As a kid, I had known a fellow science fiction fan named John Keil, a little older than me, who had dropped out of society to haunt the Bowery and write for *The Hobo News*. Keil devoutly believed in hoboism, solitude, and independence. (Ah, John, what ever became of you and your projected novel with the high concept that a Lesbian and a gay fall for each other and swap sexual identities? I wonder if you died in a blizzard in some alley, your head upon a wine bottle.) There is probably some of

John Keil in the speaker in "B Negative." All my life, I have gravitated to lonesome people for friendship—some of them oddballs and outsiders. Anyone interested in pursuing the matter might find in my work several poems about such loners, some of them imagined: a compulsive exhibitionist, a pyromaniac. By the way, the great American poets who loved and understood such characters must be Edward Arlington Robinson and James Wright, both of whose poems I continue to love.

In "B Negative," besides empathizing with a lone sticker of wastepaper twice my age, I was having a good time feeling sorry for myself— at least, for the part of me that felt like a loner too. But let me not leave claim that the poem is confessional. People are always expecting poems to be pure autobiography. Oftener, poems tell only part of the truth; the rest is sheer invention. The character in the poem isn't me.

The other terrible blast that "B Negative" received, from Randall Jarrell, was directed at the form it is written in. This is the quatrain of Edward Fitzgerald's glorious mistranslation of *The Rubaiyat of Omar Khayyam*. I wonder to what extent poets of today read *The Rubaiyat*; anyhow, it was a holy text to me. I grew up during the Depression in a family for whom books were a luxury. Yet somehow, by a stroke of luck, our household library, all two shelves of it, had a selection from Whitman's *Leaves of Grass*—including sexy parts omitted from my school literature book—and the whole of Fitzgerald's *Rubaiyat*, in two Haldeman–Julius Little Blue Books. These were primitive paperbacks that served up butchered editions of the classics and used to sell for a nickel. From their rottenly printed pages, I devoured both Whitman and Omar, two poets who couldn't differ more widely in their outlooks: Whitman, the expansive and all-embracing and formally shaggy cheerleader, positive at the top of his voice; Omar, the cynical sybarite, locking his nihilistic thoughts into terse rhyming stanzas—at least, as Fitzgerald renders him. Omar preached the doctrine of getting drunk and making love and so forgetting our lamentable human condition. At the time, I hadn't ever got drunk or made love, so his doctrine seemed novel and interesting.

Because I was wrestling to escape from Catholicism, Omar sent a thrill down my spine. Here was a guy who dared claim that, if God even existed, He didn't give a damn about us whatsoever.

> And that inverted bowl they call the sky,
> Whereunder crawling cooped we live and die,
> Lift not your hands to *it* for help, for it
> As impotently moves as you or I.

Powerful stuff for a would-be poet of thirteen! I committed fistfuls of Omar to memory. As much as anything, it was the music of Fitzgerald's translation that snared me—the sumptuous word-music that had made it the most widely read and quoted English poem of the nineteenth century:

> I sometimes think that never blows so red
> The rose as where some buried Caesar bled,
>   And every hyacinth the garden wears
> Dropped in her lap from some once lovely head.

To this day, those lines still strike me as miraculous. Besides the ingenious verbal melody of those alliterations and assonances, I love the precision of the form—the way the end of a sentence falls gracefully into the hammock of its final line. And so, when I came to write "B Negative," I found my thoughts coming out in Fitzgerald-like quatrains, and was glad of it.

Unluckily for me, Randall Jarrell detested *The Rubaiyat*—a fact I found out the hard way. In the fall of 1962 when I went to Greensboro to teach at the Woman's College of the University of North Carolina, Jarrell was the star of the faculty. Because I had recently published a book of poems, I was invited to give a reading to the college community. To my joy, the great man himself came. But shy as he was sometimes, Jarrell was never shy about expressing his judgments. When I told the audience that "B Negative" was written in the quatrain of *The Rubaiyat*, from out of the darkness came a loud, retching "Ugh!" in Jarrell's unmistakable voice. My God, what a blood-chilling moment. I had hoped, of course, that Jarrell would approve of my stuff, but at his unexpected reaction I stood there, shaken to the core. It was a struggle to go on and read the poem, and indeed, to get through the rest of the evening. I kept wishing myself a thousand miles away. Later, when I had come to know him better, I learned that Jarrell disliked poetry that tried to show off—anything too swaggeringly and ingeniously made. A. E. Housman and Elinor Wylie, also some of my favorites, were among his other antipathies. So I had baited him, without intending to, and my dream of being one of his favorite young poets and having him make my reputation overnight with one laudatory review, as he did for Robert Lowell, had been shattered by that devastating "Ugh!"

Still, if you're any kind of a poet, all you can be is whoever you really are. Try to make yourself over in the image that a critic will approve, and you end up a scarecrow on a stick. Better to be an honest William McGonagall or an authentic Julia Moore, the Sweet Singer of Michigan, or the aspirant who comes in five-thousand-and-ninth in the Yale Younger Poets contest but who goes on with his own work just the same.

Today, Randall Jarrell's contempt for polished stanzas continues to be widely shared. Me, I remain in love with such containers, provided that the poet who writes in them has sufficient energy to fill them all the way. It is better yet if the damned containers practically explode from the force of emotion trying to burst out of them. Well, let the reader decide whether "B Negative" speaks with enough feeling to overcome the constricting effect of those *Rubaiyat* quatrains. If a poem in tight stanzas lacks passion, I know, then it is stillborn—hollow and thin, like the tinkling of a row of symmetrical music boxes.

MAXINE KUMIN

Poem for My Son

Where water laps my hips
it licks your chin. You stand
on tiptoe looking up
and swivel on my hands.
We play at this and laugh,
but understand you weigh
now almost less than life
and little more than sea.
So fine a line exists
between buoyance and stone
that, catching at my wrists,
I feel love notch the bone
to think you might have gone.

To think they smacked and pumped
to squall you into being
when you swam down, lungs limp
as a new balloon, and dying.
Six years today they bent
a black tube through your chest.
The tank hissed in the tent.
I leaned against the mast
outside that sterile nest.

And now inside the sea
you bump along my arm,
learning the narrow way
you've come from that red worm.
I tell you, save your air
and let the least swell ease you.
Put down, you flail for shore.
I cannot bribe nor teach you
to know the wet will keep you.

And cannot tell myself
unfasten from the boy.

On the Atlantic shelf
I see you wash away
to war or love or luck,
prodigious king, a stranger.
Times I stepped on a crack
my mother was in danger,
and time will find the chinks
to work the same in me.
You bobbled in my flanks.
They cut you from my sea.
Now you must mind your way.

Once, after a long swim
come overhand and wheezy
across the dappled seam
of lake, I foundered, dizzy,
uncertain which was better:
to fall there and unwind
in thirty feet of water
or fight back for the land.
Life would not let me lose it.
It yanked me by the nose.
Blackfaced and thick with vomit
it thrashed me to my knees.
We only think we choose.

But say we choose. Pretend it.
My pulse knit in your wrist
expands. Go now and spend it.
The sea will take our kiss.
Now, boy, swim off for this.

Word for Word

This summer, watching my six-year-old grandson conquer his instinctual fear of the water, I find myself remembering word for word a poem I wrote almost forty years ago, titled "Poem for My Son." The stanzas come back in my head intact, and the feelings that accompanied my writing it recur with the language of the poem.

Today I look at this child's father, a robust and hirsute 43-year-old who began life in an oxygen tent, and endured several childhood bouts of bronchial croup. Born into a family of swimmers, he struggled mightily to learn that although he was skinny and lacked the natural buoyancy of his sisters, he could indeed float face down, add overhand strokes, and kick his way to shore.

The poem, in quite rigidly adhered to trimeter, comprises nine- and thirteen-line stanzas; the final stanza, five lines. Throughout, the rhymes run along in a seemingly artless abab, cdcd scheme, with reliance on a fair amount of slant rhyme (hips/up; weigh/sea, and so on). The odd-numbered final line of each stanza rhymes with the penultimate line to form a sort of recurring coda.

I don't remember how much difficulty this invented form presented at the time. I do remember my determination to make the rhymes appear effortless, unavoidable, and perhaps not too obvious, for much as I love and lean on rhyme, I abhor the overt, in-your-face variety. And I certainly remember the relief I felt working within the constraints imposed by a three-beat line and a predetermined rhyme scheme, for here, paradoxically, freedom resided. Once boxed in, I could say, it seemed, anything! Working in form has consistently been my salvation. I cling to it especially when confronting intimate subject matter—the death of a sibling, the love of a child, the loss of a close personal friend, for the demands of the schema drive me to a level of metaphor, an outreach of rhyme I would be hard pressed to arrive at in free verse.

Recently, as my editor at W. W. Norton and I conferred on the table of contents for my *Selected Poems 1961–91* to be published in the spring of 1997, I argued for the inclusion of this poem. I feel it represents not only my early "tribal poems" of kinship but also the preoccupation with swimming that caused an early reviewer to tag me virtually amphibious. With considerable regret I finally withdrew it from the very small group of poems saved from my first collection, *Halfway*; there just wasn't room.

Now, looking back at "Poem for My Son," I reenter the struggle against the soft edge of sentimentality that I fear flaws many of my early poems. I have spent 35 years paring expressions of love and commitment down to the bone. Today, I would never permit myself the next-to-last line of the poem. I doubt I'd allow the easy vocative address of the final line. I recoil from what appears to be facile, even glib, in this ending.

While the first three stanzas still look clean and workable to me, when I come to the fourth with its presumptuous clairvoyance of "war or love or luck," I begin to lose my appetite for this poem. The statement that "time will find the chinks / to work the same in me," alas, feels not only obvious but self-indulgent.

The narrative content of the penultimate stanza, however, still seems acceptable, even interesting. Does one need to be a deeply fatigued long-distance swimmer or marathon runner to have experienced this ambivalence toward finishing the task? For the climber, even staying alive, say, at 22,000 feet requires prodigious effort. Still, giving up is not an option. What physical exhaustion teaches is, "We only think we choose."

One other small item of self-congratulation about this poem: I continue to admire a reprise from stanza to stanza, which I think was a gift from the muse, for I was not conscious of its occurrence until well after the poem was written: in the last line of the first stanza, "to think you might have gone" is picked up in the first line of the second as "To think they smacked and pumped. . . ." The last line of the second stanza poses "outside that sterile nest" and answers it with its opposite, "inside the sea" in the first line of the next stanza. At the end of that stanza, "I cannot bribe nor teach you" is answered in the opening line of the next with "And cannot tell myself. . . ." Finally, "We only think we choose" reprises in the first line of the last stanza as "But say we choose."

Perhaps without my knowing it, these wraparounds were preparation for writing a crown of sonnets (see "Letters" in *Connecting the Dots*), where the last line of the first becomes the first line of the second, and so on. Reusing, rephrasing, regrouping a line makes for heady sport in a variety of forms from the villanelle to the pantoum, ghazal, and triolet.

And in a way, that supplies my credo when it comes to writing in form. I believe it is my option, even my duty to rhyme without recourse to predictable love/doves or fire/desires; to remain metrically precise without lulling the reader to sleep with a singsong lullaby; to rephrase and reuse the line in surprising permutations; to play the intricate game of poetry by stretching language in all possible directions while at the same time compressing it into apt yet unsettling images.

Formal poetry exhibits freedom and elasticity within agreed-upon confines; as in swimming, you must let the water keep you and yet bend it to your uses. Thus, while "Poem for My Son" is not quite the poem I would write today, I continue to cherish it.

To the Young Woman Looking for the Eating Disorder Workshop Who Found a Poetry Reading Instead

In any case, come in.
   I know this isn't exactly what
you were looking for, that

it isn't easy walking into a room
   of strangers who look happy
enough and yet are waiting to be

fed. Sometimes I think of words
   as food and yet, like you, must give
back what I take in—like the thought

I can hold a word in my mouth
   to keep the world together,
to put food in those mouths

that appear nightly like gaping
   sparrows. I wasn't going to say this
but, in my other life, I talk

with girls who starve themselves
   or give up their food, in the hope
that talking—when it comes down

to it, two mouths giving and taking—
   will let the world take care of itself
so those girls can begin feeding

themselves again, sitting at the table.
   By now you may realize this is
no workshop to solve this, or, to use

the words, I'm afraid, on the tip
   of my tongue, no fast food solution.
I'm not sure your listening here

will change anything, sitting in between
    the rows of these stanzas, but perhaps,
after the reading, before we both must

leave, we will have a chance
    to say a few words to each other, our sweet
luck by which to remember this hour.

Perhaps Before We Both Must Leave

OI.

nce, a few years ago, I arrived early to prepare for a poetry reading at the former estate of Henry Ford in Dearborn, Michigan, more recently a satellite campus of the state university. I found the room where I was to read my poems, one of which referred to the Detroit riots of the late sixties, one night of which a friend and I, in town for a conference, escaped the National Guard's imposed curfew to drive across the border to listen to music in Windsor, Ontario.

I was the first to arrive. Soon after, a young woman walked tentatively in, and seeing the rows of empty chairs, the lectern and microphone, quietly asked me, "Is this the eating disorder workshop?" I smiled, hopefully to myself, and said it wasn't, that it was a poetry reading and that she was welcome to stay. Students and faculty, a few older Dearborn residents came in and sat down. She stayed, too, and after the hour's reading shyly approached me with a few words of thanks.

She didn't know I was a counselor on my home campus in Middlebury, Vermont. She didn't know I counseled young women who weren't eating, not eating enough, or sometimes vomiting their food away. She didn't know, in the seventies, out of intuition and frustration, our school psychiatrist and I gathered a group of these women together, so they didn't have to be isolated in their own obsession, so we didn't have to be alone with our ignorance, so we could talk together. It may have been one of the first group therapies with eating-disordered college students, at that time, where all we had was our words.

Over the years, this Dearborn woman stayed with me—her apparent loneliness and courage, her willingness to let something new—those poems, that event—fill time and perhaps, in that moment, part of herself. She filled me with memory and feeling and then, unpredictably, in a series of associated images, which found their voice in a poem. "In any case, come in."

2.

I didn't know I wanted to speak, over the years, back to her. Or that, eventually, this poem would find its form in addressing her and, by extension, its readers. But I did have the mentors of e.e. cummings and William Carlos Williams in my literary and clinical heritage.

Once, a reporter asked cummings if he was a painter or poet. He responded in writing a poem for the catalogue to his exhibit at the Rochester Memorial Art Gallery in 1915, in which he refused to define himself in singular categories. He wrote, "Tell me, doesn't your painting interfere with your writing? / Quite the contrary, they love each other dearly." We remember, Williams drafted poems after house calls, on his prescription pad. And the Greeks had their pantheon of gods and goddesses who, in their multiplicity, were us. So, too, the poets who are teachers and psychologists, priests, lawyers, and insurance executives.

This complexity of human urge and roles is mirrored in language itself—how speaking in one voice, tone, and diction carries the depth and nuance of other voices. The word, and the image or action it stands for, holds the history of its own use, as well as history. The word disappears into its own silence and space, and also stays on the page, in the ear, implying, creating its future. "In any case come in."

3.

A poem needs to find a way into itself. In this case, my poem found a way to talk back to/remember the young woman in Dearborn, to speak to the women with whom I was currently working, to contemplate what words do and don't do, the necessity and helplessness we sometimes feel in speaking and being talked to. This poem wanted to hope for and think about recovery—a kind of healing—at the same time it realized, acknowledged the uselessness sometimes of fast solutions, of treatments, of language. Sometimes all we can hope for is acknowledgment and human recognition in a voice that is familiar. Those few words, at the end of an hour, are a remembrance and never a cure, they are something fixed, unmoving. "I know this isn't exactly what / you were looking for."

So the poet-counselor, the speaker of this poem, begins speaking back to her and to himself, in a tone that is both casual and considered, that talks itself into and to its terrors and knowledge. The poem comes to surprise—the moment of fear and astonishment, some realization—in the image of the gaping sparrows, the starving poor and the rich who starve themselves, whom the speaker wishes to feed with food and words and yet realizes the he, the poem, cannot do this *for* anyone else. We ultimately learn to feed ourselves.

The poem comes to surprise, too, when the speaker surprises himself with his own disclosure, revelation—"I wasn't going to say this, but, in my other life. . . ." The poem cannot expect truth in its saying, if, in any case, it cannot speak truthfully about and to itself. The young woman, this poem's muse, took the speaker by surprise, astonished him in her willingness to connect through listening and brief gratitude. Yet, as in any poem, the surprises that remain in the writing, the revising are chosen. We choose what we let be seen of ourselves, at the same time we can't hide who we are. "I wasn't going to say this, but, in my other life. . . ."

4.

Finally, the poem needs to say what it isn't—"no workshop," "no fast food solution." It is only its own remembrance, its wish, its moment of expression and contemplation. The poem knows what the speaker sees and thinks and what it doesn't know, what the speaker cannot fix or cure. Saving or salvation is then in the speaker's hope for the "you," the listener, that she realizes what the poem isn't, what words can't guarantee, what faith can only exist in *perhaps*, in a word like *perhaps*. And in that point of connection, exchange, even in leaving. "Perhaps, / after the reading, before we both must / leave, we will have a chance / to say a few words to each other, our sweet / luck by which to remember this hour."

Quid Pro Quo

Just after my wife's miscarriage (her second
in four months), I was sitting in an empty
classroom exchanging notes with my friend,
a budding Joyce scholar with steelrimmed
glasses, when, lapsed Irish Catholic that he was,
he surprised me by asking what I thought now
of God's ways towards man. It was spring,

such spring as came to the flintbacked Chenango
Valley thirty years ago, the full force of Siberia
behind each blast of wind. Once more my poor wife
was in the local four-room hospital, recovering.
The sun was going down, the room's pinewood panels
all but swallowing the gelid light, when, suddenly,
I surprised not only myself but my colleague

by raising my middle finger up to heaven, *quid*
pro quo, the hardly grand defiant gesture a variant
on Vanni Fucci's figs, shocking not only my friend
but in truth the gesture's perpetrator too. I was 24,
and, in spite of having pored over the Confessions
& that Catholic Tractate called the Summa, was sure
I'd seen enough of God's erstwhile ways towards man.

That summer, under a pulsing midnight sky
shimmering with Van Gogh stars, in a ructive,
cedarscented cabin off Lake George, having lied
to the gentrified owner of the boys' camp
that indeed I knew wilderness & lakes and could,
if need be, lead a whole fleet of canoes down
the turbulent whitewater passages of the Fulton Chain

(I who had last been in a rowboat with my parents
at the age of six), my wife and I made love, trying
not to disturb whose ever headboard & waterglass
lie just beyond the paperthin partition at our feet.
In the broad black Adirondack stillness, as we lay

there on our sagging mattress, my wife & I gazed out
through the broken roof into a sky that seemed

somehow to look back down on us, and in that place,
that holy place, she must have conceived again,
for nine months later in a New York hospital she
brought forth a son, a little buddha-bellied
rumplestiltskin runt of a man who burned
to face the sun, the fact of his being there
both terrifying & lifting me at once, this son,

this gift, whom I still look upon with joy & awe. Worst,
best, just last year, this same son, grown
to manhood now, knelt before a marble altar to vow
everything he had to the same God I had had my own
erstwhile dealings with. How does one bargain
with a God like this, who, *quid pro quo*, ups
the ante each time He answers one sign with another?

Quid Pro Quo

Randall Jarrell once commented to the effect that a poet, prepared to stand in an open field over a lifetime of waiting, would be lucky to be struck by lightning half a dozen times. He was talking about the vast disparity between preparedness—keeping one's pencils sharpened and erasers at the ready as one went through the daily exercise of writing—and the times when the poet believes inspiration had arrived. By inspiration I suppose Jarrell meant something like the welding of music to the precise curves of a complex, shimmering emotion. It's the way I feel about "Quid Pro Quo."

Like you and you, I too have spent weeks and months sweating over a particular lyric, trying to get the thing right. One poem I wrote two years ago, called "Then," is just such an example. Originally it had a complex Rilkean scaffolding and three days of intense talks with Robert Bly—at U Mass for a conference on Rilke—holding it up. In its early states it was hung with Rilkean angels and attitudes before I finally eased all of them out of the poem in the name of a New World pragmatic simplicity. "Quid Pro Quo," on the other hand, came to me largely in a single sitting for reasons I can only guess at. And it's because the poem still haunts me (and apparently others) that I want to talk about it in the hopes that I too will better understand it.

Here's how I remember the poem's psychogenesis. In the spring of '95 my wife and I were reading through St. John's Gospel, a short passage each morning. We'd been at this for nearly two months when, one Sunday morning towards the end of Lent, sitting at the kitchen table, we came to the passage in John 13 where Jesus tells his disciples that he is about to be betrayed by someone close to him. Suddenly a shiver went through me and I was remembering an incident which had occurred thirty years before at Colgate. It was something I don't believe I'd ever told anyone about.

I was twenty-four then and had been married just seven months. I was a struggling instructor of English then—teaching four sections of freshman English for a small-enough salary. My wife was in the local (twelve bed?) hospital in Hamilton recovering from her second miscarriage and I was sitting in an empty classroom late one afternoon with my friend, Mike Begnal, a freshman instructor and budding Joyce scholar. It was a late winter's day, and there was the glacial feel of Siberian winter over everything. I remember Mike looking at me with that characteristically bemused, inquisitorial glint of his through steel-rimmed glasses like the spoiled Irish priest I imagined him to be, and his asking me what I thought *now* of God's ways toward men.

I was broke, terrified of being unable to go on with my education—the one way I saw out of my working-class background—and completely unprepared emotionally or economically to become a father. My wife and I were serious Catholics and here, for the second time in little more than half a year, the rhythm method of birth control had inexplicably failed. No one at a liberal Protestant bastion like Colgate, I believed, could really understand how a young graduate student would allow himself to get into such a predicament as I now found myself. In truth, as sad as I was at this second miscarriage, something in me felt relieved *and* guilty, though thirty years later I still find myself mourning for the babies that might have been and must remain forever now mere possibility.

And so, when my friend quoted Milton's tag about my justifying God's ways now to men, without thinking about it I raised my middle finger up to the heavens. Lapsed Irish Catholic though he was, his face registered a sort of bemused shock at what I'd done, followed by nervous laughter on both our parts. My own reaction was more complex. Had I really just done such a thing? And if I had, had I meant it? Could I now erase the gesture? Those feelings would quickly sink underground, to surface now and then over the years. As on the particular Sunday morning which I mentioned earlier, when I read the words, *One of you will betray me.*

In the fall of '64 I began graduate studies at Hunter College in midtown Manhattan. One of the first courses I took was with the noted translator and poet Allen Mandelbaum. He was thirty-seven then, dressed impeccably after the Italian fashion, had just joined the Hunter faculty after a thirteen-year sojourn in Florence and Rome, and was already preparing his brilliant translation of the *Commedia*. It was in his class that I came across the passage in Canto XXV of the *Inferno* where the tormented thief makes "figs / of both his fists, and raising them, cried, / 'Take that, God, these are both for you!.' " Reading those words, the classroom at Colgate reemerged from the glacial depths for a moment, then sank back again.

The question one has to consider—and it is the same question Job's God responds to—is just who is this poor forked yammerer, this piss-poor inquisitor who insists on knowing God's deepest designs. Is this metaphysical questioner the same who had lied to the owner of that camp for boys up in the Adirondacks that he was no less than an expert canoeist so that he and his wife might have a rent-free place for the summer and meals and rent money at summer's end for a small apartment in Flushing? The same who allowed the owner to talk him into taking a too-huge group of boys down the splendid lakes that make up the Fulton Chain, including some too small to portage their own canoes, a miscalculation that led on the second day of the trip to the leader's trying to shoot the rapids with his charges in tow rather than try yet another time-consuming portage, and this with summer dusk coming on?

There is one moment that still sticks out vividly in my mind. We are between sections of punishing whitewater, and have turned a bend in the river. It is about eight in the evening and a doe has come down to the water's edge to drink. As I approach in the lead canoe, having signaled to the boy in front not to stir, and with the others straggling behind and out of sight, the doe looks up at me with its large round feminine eyes and will not scare. And then, as I come within feet of it, the ten canoes straggling behind me, each with its two or three boys paddling and laughing as they follow this twenty-four-year-old who has put their lives in jeopardy, the doe slowly turns and disappears into the darkening shadows.

And then the reality of the present situation is back with us again. Bats circle and dive above us, the swirling silver-flecked waters grow darker and darker. We are all of us pretty much soaked through by now, and there are still those last rapids to negotiate, and I am praying to the same God whom I had earlier signed to to please—*please*—get us through this and out onto the stillness of the lake without anyone capsizing or getting hurt.

And though we are soon in the midst of the rapids, we somehow make it through without mishap—a miracle in itself—and then we are out on the still black waters of Long Lake under a beautiful rising moon. As soon as we can make a ridge, we camp for the night, build small fires, eat the packaged stew we've brought, and sleep soundly. In the morning there is a storm louring on the horizon, and when I ask my young charges if they want to continue on like troopers or admit defeat and go back to camp, they opt for camp. Who can blame them?

Sed quaeritur: Is the speaker in this poem any more prepared—than the reader, say—to receive a sign from God that he will read aright? Does he—this young husband and soon-to-be-father—understand even the human relationships he's in, much less his relation to the divine? This drama I have tried to capture in the mesh of language itself: the headstrong overrove syntax, the nervous asides, the comic appeal to the speaker's Catholic intellectual credentials. Underlying all of this shuttling back and forth of language, however, there still remains the underlying seriousness of the question.

Then there is the question of the speaker looking back now through the lens of Hopkins and Van Gogh on the sheer beauty of that particular moment in the Adirondacks, of the hole in the cabin roof through which all that starry beauty—which had always been there, mind you—seemed to look down on the young speaker and his younger wife, when the gift of conception was granted. Not of course that the young man would have understood this at the time, for the reality of that night and the morning of his first son's birth (Passion Sunday, April 4th, 1965) still has the power to awe this speaker. So this is the grace that has been granted in spite of the speaker's impatience and rebellion and gracelessness: the mystery of fatherhood. And so much more.

More time elapses. In the wink of an eye a quarter century falls away, and the embryonic drama continues to unfold, right up to the present. The speaker, older now, but essentially one with that younger self, watches as his son and namesake kneels before a small altar in a Jesuit chapel in Los Angeles with a group of other young men—Irish, Italian, Vietnamese, Filipino, Latin American—and humbly, gladly, prepares to turn over his life to the same God the speaker had once had his own awkward dealings with.

* * *

The poem consists of nine sentences, some of them short declarative statements, some of them baroque in their twisted convolutions the way Stevens, say, is in *The Comedian as the Letter C*. Eight sentences are followed by a final open-ended question, for which the reader—like the speaker—will have to provide his or her own answer. There are seven isostanzaic stanzas, each seven lines long, and someone who knows more about sacred numerology than I do will have to say what seven sevens might represent. For me the pattern satisfies, and gives a sense of completion and of rest, perhaps from my reading of the first creation mythos in Genesis of the Lord who creates the world in six days and rests on the seventh, his work week completed.

Another thing. For all the poem's speed and rush of syntax, there's a grand stillness in the poem, as if it were the equivalent of an ikon of some sort: the speaker's restlessness countered by God's hand supporting him and his young wife. For me the poem feels as if it had somehow captured the essence of at least four relationships: the man and the woman who open the poem, the young father and his infant son, the speaker young and the speaker older, looking back on his brash younger self, though not exactly in Wordsworthian tranquility.

Finally there is the relationship of the speaker to his God, the same whom he has underestimated more than once, trying to make the Lord of subatomic particles *and* the Lord of exploding new galaxies (new proof of which Hubble is just now flashing back at us at an awesome rate) over into *his* own sorry image. There's a lesson here, not much different from the one Dante and Milton and Herbert and Berryman—to compare great things with small—have also given us, but a lesson worth repeating.

People Like Us

When the ox was the gray enemy
of the forest and engine of the plow,
the poor drifted across the fields,
through the sweet grasses and the vile,
and tendered bare bowls at our doors.
We hoarded and they begged. We stacked
our hayricks high and they slept there
like barncats or cuckoos.

When we sluiced the maculate streets
with fermenting slops, and strode to our jobs
furred by coaldust, didn't the poor
punctuate our routines with cries
for alms? Our sclerotic rivers
turned the color of old leather
and the poor fished them anyway
and slept under their bridges.

Now they come flaring up the stairs
and up the fire escapes. Open our door
to them and then they're us,
and if we don't we're trapped inside
with only us for company
while in the hall they pray and sing
their lilting anthems of reproach
while we bite our poor tongues.

"People Like Us"

I wrote what turned out to be an early version of "People Like Us" while I was working on *Time & Money* (1995), and published it, under a different title, in *Hubbub*, an excellent magazine in Portland, Oregon. I try not to let a poem get loose before I'm sure I've made of it all I can, but in this case I failed.

These days I store my poems in a computer. I can't compose poems on one, I like to say; this formula may be no more than a sour Luddite pride. It seems to me that poems in the magazines are about 20% longer since the computer has been in wide use among poets than they were before, and perhaps I don't compose poems on mine as a prophylaxis against windiness.

In any case, I sent my earlier version into cyber-darkness when I re-wrote the poem late in 1995. Keeping my own drafts seems to me both a clutter and a vanity. I'm not sure that comparison of my early version to this one would prove instructive, but it's impossible.

The first stanza seems to take place in rural England, the second in London, and the final stanza in a city rather like the one I live in, New York. Perhaps the eras in which the three stanzas happen are more important than the exact settings, for the poem makes little fuss about identifying those settings.

In the first stanza the industrial revolution feels a long way off. Work means converting forests to tillable fields. There's an odd mixture of tones in the stanza: "the sweet grasses and the vile" has a Book of Common Prayer sound to it, and perhaps I had the phrase "vile bodies" not so much "in mind" as in my memory's "ear." A similar tone is struck by "tendered." On the other hand, "the poor drifted across the fields" calls to mind, now, though not when I rewrote the poem, a scene out of "The Night of the Living Dead." The word "drifted" suggests snow more than any physical menace. Perhaps the major threat the poor can offer here, as elsewhere in the poem, is to represent the human cost of the prosperity that the ants in the poem (the poor, then, are the grasshoppers) enjoy. It will be to insulate the ants against this constant reminder that, many years after the era depicted in the first stanzas, suburbs will be built.

The poem has some sound patterns in it that don't quite constitute end-rhyme, but that are faintly audible all the same. In the first stanza, "doors" and "there" look forward to "poor" in stanza two and "door," again, in stanza three. In stanza two, "rivers" has a faint link both to "bridges" and "leather." And in the third stanza "sing" and "tongues" chime softly. I'll leave the investigation of internal rhyme to the curious reader.

The beginnings of the three stanzas are linked: "When" (stanza 1), "When" (2), and "Now" (3). All three stanzas are end-stopped; they're complete units. The sentence that ends each stanza is always longer than the one that ends the previous stanza. If this effect contributes anything to the impression that the poem has grown into its own conclusion, as I think it might, it's the sort of effect that can't be planned. The decisions that produce it are made subliminally. It's possible that one major function of revision is to keep the poet in touch with the poem's possibilities long enough for such subliminal patterning to occur. If so, what went wrong with the early version I published in *Hubbub* may well have been the result of not handling the poem long enough.

Of course, it's possible to handle a poem too much. Then the moment comes when the poem goes inert, like dough kneaded too long, and the poet has handled the poem to death.

I notice that things tend to get paired in this poem: "gray enemy" and "engine," "sweet grasses" and "vile," "hoarded" and "begged," "stacked" and "slept," and "barncats" and "cuckoos" are all from the first stanza alone. "And" appears three times in the second stanza and four in the third. They all refer to a larger yoking together that keeps on not getting made, between the poor and the prosperous, the drifters and the workers, between people like us and those on whose bad fortune our good fortune has been built.

In this context we hear the title as heavily ironic. In ordinary social life the phrase "people like us" is used not only to characterize similarity but also to exclude, and the poem keeps suggesting that the excluded are far more like us than we like to think.

There's a fastidious, precisionist diction running through the poem that I associate, looking at the poem now, with an urge toward tidiness and exclusion: "tendered," "maculate," "sclerotic," and perhaps "punctuate" and "reproach." A tonic and uncontrollable messiness also infests the poem: "barncats," "slops," "flaring" (I like its proximity to "fire escapes"), and "bite our poor tongues." The attachment of the adjective "poor" to the tongues of the silent, prosperous folks unsettled by the messy and vocal poor suggests an identity the poem has been hoping to assert to the speaker all along. It may be a happy irony of the poem that this moment can only happen if the speaker voices it himself, and once he does, the poem's work is over.

J. D. MCCLATCHY

My Mammogram

I.

In the shower, at the shaving mirror or beach,
For years I'd led . . . the unexamined life?
When all along and so easily within reach
(Closer even than the nonexistent wife)

Lay the trouble—naturally enough
Lurking in a useless, overlooked
Mass of fat and old newspaper stuff
About matters I regularly mistook

As a horror story for the opposite sex,
Nothing to do with what at my downtown gym
Are furtively ogled as The Guy's Pecs.

But one side is swollen, the too tender skin
Discolored. So the doctor orders an X-
Ray, and nervously frowns at my nervous grin.

II.

Mammography's on the basement floor.
The nurse has an executioner's gentle eyes.
I start to unbutton my shirt. She shuts the door.
Fifty, male, already embarrassed by the size

Of my "breasts," I'm told to put the left one
Up on a smudged, cold, Plexiglas shelf,
Part of a robot half menacing, half glum,
Like a three-dimensional model of the Freudian self.

Angles are calculated. The computer beeps.
Saucers close on a flatness further compressed.
There's an ache near the heart neither dull nor sharp.

The room gets lethal. Casually the nurse retreats
Behind her shield. Anxiety as blithely suggests
I joke about a snapshot for my Christmas card.

III.

"No sign of cancer," the radiologist swans
In to say—with just a hint in his tone
That he's done me a personal favor—whereupon
His look darkens. "But what these pictures show . . .

Here, look, you'll notice the gland on the left's
Enlarged. See?" I see an aerial shot
Of Iraq, and nod. "We'll need further tests,
Of course, but I'd bet that what *you've* got

Is a liver problem. Trouble with your estrogen
Levels. It's time, my friend, to take stock.
It happens more often than you'd think to men."

Reeling from its millionth Scotch on the rocks,
In other words, my liver's sensed the end.
Why does it come as something less than a shock?

IV.

The end of life as I've known it, that is to say—
Testosterone sported like a power tie,
The matching set of drives and dreads that may
Now soon be plumped to whatever new designs

My apparently resentful, androgynous
Inner life has on me. Blind seer?
The Bearded Lady in some provincial circus?
Something that others both desire and fear.

Still, doesn't everyone *long* to be changed,
Transformed to, no matter, a higher or lower state,
To know the leathery D-Day hero's strange

Detachment, the queen bee's dreamy loll?
Oh, but the future each of us blankly awaits
Was long ago written on the genetic wall.

V.

So suppose the breasts fill out until I look
Like my own mother . . . ready to nurse a son,

A version of myself, the infant understood
In the end as the way my own death had come.

Or will I in a decade be back here again,
The diagnosis this time not freakish but fatal?
The changes in one's later years all tend,
Until the last one, toward the farcical,

Each of us slowly turned into something that hurts,
Someone we no longer recognize.
If soul is the final shape I shall assume,

(—*A knock at the door. Time to button my shirt*
And head back out into the waiting room.)
Which of my bodies will have been the best disguise?

On "My Mammogram"

Most poems are willed into being, worked up. Their subjects are traditional or appropriate or trendy. I may decide, for instance, that it would be a good idea to write about my mother's childhood or my father's death, about Auden's dictionary or the pope's penis. I might decide, putting a collection together, that for the sake of balance or surprise my book needs another nature poem or perhaps some lovelorn haiku about an ex. But at rare moments—probably those moments described by Randall Jarrell as standing forever in the rain and finally being struck by lightning—it is not your call: a subject takes hold of you. I don't mean to indulge any romantic sense of the poet-as-vessel. The experience is altogether more mundane and practical than that. Still, there is an unusual exhilaration attached to the moment you realize a poem you hadn't anticipated suddenly demands that you write it down. That happened with "My Mammogram."

I should say, first of all, that a few years ago I did indeed have a mammogram, and that the event's combination of terror and incongruity at once prompted the poem. The procedure itself, less rarely undergone by men than is commonly assumed, raises all sorts of what are now clumsily called "gender issues." The staff and doctors, the waiting and examination rooms, the Inspirational Material taped to the walls—everything anticipates a woman's visit. And at the same time, as a man I had no idea of the unholy fear intelligent women endure at regularly scheduled intervals. The only part of the poem that closely corresponds to what actually transpired is the second section, the x-ray itself. The rest has all been exaggerated. Take the first section, for instance. Yes, there was an anomalous gynecomastia, but no discoloration or pain; and I don't go to a gym. But at the poem's outset, I felt I needed to strengthen the melodrama of symptom and anxiety, as well as nervously introduce a sexual note. If a narrative poem doesn't start vividly—the telling detail in high relief—the odds of its story engaging the reader are handicapped. And later, to keep the narrative voice lively, and steady the focus not on events themselves but on my feelings about the turn of events, I made mild caricatures of both the nurse and the doctor. The diagnosis is entirely fabricated—because it suited my purposes. (I'd hope by now I needn't even mention that I don't drink Scotch.) I wanted a comic interlude before steering the poem toward its more somber conclusions, and the only humor with bite is self-satire.

The problem with material of this kind is that any treatment of it can turn sensational or sentimental. How then to move the narrative along and at the same time rein in the tone? It occurred to me almost at once to cast the poem into a sequence of sonnets. To discourage a plodding or overdetailed narrative, I thought that the self-contained unit of each sonnet would dramatize—rather like a cartoon panel—a section of the story, and the sequence would move the narrative briskly along. The hallmark of the sonnet has always been its sense of limited freedom, a *constraint* that marks the form and is usually its very subject matter. Certainly that suited my circumstances. And over all the centuries sonneteers have been busy, the themes of the form have remained basically the same. Time (or mortality), art (or eternity), and love or beauty as the crossroads between them—again and again, from Petrarch to Shakespeare, from Keats to Frost, these same themes are enfolded, so that one must conclude there is an intrinsic bond between this form and that content. And by choosing to cast the poem as a sequence of sonnets, I was counting on the form to isolate those themes and thereby help shape my material. I had written a crown of sonnets, called "Kilim," that appears in *The Rest of the Way* (1990); it was of a scale and intricacy much beyond what I wanted here. I wanted now a voice that was both casual and alert, intimate but wry, febrile. I needed a tone that could shift gradually from the nervous humor at the start to a darker, more serious meditation of the final two sonnets. I kept the sonnets pretty steady; the octaves all have the same rhyme scheme (strict rhymes soon enough yielding to slant), while that of the sestets is varied. The effect, I hoped, was of a looser scaffolding than that of "Kilim": the look of structure, but open. The tighter the structure, the more intense but monotonous the voice. The two contrasting methods I've come to prefer for my poems—sharply jump-cut images and the discursive ramble—can be more fluently combined in a longish poem less rigorously organized than, say, "Kilim." The artist Saul Steinberg once said that drawing was his way of thinking on paper. That's what I want my poems to do: work their way by reflection, digression, guess, and surprise through a heady thematic set of givens toward an elusive emotional point, and in a voice with its own personality—rueful, dubious, aware, vulnerable, whatever.

(Let me interject a note about the parentheses in the last sonnet. Those two lines had originally been at the end of the poem. When I showed the poem to the late James Merrill and asked—as I used to do with nearly every poem of mine—for suggestions, he urged me to move the lines back into the body of the concluding sentence. I took the suggestion, but when I have read the poem in public, I regress to the earlier version. The printed version is more elegant; the spoken version easier to understand.

Perhaps a further word about one's first readers. There are two or three to whom I send everything, and there is nothing I have written that hasn't in ways great or small been improved by their help. I don't send preliminary drafts for fear of taxing their patience; it would be like telling someone your dream every morning—we have to pay professionals for that! Besides, at that point in the process I can see pretty clearly myself. It's only later, near the end, when I've grown half-blind and self-satisfied, that I need a cold eye cast on things. It's then I can't see the lapses and contradictions, the smudged phrases, botched rhythms, weak rhymes, distracting images. The best criticism is the sort that tells you what you already know but had been reluctant to accuse yourself of. I think my case is fairly typical. In fact, I don't know of a poet who *doesn't* send his work around a circle of close readers, less eager for praise than for practical help.)

I almost never start a poem without a subject in mind—and usually a title and some sort of scheme. So a lot of my "conscious" effort precedes the actual writing. While I'm at work on a poem, I hope for accidents along the way. Any writer knows, I think, the sensation of what laymen call "inspiration." My sense of that experience is this: when hard at work on a poem, help comes from everywhere—things you read or overhear, the lull of the subway, the newspaper, the bedside book, the rock song on the radio, the odd memory . . . everything suddenly feeds into what you have cooking. *Feeling* and *authenticity* are precisely the parts of a poem I'm most "conscious" of—that is to say, I most try to manipulate. The actor learns how to hesitate or stutter or fall silent at just the moment when that gesture will clinch what he is saying. So too, I try to watch how and where I place, say, a slang word, or a shocking detail, or a sweeping moral.

"My Mammogram" is finally about change, and all change in the end is tragicomic. I wanted to talk about change in a form that hasn't itself much changed over the centuries. I wanted, naturally, to mock the change I feared, and to brood on what change is inevitable. If the poem has patron saints, they would be Ovid and Yeats. Oh, but how things have changed since their glamorous, large-souled examples!

LYNNE MCMAHON

For Gabriel, Falling Through Glass and Ice

As if all matter separating us from the angelic orders
were transparencies, beautifully bloodying
the trumpet lips, sheering the now vectorless wings
spiraling down through spidered light,
crazed mirrors, shards of hardened water,
he falls continually through glass and ice
that we might see him, beckoning welcomer
of the Final Judgment, in the staggered
stop-action of a serial Duchamp,
facets of not-us-ness catching the light,
raying out into the stone air and off our hard
human hearts whose immortal diamond, Hopkins
heart-stoppingly held, is immortal diamond.

"For Gabriel, Falling Through Glass and Ice"

Our son Zach, who just turned seven, has long been interested in the idea of God and Heaven and angels and Jesus. When he was three, he was told by a playmate expert in such matters that Jesus was married to God and Christ was their nephew. Zach thought the word "nephew" sounded like a sneeze—not a bad Creation analogy, I suppose—and my husband and I, perhaps wrongly, failed to correct him. Nor did we dispute his claim that he could reach the floor of Heaven if he stacked up all the shoes in Missouri. Any shoes, he emphasized, they didn't have to be the golden ones. For the next four years, he went in and out of Explanation phases, much to the dismay of his older brother Ben (who doesn't believe us when we tell him he said the same sorts of things at Zach's age). The angelic orders are still on Zach's mind, but now they have become conflated with the more human order of "naming." Now he wants to know why he is Zachary McMahon Santos. Can he rename himself? he asks us. He prefers Jamie or Conor or (this is from his first grade yearbook) Bibkudeep LaZomba. He doesn't mind McMahon so much (Mc means "son of," his grandfather told him, and "Mahon" is pronounced "man"—Son of Man makes sense to him) and he likes Santos ("saint," which means holy person, which means Good, Ben told him, which means you'd better be). He likes the marriage of Man and Saint; he's already testing the waters with the soles of his feet. But "Zachary"? Where did we come up with that? We told him our list of possible names—Jack, Max, Sam—rhymes or near-rhymes with Zach. Not bad, he told us, those would have been okay. It was a good thing we didn't call him Dustin, he said, because Dustins are shy. And Justins have big chests and are bullies. Actually, my husband said, we almost called you Gabriel. Zach's reaction was immediate: *Not Gabriel*, he said, *Gabriels are always falling through glass and ice.* Do you know any Gabriels?

Rod asked him. At your school? But he didn't, had never met one, he just knew they fell through glass and ice.

So that was the genesis of my poem, the phrase itself becoming bound up in the whole notion of the demands of faith in a secular time. The poem may owe something to James Merrill's metaphor, near the end of *The Changing Light at Sandover*, of the photographic darkroom in which the archangels Michael and Gabriel represent the positive and negative images on the template of human capabilities, but the more immediate influence lay in my preparations for class. I had been reading most of the summer for a seminar on Hopkins and an undergraduate survey on British literature beginning with Blake, and I was dizzy from contemplating the effect of one poet on another. Then I came upon Blake's illustrations for his prophetic work, *Milton*. In one relief etching, titled "William," a beautifully muscled and young William Blake is shown arching backward in an ecstasy, waiting for the spirit of Milton, in the form of a star, to enter his left foot. In another more famous plate, a naked Blake is shown on his knees before a naked Milton in what could be construed as an act of fellatio. (Blake, after all, did think Milton was enchained by his own repressive sexual ethic, so part of his poetic mission was to break Milton free of his self-divisions.) The illustrations were clear: the seed of one poet passing into the mouth of another. The cadence of one passing into the foot of another. And the horizontal line of poetic lineage and influence intersecting at some point with the vertical axis of hierarchic divinities, even if those divinities, as Blake held, were interior, in the mind of mortal man himself.

What Zachary said to us—Gabriel falling through glass and ice—began to seem a recasting of Blake's recasting of the Fall. Except that this time the Fall was entirely outside us. Gabriel falls so that we might see him, know that the angelic orders exist. We see him in the staggered stop-action of a serial Duchamp—in bits, for to see him whole would blind us. And here I lifted a phrase from one of my husband's poems, "not-us-ness," because it was the most economical way I could find to get to the heart of the poem—that the angels are made of different stuff, and that their medium, glass and ice, is less durable and precious than the stuff of our hard hearts. This is the paradox that Hopkins struggles with in his poem "That Nature is a Heraclitean Fire." After detailing the bounties and immensities of Nature, and lamenting the brief mark of man ("how fast his firedint, his mark on mind, is gone!"), Hopkins takes comfort in the Resurrection: "Away grief's gasping, joyless days, dejection. / Across my foundering deck shone / A beacon, an eternal beam. Flesh fade, and mortal trash / Fall to the residuary worm; world's wildfire, leave but ash; / In a flash, at a trumpet crash, / I am all at once what Christ is, since he was what I am, and / This Jack, joke, poor potsherd, patch, matchwood, immortal diamond / Is immortal diamond." Hopkins in a flash sees that "Christ was what I am"—at once matchwood and immortal diamond. His flesh will fall to the residuary worm, but his soul shall never die. It is a hard-won consolation for Hopkins; how often he felt himself to be the Jack, joke, poor potsherd, how rarely the blessed and saved. Hopkins uses the diamond, I think, not only for its preciousness and indestructability, but also for its origin as allotrope of carbon, and the extremes of pressure the carbon undergoes. When Hopkins finally arrives at immortal diamond, he breaks the line and repeats immortal diamond. Beyond pain and grief and the desolations of abandonment, the diamond is the hard Christstuff itself. I wanted to pay homage to Hopkins, even as I lifted his image, just as I want to acknowledge my debt to my family, even as I appropriate their words. The line between thievery and influence thins more and more at our house. Sometimes life makes him feel sad, Zachary said to us last week, but not as sad as you would be *at the wedding of your death*. And there was a rustle of wings in the corner.

CHRISTOPHER MERRILL

The Hurricane

As if a guest overturned the sea's glass tabletop, then made off with
the buoys and floats, leaving the servants in a frenzy.

As if anyone could have stopped the surf, the tide's greedy heir,
from wrapping the beach, the dunes, the whole island in winding
sheets of sea wrack and foam.

Certainly no one on this partial list of retainers: mariners, fishermen,
lifeguards, bodysurfers, sunbathers, scrimshawers, seascapists,
weathermen, widows, walls . . .

Nor the sailors manning the warships perched on the horizon—birds
tensed on a wire stretching around the world.

Nor even the evangelist bellowing in the television studio.

Not while sand swarmed up the road, clogging the exhaust pipes and
engines of the cars and trucks headed for the mainland.

And over the canal the drawbridge opened, opened and swayed, its
crossbars snapping like garters, its tender fleeing on foot.

And a bulkhead slid into the water, ripping off its salt-soaked
planks,

Like an old lecher unbuttoning his coat, begging for release.

* * *

As if this uninvited guest despised our offerings—our weather maps
and balloons, our sandbags and stilts, rickety stairways anchored in
the dunes, rockets unleashed at the moon, barges spreading garbage
all over the sea.

Because as hosts we had neglected our duties and thus upset the
order of the universe.

An order we never understood nor successfully replaced.

For we couldn't waken from our sun-stunned drowse, couldn't tear ourselves away from the sand castle competition, the dune buggy races, the cockfights at the club.

Not even when the lifeguard raised the red flag, and saluted the storm clouds, and whistled in the swimmers and the end of summer.

Then the jetties, those long sleeves of rocks, gathered trawlers, steamers, and yachts, like lint.

And a sinking schooner wadded its sails, its handkerchiefs.

And the sea, mad dog, foamed at its mouth, this tidal inlet, then started chewing up the shore.

—All we could do was clap our hands . . . and wait for the help to come.

* * *

Yet there were those who called the hurricane a rite of passion, believing it would turn them in its four winds, would sweep their souls clean.

And some who tried to read its treatise nailed to the church door, while others prayed to learn where it got its marching orders and why it spurned our gifts.

And one who hoped its waves would hollow out the shells of words worn smooth on the lips of the crowd.

—They were the first to notice its open eye, the calm center of its fury.

But once the sand settled in the road, the skittish boats stopped straining to bolt from their slips and docks, and a boy, blinking away his mother's warning, scrambled up a dune to launch his kite.

A mote in the eye of a god, a surf-caster chuckled on his way to his favorite perch.

While an old man paced the vanishing shore, mumbling the names of all the women in his life.

Certain he could tame the winds gathering on the horizon.

—Then the eye closed, and the nightmare began again.

*   *   *

The summer houses propped up on the dunes, governments support-
ed by a foreign power and subject to its shifting sense of priorities—
toppled quickly, they embraced the harsh directives of wind and
water, opening their doors and windows to the new order.

Like a coach with a drunken driver—that's how one cottage rode
out to sea, spilling clothes, books, clocks, chairs, Persian rugs, and
all the family secrets across the trail of a long high wave.

The same wave that towed abandoned cars up the canal and pushed
a bungalow, like a baby stroller, across Dune Road then into
Shinnecock Bay, where it stalled on an island of its own making.

A sandbar, really, with dashes of dune grass, macadam, stilts, and
nails thrown in for support, around which a woman crazed by the
winds would swim the next summer.

Singing, *There was a house, and then a hurricane . . .*

A place where the sun would rattle its keys and the conch shell own
up to its white lies.

Where a poet learning to praise the winds might find a storm of
words coming to rest.

Where lovers stranded on a reef of flesh and spirit could dream of
making a fresh start.

Where the tide would slip in, like a familiar guest . . .

Seaglass: Notes on "The Hurricane"

The vase was filled with seaglass—pieces of white, brown, bottle green, and blue glass buffed in the Atlantic—collected over the years. My mother, it was true, had found most of the glass on her morning walks—she scoured the beach with the same furious energy of a sandpiper, prizing in particular the rare bits of blue (from *Milk of Magnesia* bottles) washed up among the shells, seaweed, and driftwood. And when our house was swept out to sea in a hurricane she grieved more than anyone over the missing vase, which was for her a symbol of our life on the south shore of Long Island. Though the house was rebuilt—this time behind the dunes—and refurnished, my family was left with a powerful sense of dispossession, which found its most vivid expression in the new seaglass collection my mother put together. That was what she saved when, six years later, we sold the house and moved away.

"The Hurricane" was composed, over the course of several days, in October 1987, though it may be more accurate to say the poem was twenty-five years in the making. Certainly I had tried to write it for some time. Nothing from my childhood haunted me more than that hurricane (I was only five when it struck), and from my earliest apprenticeship into the craft of writing I had wanted to explore the ways in which a storm can shape a life. I filled pages with descriptions and memories of that hurricane. Here were lines in various measures, formal and free; streams of automatic writing; prose paragraphs; Anglo-Saxon hemistitches. It was instructive to gather poetic materials in so many different forms, but I despaired of ever finishing my poem. Indeed, when I packed up my study in August 1987, preparing to move from a rented house in Salt Lake City, I was tempted to throw out the ream of legal pads on which I had scribbled "The Hurricane" across the top. Then I put them in a box marked *Save* and drove to my new home.

I carry it with me everywhere—the work, the example, of St.-John Perse, the French poet and diplomat. "Poetry is not only a way of knowledge," he declared in his Nobel address; "it is even more a way of life—of life in its totality." This is precisely what I seek in poetry, which offers its devotees the richest experience imaginable—the chance to see the world afresh, in its suffering and glory, its marvels and mysteries. Nothing is alien to a poet blessed with courage, vision, and understanding. St.-John Perse was such a man—after all, he stared down Hitler at the infamous Munich Conference—and his poetry, much of which dates from his years of exile in America, reflects his complete engagement with life. What better illustrates his belief that the poetic image "rekindles the high passion of mankind in its quest for light" than his own work? In my darkest moments I turn to it in the same spirit as that of a lost mariner glimpsing lights on a distant shore. Here is how the sixth section of his long poem, *Winds*, opens:

> . . . These were very great winds over the land of men—very
> great winds at work among us,
>   Singing to us the horror of living, and singing to us the
> honour of living, ah! singing to us and singing to us from the
> very summit of peril,
>   And, with the savage flutes of misfortune, leading us,
> new men, to our new ways.

Suffice it to say that by the fall of 1987 it had become clear to me that I must find a new way of living.

Only my bedroom was spared by the hurricane—it remained anchored in the sand, along with the houses on either side of ours. When I told this to a group of friends, one who had lived in the Alaskan bush said, "A Koyukon elder would say you're destined to witness chaos from your bedroom."

"*In* your bedroom," said another.

My academic career was over—I had just flunked out of a doctoral program—and my marriage was in trouble. My wife and I realized our hasty decision to move to New Mexico and live as caretakers on an estate bordering the Santa Fe National Forest had not solved our marital problems. Nor had we discovered new lives in the high desert, notwithstanding the example of countless migrants who had reinvented themselves there. In "The City Different," as Santa Fe is called, we were learning we could neither escape our past nor easily surmount our present difficulties, especially since we had no money or job prospects. Our arguments grew more heated, our apologies more desperate. *Divorce* was becoming our favorite word.

Yet good things happened, too. My wife, a classical violinist, embarked on a series of lessons with a renowned teacher who would help her to remove a lingering technical defect in her playing. For my part, after a long dry spell during which I had not completed any poems, I began to write again. Suddenly I was finishing a poem a day—a remarkable rate for me. In a kind of freedom borne of dispossession we were taking chances—what did we have to lose?—and they were paying off. My wife won a position in the New Mexico Symphony. I was deep into my second book of poems, *Fevers & Tides*. One day I came across the box filled with notes and drafts of "The Hurricane." Suddenly I could see a way to write the poem, and I set to work with uncommon excitement.

Versets provided the formal imperative for "The Hurricane," the shape and structure for "a storm of words" that had been building up in me for as long as I could remember. An altogether different kind of dispossession was what I now needed to address. Unleashed by the turmoil in my present circumstances, the "storm" followed a course dictated by the requirements of an ancient form, one dear to the writer of the Psalms as well as to poets like Whitman, Perse, and Czeslaw Milosz— all decisive influences on my own work. "These were very great winds questing over all the trails of this world," Perse writes. I followed one back to another time and place, in order to understand a new storm raging all around and within me.

In the high desert I kept sensing the presence of the sea that once covered this land—the waves of heat, the taste of salt, the way the earth collected itself into dunes, the shells along the trail behind our house. Even the night winds sounded like the distant roar of the ocean. Unaccountably, I began to feel at home. Little by little, my wife and I rebuilt our marriage. Stranded on a reef of flesh and spirit, we had dreamed of "making a fresh start"—and here we were, finding new ways to live. It is safe to say that "The Hurricane" played a role in those discoveries.

Edward Hopper's Nighthawks, 1942

The three men are fully clothed, long sleeves,
even hats, though it's indoors, and brightly lit,
and there's a woman. The woman is wearing
a short-sleeved red dress cut to expose her arms,
a curve of her creamy chest; she's contemplating
a cigarette in her right hand, thinking that
her companion has finally left his wife but
can she trust him? Her heavy-lidded eyes,
pouty lipsticked mouth, she has the redhead's
true pallor like skim milk, damned good-looking
and she guesses she knows it but what exactly
has it gotten her so far, and where?—he'll start
to feel guilty in a few days, she knows
the signs, an actual smell, sweaty, rancid, like
dirty socks; he'll slip away to make telephone calls
and she swears she isn't going to go through that
again, isn't going to break down crying or begging
nor is she going to scream at him, she's finished
with all that. And he's silent beside her,
not the kind to talk much but he's thinking
thank God he made the right move at last,
he's a little dazed like a man in a dream—
is this a dream?—so much that's wide, still,
mute, horizontal, and the counterman in white,
stooped as he is and unmoving, and the man
on the other stool unmoving except to sip
his coffee; but he's feeling pretty good,
it's primarily relief, this time he's sure
as hell going to make it work, he owes it to her
and to himself, Christ's sake. And she's thinking
the light in this place is too bright, probably
not very flattering, she hates it when her lipstick
wears off and her makeup gets caked, she'd like
to use a ladies' room but there isn't one here
and Jesus how long before a gas station opens?—
it's the middle of the night and she has a feeling

time is never going to budge. This time
though she isn't going to demean herself—
he starts in about his wife, his kids, how
he let them down, they trusted him and he let
them down, she'll slam out of the goddamned room
and if he calls her *Sugar* or *Baby* in that voice,
running his hands over her like he has the right,
she'll slap his face hard, *You know I hate that: Stop!*
And he'll stop. He'd better. The angrier
she gets the stiller she is, hasn't said a word
for the past ten minutes, not a strand
of her hair stirs, and it smells a little like ashes
or like the henna she uses to brighten it, but
the smell is faint or anyway, crazy for her
like he is, he doesn't notice, or mind—
burying his hot face in her neck, between her cool
breasts, or her legs—wherever she'll have him,
and whenever. She's still contemplating
the cigarette burning in her hand,
the counterman is still stooped gaping
at her, and he doesn't mind that, why not,
as long as she doesn't look back, in fact
he's thinking he's the luckiest man in the world
so why isn't he happier?

"Edward Hopper's Nighthawks, 1942"

The *he attempt to give concrete expression to a very amorphous impression is the insurmountable difficulty in painting.*

These words of Edward Hopper's apply to all forms of art, of course—certainly to poetry. How to evoke, in mere words, the powerful, inchoate flood of emotions that constitute "real life"? How to take the reader into the poet's innermost self, where the poet's language becomes the reader's, if only for a quicksilver moment? This is the great challenge of art, which even to fail in requires faith.

Insomniac nights began for me when I was a young teenager. Those long lonely stretches of time when no one else in the house was awake (so far as I knew); the romance of solitude and self-sufficiency in which time seems not to pass or passes so slowly it will never bring dawn.

Always there was an air of mystery in the insomniac night. What profound thoughts and visions came to me! How strangely detached from the day-self I became! Dawn brought the familiar world, and the familiar self; a "self" that was obliged to accommodate others' expectations, and was, indeed, defined by others, predominantly adults. *Yes but you don't know me* I would think by day, in adolescent secrecy and defiance. *You don't really know me!*

Many of Edward Hopper's paintings evoke the insomniac's uncanny vision, none more forcefully than *Nighthawks*, which both portrays insomniacs and evokes their solitude in the viewer. In this famous painting, "reality" has undergone some sort of subtle yet drastic alteration. The immense field of detail that would strike the eye has been reduced to smooth, streamlined surfaces; people and objects are enhanced, as on a lighted stage; not life but a nostalgia for life, a memory of life, is the true subject. Men and women in Hopper's paintings are somnambulists, if not mannequins, stiffly posed, with faces of the kind that populate our dreams, at which we dare not look too closely for fear of seeing the faces dissolve.

Here is, not the world, but a memory of it. For all dreams are memory: cobbled-together sights, sounds, impressions, snatches of previous experience. The dream-vision is the perpetual present, yet its contents relate only to the past.

There is little of Eros in Hopper's puritanical vision, *Nighthawks* being the rare exception. The poem enters the painting as a way of animating what cannot be animated; a way of delving into the painting's mystery. *Who are these people, what has brought them together, are they in fact together?* At the time of writing the poem I hadn't read Gail Levin's definitive biography of Hopper, and did not know how Hopper had made himself into the most methodical and premeditated of artists, continuously seeking, with his wife Jo (who would have posed for the red-headed nighthawk), scenes and tableaux to paint. Many of Hopper's canvases are elaborately posed and their suggestion of movie stills is not accidental. This is a visual art purposefully evoking narrative, or at least the opening strategies of narrative, in which a scene is "set," "characters" are presented, often in ambiguous relationships.

Nighthawks is a work of silence. Here is an Eros of stasis, and of melancholy. It is an uncommonly beautiful painting of stark, separate, sculpted forms, in heightened juxtapositions, brightly lit and yet infinitely mysterious. The poem slips into it with no transition, as we "wake" in a dream, yearning to make the frozen narrative come alive; but finally thwarted by the painting's measured void of a world, in which silence outweighs the human voice, and the barriers between human beings are impenetrable. So the poem ends as it begins, circling upon its lovers' obsessions, achieving no crisis, no confrontation, no epiphany, no release, time forever frozen in the insomniac night.

Her Story, My Daughter Beatrice

Beatrice Cenci, 1856

The Secret Archives of the Vatican contain
a manuscript from 1599—the trial
for parricide of Giacomo and Beatrice Cenci
the ill-used children, and their stepmother Lucrezia.
The Pope shows poorly in this daughter's tale
of incest. She wrote him more than once
complaining of her father's treatment. No response.
The same Count Cenci her father, convicted
sodomist, bought pardons and enriched the Church.

How many ways for a daughter to be abused—
by lustful gods, by errant husbands—even
by her father. The Count with threats and force
took Beatrice to his bed, telling her
this new heresy: that when a father
used his daughter thus, the saints were born.
Sometimes he moved the family to a grim
outpost-castle in a rock, La Rocca Petrella,
where he locked them, used them as he willed.
No earthly rescue but what they'd themselves devise:
the murder of him who kept them in his hell.

> *We do but that which 'twere a deadly crime*
> *to leave undone.*

But the murderers were found, the plotters condemned.
Even Farinaccio's defense
based on the Count's incestuous abuse
failed to save Beatrice's life.
Beheaded, she and Lucrezia;
Giacomo clubbed to death:
such the clemency of Clement VIII.
The Church put in its thumb,
pulled out the rich Count's plum,
and said What a good boy am I.

My marble daughter's figure speaks her piece:

Now he is dead I can sleep face down
my back turned on all possible harm.
I have not slept so easy since before I bled.
I sleep soundly though tomorrow I wake
to my last dawn, last clover-sweetened air.
I fold one leg to my chest as in the womb,
the other stretches out, toes at the edge
of my world. One slipper shows, trimmed
with lace and ribbons. These slippers I will leave
before I climb the stairs to my beheading.
My gown slips like water off one shoulder,
its folds cascade down my terraced pallet.
A mother gave my head a pillow
and I give myself human comfort, my right
hand beneath my cheek. The other
holds a rosary. My faith is strong. I know

> *The crimes which mortal tongue dare never name*
> *God therefore scruples to avenge.*

I therefore sleep. You, watching—grant
the mercy that my judges have denied.

Merely Dead, Not Absent

Planting hosta today in a shady corner of the garden, where I will later see them from my desk—which I am avoiding by planting said hosta (plantain, lilies, *Liliaceae, Hosta lancifolia*)—I remember Howard Nemerov's injunction to poets to get them a garden and a dog, and wonder why I am having such trouble making a poem of my own the focus of a short essay, when I would have no difficulty warming to the subject of another poet's work. Again, Howard: "Being unable to write, you must examine in writing this being unable, which becomes for the present—henceforth?—the subject to which you are condemned. The first thought is this: fear. I cannot write because I am afraid. Of what?"

The matter at hand: to wit, *this* hand, with this pen in it, a fountain pen of bold stroke and flashy nib. This pen with which I almost always write the first version of the poem to be altered and fitted later, and finally displayed by other instruments less intimate with my fingers, arm, vena cava, islets of Langerhans, brainfolds, neural backroads. The matter of public poetic *self*-contemplation. This only a personal matter, for I am intrigued by other poets' disquisitions on their own work. What to do? put the roots deep and plant where conditions for generation are favorable. Afraid of self-aggrandizement, I remain still the girl child who sang songs to her audience from under the kitchen table, a room away from where they sat. Perhaps all this is not unrelated to the nature of the project I choose here to describe. As I stated for a possible panel focusing on collaborations, "I like to walk around in someone else's life and so began my current project: a book of poems based on the life of American sculptor Harriet Hosmer (1830–1908). Such writing requires research—or more accurately collaboration with the subject, in this instance Hatty. It also works together with personal history in ways that become clear only as the poems are made."

The poem I will discuss (in an admittedly, I hope usefully, circuitous manner) appears in the collection in-process, a book that situates the author inside the life and time of a character she encountered about a decade ago while working on *Night Watches: Inventions on the Life of Maria Mitchell*, the first American woman astronomer. Maria's travels in Rome brought her—and me—to the studio of Harriet Hosmer. At first put off by Hosmer's manner, Quaker Maria was gradually won over. For a long time, Hosmer's legendary eccentricities stayed with me, making her the possible subject of a full-length book of poems. Last spring, on a leave granted by my university for the express purpose, I re-entered Hosmer's world and wrote about what I found and did not find. Like the earlier book, this work-in-progress led me to travel literally as well as in imagination to places significant in Hosmer's life—her birthplace (the house now gone); her grave in Mt. Auburn Cemetery; the locations of her various studios, residences, and extant sculpture in a church in Rome.

One way to describe the process of writing this kind of book involves three essential stages: identification, immersion, and transformation, each with its own proportion of mystery and imponderables. For the first, identification, I can only guess at some of the reasons for my identification with Hosmer sufficient to have carried me through stages two and three. My own father was an architectural sculptor, schooled by carvers such as those who helped execute Hosmer's sculptures in Italy; poets carve forms from blocks of language; as a woman, women's lives and work have particular magnetism for me. Perhaps just as important, the ways in which Hosmer, notorious for her mischief, enacts my unsatisfied wish for naughtiness. Written out, though, these explanations sound to me superficial and inadequate. Here I allow mystery the last word, or the silence.

In the second stage of my process, immersion, I began by reading two biographies of Hosmer, one authorized and published shortly after her death, the other published in 1991. Next, I spent several weeks in Cambridge at the Schlesinger Library at Radcliffe College and the Watertown Public Library, where voluminous microfilms and original documents reside. I lived and breathed Hosmer till the contemporary acts of my own life were refracted through the lens of Hosmer's—she who now inhabited me, a beneficent guest.

The third part of the process unfolded at my desk, the selfsame one I was avoiding yesterday in my garden by falling to my knees. For ten weeks I wrote three poems weekly, primarily forging on without stopping to revise, but to come as close as possible to finishing a first draft of the manuscript. Throughout the months of my work on the book, I tried to remain open to the demands of my current subject that might differ significantly from those of the Maria Mitchell poems, hence manifest themselves in alternate poetic forms and strategies. For example, noting in a journal some struggles and observations concerning process, I wrote:

How I have to overcome my resistance to certain aspects of HH's personality and life. How my uneasy identification with her is more like a relationship with a living being than mine with Maria Mitchell. MM easier to idealize—a benefit death normally confers. But the darker sides of HH—or at least the less admirable—poke through even death.

In these poems, unlike the MM book, I do not indicate HH's ghost speaks when anachronisms are to enter the poems. Rather I let her spirit float free in time; since she is so present to me as I write, I do not allow the fact that she is merely dead to portray her as absent—i.e. speaking from some arbitrary unknown distance.

How, once my personal connections with the subject begin to surface, I admit them, along with anachronisms, into the writing—all of which I accept as part of the adventure of this kind of book. Sometimes I wonder, like Calvino, "if I am destroying the past, or saving it" (RtSG, 84); sometimes I believe I am doing both.

How perhaps my own interventions serve as substitute/other for H's ghost, i.e. to convey the presence of Hatty now. Or that she, unlike Maria, doesn't need a ghost because she can speak now.

No single poem I might choose for discussion will illustrate all I've suggested about the book-in-progress. Try this one, though, in which Hatty tells the story of Beatrice Cenci, quoting twice from Shelley's tragedy, "The Cenci." Hosmer loved poetry, spent many happy hours in the Brownings' company, and was especially fond of Tennyson's poems. The other speaker in this poem is Hosmer's statue, Beatrice having her turn. This poem is one of several focused on the sculptures that Hosmer, unmarried and childless, called her children.

This poem allows me to call attention to Hosmer's work, and beyond that to a particular aspect of it which I found essentially Hosmer. Taking themes traditionally associated with women at the center of familiar myths or in this case an actual event, Hosmer characteristically gives them an untraditional treatment. I choose this poem and this sculpture, because as one of Hosmer's first full-length statues, the Beatrice demonstrates some of the signal ways Hosmer's presentation of women differs from that of her male contemporaries. Significantly, Beatrice reclines in a horizontal, inward-turning pose of privacy and reflection, rather than standing upright and exposed or nude. Against conventional notions of the time—family as moral stronghold—Hosmer works with this story that shows family as locus of evil, not sanctuary. An artist who called her creations her "children," here Hatty provides nurturance in the very posture she gives the figure Beatrice, and in the pillow she places under her "daughter's" head. At the beginning of stanza two, Hatty alludes to several of her other sculptures, Daphne, Medusa, and Oenone—whom a reader of the sequence would have encountered in earlier poems. When Hatty lets her marble daughter speak her piece, she is also speaking her peace. At the close of the poem I want to convey that a dimension of her peace depends on the viewer/reader to vindicate Beatrice, as the ecclesiastical and judicial powers of her time did not. It takes art—Shelley's poetry, Hosmer's sculpture—to accomplish such rescue. Two visitors to Hosmer's studio who saw the statue in progress had this exchange: " 'How well she sleeps.' . . . 'No . . . How well she dreams.' "

I'm not through with Hatty yet, nor she with me. As my previous experience with Maria Mitchell would indicate, I may even be finding ways to delay finishing. I become reluctant to part company with a character who has lived with/in me for many months—by one reckoning, for a decade, at the level of that aura writers trust. From my desk now, the first week of classes over, I see that the hosta planted six days ago are thriving. The essay is writ. The hand slips a new cartridge into the mystic pen, and tries *From 28 Via Gregoriana, I turn up . . .*

The Trees Will Die

> An increase of one degree in average tempera-
> ture moves the climatic zones thirty-five to fifty
> miles north. . . . The trees will die. Consider
> nothing more than that—just that the trees will
> die. —Bill McKibben, The End of Nature

Late in Vermont let me consider
some familiar trees I've lived among
    for thirty years of sleet and snow,
    of sun and rain: the aspens
quaking silver when the wet winds blow,

    the white oaks, with their seven-lobed leaves
        and gently furrowed bark,
whose April buds sprout reddish-brown;
    and I'll consider pin oaks,
    their stiff branches sloping down

asserting their own space, and sculpted leaves,
    flaming vermilion in the fall,
holding on even when they're curled and dry,
    through freezing winter storms
    in which we huddle, you and I,

around a fire that woos us back to feel
    what our ancestors felt
    some sixty thousand years ago;
and I'll consider red oaks with their pointed leaves,
    shiny dark trunks that seem to know

    the secret of slow growth,
    a message safe to pass along.
And then, considering the plenitude
    of maples here, I'll start with sugar
for its syrup and its symmetry, its brood

    of tiny yellow flower clusters
in the spring, and in the autumn such a blaze
    of orange, gold, and red,

whatever gloom might form the drizzling weather
    in my doom-reflecting head,

relief comes from the self-forgetfulness
    of looking at what's there —
the trees, the multitude of trees.
I stop here to consider in the brief years left
    to praise them and to please

    you who have loved their scented shade,
their oceanic choiring in the wind. And so I'll list
    a few more that I know:
the silver maple and the willow and the birch,
    box elder, basswood, and the shadblow

    whose pinkish-white flowers
quicken the awakened woods
and quicken me. And then the spruce and pines,
    their slender, tapered cones
    glimmering intricate designs

that tempt astonished eyes to contemplate
    how an indifferent force —
just evolutionary randomness,
    yet so like old divinity —
could wrest such pattern from initial emptiness.

    Before our history began,
        the void commanded
there be congregated trees and creatures filled
        with words to mimic them
    and represent the moods that spilled

out of the creature's thoughts into the world
    so that the trees and names for trees
        would then be joined as one:
the melancholy hemlocks in the humming dark,
    the tamaracks which flare gold in the sun

    as if to hold the light
of wavering October in their arms
    a little longer, as I do —
yet though they're evergreens at heart,
    like me, my dear, and you,

they lose their needles when the cold comes on.
And as the tilted planet turns
to offer us fresh colors that embellish speech,
more names rush into view:
the sycamore, the cedar, and the beech,

horse chestnut, butternut,
the hickories, black walnut, and of course
the cornucopia of fruits—
apple and cherry, pear and plum and peach—
each with a tang that suits

the palate of whatever taste
one might have dreamed of ripened paradise.
When I consider how
a man-made shift in climate of a few degrees
reveals the rebel power we now

have learned to cultivate
in order to subdue the animals
and take dominion, like a curse,
over the fields, the forests, and the atmosphere—
as if the universe

belonged to us alone—I wonder
if consideration of the family of trees
might give us pause
and let us once again obey the sun,
whose light commands all human laws.

Naming the Animals

Two accounts of the creation of human beings in the Book of Genesis address the question of the proper relationship between humans and the natural world: how can we simultaneously both subdue nature and celebrate it? In the first account, an androgynous God "created man in his own image, in the image of God created he him; male and female created he them." God's first commandment to Adam and Eve is to reproduce: "Be fruitful and multiply, and replenish the earth, and subdue it: and have dominion over the fish of the sea, and over the fowl of the air, and over every living thing that moveth upon the earth." This Darwinian injunction has been taken to heart, so to speak, by every gene in every human, animal, and plant ever since. Evolution has been driven by the principles of replication and survival. Humankind's dominion over nature represents a distinction between people and animals, but only in terms of power. The earthly hierarchical chain of domination ends with us, yet a limit as to how we appropriate other life is implied by the close linking of human beings with the rest of creation.

In the second account of creation, however, the first act that God requires of Adam, the naming of the animals, represents a very different kind of power: not that of appropriation, but of appreciation. The history of poetry, one might say, begins here with the annunciatory power of language, and it follows that human creativity, by virtue of the gift of speech, will evolve in response to the natural world: "And out of the ground the Lord God formed every beast of the field, and every fowl of the air; and brought them unto Adam to see what he would call them; and whatever Adam called every living creature, that was the name thereof." Humankind's ambivalence toward nature—the desire to subdue nature and to celebrate it—begins mythically with our Biblical origin.

In time, as we now witness to our dismay, appropriation would exceed its original limit of survival and become exploitation, and celebration would shift from acknowledging the otherness of nature as a resource for the imagination—our capacity as namers—and diminish into indulgent subjectivity. The ultimate irony that we must now confront is that as a species we may very well fail by succeeding: by subduing the earth and by multiplying beyond any expectation of the Biblical imagination, we may destroy the resources upon which life depends. What once appeared to be God's and therefore nature's infinitude, its capacity to be cultivated without ever finally being subdued, now appears as a revelation of limits requiring a new commandment of both sexual and acquisitive restraint—a restraint that our genes are not designed to comprehend or enact.

A respect for nature's otherness, its long evolutionary history preceding ours, should, however, prevent us from being sentimental about nature's awesome beauty. Nature's cruelty and indifference to suffering and loss, and thus the need to subdue its forces, were well understood by the Biblical imagination and have been restated with great vividness many times subsequently. In Darwin's words: "As more individuals are produced than can possibly survive, there must in every case be a struggle for existence, either one individual with another of the same species, or with the individuals of distinct species, or with the conditions of life." John Stuart Mill, in his unflinching essay, "Nature," expressed the same realization: "Nature impales men, breaks them as if on a wheel, casts them to be devoured by wild beasts, burns them to death, crushes them with stones like the first Christian martyr, starves them with hunger, freezes them with cold, poisons them by the quick or slow venom of her exhalations, and has hundreds of other hideous deaths in reserve."

The contemporary historian of the changing concepts of nature, Roderick Nash, in *Wilderness and the American Mind*, emphasizes that the modern idea of wilderness, usually ecstatically positive, as in Gerard Manley Hopkins's lines, "What would the world be, once bereft / Of wet and wildness? Let them be left, / O let them be left, wildness and wet; / Long live the weeds and the wilderness yet," differs radically from that of the "ancient Hebrews [who] regarded the wilderness as a cursed land and associated its forbidding character with a lack of water." And, conversely, as Nash points out, "when the Lord wished to express his pleasure, the greatest blessing he could bestow was to transform wilderness into a 'good land, a land of brooks and water, of fountains and springs.'" It would appear that only because nature and wilderness had already been largely subdued by civilization was Thoreau free to declare in his essay, "Walking," that "Wildness is the preservation of the World" or that

"The most alive is the wildest. Not yet subdued to man, its presence refreshes him." Wilderness "refreshes" for Thoreau because it carries with it the association of water rather than the desert's association with barrenness. Yet the case for emphasizing humankind's primary role as the bringer of civilization, particularly as artistic namer, against the random flux and purposeless destructiveness of nature, may be seen as epitomized in Nietzsche's succinct declaration that "We possess art lest we perish from the truth."

In the course of civilization, however, and with unprecedented intensity in the nineteenth century, poets have depicted the power of the human mind as equal to or predominant over the power of nature. Yet these literary namers often failed to acknowledge that artistic creation depends upon a physical world of things and creatures that have existed *prior* to them. Indeed, the forms that nature has evolved are more various than poets could have contrived from their most fervid imaginations. Nature provides the images from which poets make their metaphors, so a world where fewer creatures thrive diminishes the resources that inform our capacity to invent symbols. Without the snake, for example, our ability to evoke a sense of evil would be lessened. With industrialization and technology—in opposition to which writers like Hopkins and Thoreau eulogized wilderness—there is an arrogance in asserting human dominance over nature, to the point where the balance between domination and appropriation on the one hand and celebration and naming on the other has taken a fatal shift.

The prophetic passage in the Bible that perhaps anticipates that fatal shift toward aggressive domination can be found in Genesis Chapter 9. After the flood has abated and Noah leaves the ark to make his residence again on the land, God reaffirms His covenant with Noah and gives him the same Darwinian commandment He gave to Adam, "Be fruitful, and multiply, and replenish the earth." But now, perhaps in recognition of some endemic predatory instinct in human nature, God chooses to permit human beings to eat animals as well as plants, thus establishing a terrible separation between humankind and the rest of the animal kingdom: "And the fear of you and the dread of you shall be upon every beast of the earth, and upon every fowl of the air, and upon all that moveth *upon* the earth, and upon all the fishes of the sea; unto your hands are they delivered. / Every moving thing that liveth shall be meat for you; even as the green herb have I given you all things."

We would do well, through an empathetic act of imaginative projection, to contemplate the "dread" of the animals today. Despite the immemorial and necessary project of civilization to mitigate the random cruelty of nature, what Mill asserts as the "undeniable fact that the order of nature, in so far as unmodified by man, is such as no being, whose attributes are justice and benevolence, would have made," we are destroying our resources of metaphor and therefore limiting our capacity as namers, our Nietzschean power to truly strengthen ourselves through the possession of art. Species in the animal and plant kingdom are now being brought to extinction throughout the planet at a rate thousands of times faster than in the previous 65 million years. These species, we should remember, took millions of evolutionary years to create. Among the natural catastrophes that brought destruction to life on this planet, such as the asteroid that, colliding with the earth, scattered dust that obscured the sun and killed off the dinosaurs, we, the human species, are the earth's preeminent catastrophe. Our dreadful capacity to subdue, to dominate and destroy, always has been inextricably bound to our artistic capacity to name and celebrate, and our salvation as a species lies in the desperate hope that the uses to which the aggressive instincts may be put remain within the scope of the human will—the will to make civilization itself a work of art that names and celebrates nature rather than replacing nature only with self-reflecting human images.

Like Adam's initial act of naming the animals, the pictures on the walls of the caves of Lascaux celebrate the grandeur of the animals. They are drawn with incredible grace, compared to the few awkward representations of the human figure. In contemplating these depictions of the animals, we can imagine that we are witnessing the human invention of the idea of beauty. The Lascaux artists' personal renditions are wedded to the observed animals being hunted, just as Adam's names become the names of the animals that God "brought unto Adam to see what he would call them." But we cannot fulfill our role as namers without a world of things, of animals, beyond our own making that have preceded us and helped us define our special function within the mutual creaturely bond as namers, as celebrators, in the temporal kingdom of the living.

Naming as a response to what is *there*—naming grounded in observation and description—can, however, easily collapse into indulgent subjectivity in which self-assertion is given priority over the natural world. When language becomes a form primarily of self-expression, when it abandons its fidelity to the natural world, we no longer can assume a shared understanding about the relationship between an object and its name, or find a solid communal meaning in a text that derives from the design of named things. Communication collapses, and discourse becomes anarchic as in the city of Babel. Wordsworth clearly understood the breakdown of language as an aspect or an extension of The Fall when he claimed in his Appendix to the Preface to Lyrical Ballads (1802) that "the first Poets . . . spake a language which, though unusual, was still the language of men . . . [until] diction became daily more and more corrupt, thrusting out of sight the plain humanities of nature." Wordsworth's point is that the directness and simplicity of poetic diction must serve to highlight the actuality of objects, the specific details of divine creation, rather than draw attention to itself, since the origin of language itself derived, Wordsworth believed, from the physical sounds of the natural world:

> ... and I would stand,
> If the night blackened with a coming storm,
> Beneath some rock, listening to notes that are
> The ghostly language of the ancient earth,
> Or make their dim abode in distant winds.
> (Prelude II, 306–310)

Just as language, according to Wordsworth, derives from the "notes" of the "ancient earth," so, too, does physical creation, represented by the animals, evoke what is essential to our humanity—our ability to celebrate the natural world by giving names to its inhabitants. The animals that the Lord brought forth for Adam to name are meticulously described by the Lord Himself in the Book of Job when the Lord answers Job out of the whirlwind in response to Job's challenge that the Lord explain why evil exists in the world, why good people often suffer for no discernible cause, and why malefactions go unpunished. Replying out of the whirlwind, the Lord circumvents any discussion of the ethical issues raised by Job; rather, He recounts the scope and magnitude of His powers in having created the universe ("Where were you when I planned the earth?"), culminating in a long list of the creatures that He has fashioned—a list that (with divine irony) does not include human beings.

There is nothing sentimental in the Lord's depiction of the animals. Invariably, their behavior and their fortunes involve pain and destruction, as Darwin claimed subsequently was the inevitable design of nature, but they are awesome and beautiful nevertheless. It is as if they are there simply to be seen, as if the universe required nothing more in making creation complete than that the animals be named. The Lord describes them to Job in loving detail to reawaken in Job his capacity for wonder and celebration and to remind him of his own finitude within the larger scheme of nature—a cosmic scheme well beyond the workings of planet earth and the control of design by human beings.

> Do you tell the antelope to calve
>   or ease her when she is in labor?
> Do you count the months of her fullness
>   and know when her time is come?
> She kneels; she tightens her womb;
>   she pants, she presses, she gives birth.

Her little ones grow up;
    they leave and never return. . . .

Do you show the hawk how to fly,
    stretching his wings on the wind?
Do you teach the vulture to soar
    and build his nest in the clouds?
He makes his home on the mountaintop,
    on the unapproachable crag.
He sits and scans for prey;
    from far off his eyes can spot it;
His little ones drink its blood.
    Where the unburied are, he is.
        (Stephen Mitchell translation)

Such are the images of life, breeding and struggling to survive, given by the Lord to inspire the human imagination in its contemplation of the interdependence of creation and destruction. In preceding human existence, either according to Biblical mythology or evolutionary theory, the animals, the forms of the natural world, still hold dominion over the poetic mind, even as human greed and appetite have subdued nature's astonishing plenitude.

To exploit and destroy the plants and the animals, which our species always has done, but which we are doing now at an ever-increasing rate, is to diminish the source of beauty in ourselves, to turn the world into a cesspool of human waste. Sadly, this is true despite the bitterly ironic fact that simultaneously as we annihilate our fellow inhabitants on this planet we also pursue the legitimate work of replacing nature's indifference with human empathy upon which morality and the sense of justice are based—as in King Lear's injunction to himself, and to us all, to "Expose thyself to feel what wretches feel, / That thou mayst shake the superflux to them, / And show the heavens more just." This split between the impulse to take dominion and the impulse toward celebratory respect, I believe, constitutes the tragedy of our species.

Darwinian wisdom reminds us that we have not evolved as a species designed to solve problems that are not immediate, of our own generation; never before has this been a necessity. "Natural selection does not look ahead," says Colin Tudge in *The Engineer in the Garden*, "and in general is bound to favor short-term advantage over long-term." If being fruitful only means multiplying, then our species will be left without a morality of fruitfulness when the earth no longer can support any further enlargement of the human population. The idea of fruitfulness will have to change from numerical increase to some concept of improvement in the quality of life. We as a species need to change ourselves radically through an act of reasoned will—a change no species has ever been called upon to accomplish. The power of naming, therefore, that poets must summon today, more urgently than ever before, is to name ourselves as devourers gone berserk, as the scourge of the earth, and, perhaps, in the realization of that naming, to reinvigorate our commitment as preservers and our role as celebrators.

The need to enlarge the idea of fruitfulness, to regard it metaphorically, not only literally in numerical terms, is inherent in the Biblical text as a warning to Adam about forbidden fruit. Adam is not permitted to transcend nature, and therein lies the fundamental lesson of accepting limits. Because Adam rebelled against his bond with nature by seeking to become immortal, by violating a necessary limit, God sends Adam forth from the garden of Eden "lest he put forth his hand, and take also of the tree of life and live forever." In presuming to take dominion over the planet earth, with only human welfare and comfort in mind, our species, of course, has not mastered the universe or taken dominion over the second law of thermodynamics or, most significantly, achieved eternal life that would set the human species apart from the fate of all other creatures.

With the first human awareness of death as an ongoing state of non-being, the desperate wish not to die must simultaneously have been born, as is implied in the earliest burial sites in which possessions are placed in the grave to accompany the dead on a journey. But taking dominion, even when that effort aspires to the most glorious aspiration of civilization—to bring empathy and justice into the world—cannot mean that we can possess our bodies for long or that the Yeatsian speculation, "Once out of nature I shall never take / My bodily form from any natural thing," can ever be realized, except as a fantasy of power in which one gives birth to oneself as if to a work of art. The fantasy of transcending nature and becoming immortal is the ultimate extension of the wish to take dominion over nature and subdue it. But taking dominion over nature can only mean for our species that we will have proven that our particular genius has been the destruction of many wondrous living forms, and finally the destruction of ourselves. No doubt, bacteria and cockroaches will survive our folly, or some more adaptable life form will emerge in another solar system. To choose to remain creatures, then, moral creatures, yes, but creatures still, is to accept limits—the limits of mortality, the limits of power and possession, and thus to remember and remain true to our evolutionary origins, not merely as multipliers, but as namers as well.

The human imagination continues to depend on natural images and natural beauty, on trees and plants and birds and animals, on the seasons and the weather; without them, the human spirit, nurtured by its own poetic expression of a world of "wildness and wet," is diminished and impoverished. Without a sense of beauty that derives from other-ness, from nature's independent existence, a prior world on which our fabricated cultural world depends, the capacity for taking delight in our surroundings will have withered away. Even before the planet becomes inhospitable to the human species, we will have died in spirit. Perhaps superintelligent creatures of our own technological creation, based not on carbon but on silicon molecules, who do not depend on food or air or a moderate climate or leisure time for reading Shakespeare, will evolve to survive us in a state of happiness that we, still the children of natu-ral laws, who live, as Prospero says, " 'twixt the green sea and the azur'd vault," have not evolved to comprehend.

JAY PARINI

A Conversation in Oxford

for Isaiah Berlin

Euphonious if not in sync the bells
beat time in amber chapel towers,
and the time has come for tea and talk.
We settle in a room of many shades,
the questions you have spent the decades turning.

"What can we assume about this world?"
you wonder, once again. "What can we claim?"
So little, it would seem. The weak foundations
of all human knowledge make one shudder
to assume too much, to claim too boldly.

"What do you believe?" you ask, so frankly
that I redden, turn, avert my eyes.
"Is consciousness itself an end or foretaste
of a fuller life? This 'oversoul' that Emerson
proposed: Whatever does it mean?"

The honeying facades along the High Street
seem impervious to dwindling light;
whole generations are absorbed
in rheumy passages and darkened cloisters
where so many questions have been put

and left unanswered. It was not a failure
not to answer. I assume that you,
over the decades, have refused to grant
those easy answers that can dull a heart,
occlude a mind, can chain a soul.

You tap your pipe and offer this:
"Real liberty is found in fine gradations,
dartings of the mind—not Big Ideas,
which are mostly preludes to deceit,
embodiments of someone's will-to-power."

I scan the rows of volumes you have filled
with annotations in the well-kept nights—
from Plato to Descartes, from Kant to Kripke.
Herzen was a friend, and Vico, too.
You say that all the best books seize us

half by chance, interrogate and turn us
loose upon ourselves again. I mostly listen,
letting what you say fill up the hour.
The room grows violet and dusky,
insubstantial, as your voice compels

and seems to quicken as your flesh dissolves.
And soon the darkness is itself complete,
consuming everything except your language,
which assumes an Old World gaiety and calm.
I feel, myself, an apparition.

"It is strange," I say. "We find ourselves
alive without a reason, inarticulate
but always trying to re-form a thought
in words that never seem quite right."
I see a flicker in your candle-eyes.

"The world is what it is," you answer strictly,
having seen enough of it to say.
"The world is what you claim it is
as well: this dwindling light, the smoke
of reason, ghostly words in ghostly air."

I claim this hour, a plum-deep dusk,
the need to pose so many questions,
late, so late—an Oxford afternoon
when everything but language falls away
and words seem all the world we need.

Conversing in Oxford with
Sir Isaiah Berlin

A few years ago I had the opportunity to renew my acquaintance with Sir Isaiah Berlin, the philosopher and intellectual historian. I first met him in 1969, at the University of St. Andrews in Scotland, where I was both an undergraduate and graduate student in the late sixties and seventies. Berlin was a visiting lecturer one term, and I was among his students. I never got to know him well, but I did linger on the fringe of his society, taking the odd cup of tea with him in a local café. I don't think any teacher ever made a more vivid impression on me. His lectures were characterized by the dazzling speed of their delivery, the vast range of historical reference, the easy allusions to thinkers from Plato to Wittgenstein (his interest in the Enlightenment was profound, and he would dwell on relatively obscure figures from that era). His knowledge of western intellectual history seemed unparalleled. One left his lectures desperate for good libraries and infinite hours to read and think.

After many years absence, I returned to Britain in 1993–1994 as a visiting fellow of Christ Church, Oxford. One of my first acts upon taking up residence was to write a note to Berlin, saying that I had not seen him in over two decades but would like to remedy that. He wrote back warmly, inviting me to lunch at his college, All Souls. (Berlin has been a fixture at Oxford since the early thirties, when he began as a lecturer in philosophy, having himself taken a degree in classics at Corpus Christi College. He has long been a Fellow of All Souls, although he once served as head of Wolfson College—one of the new colleges.)

It was thrilling to sit in Berlin's company again. He seemed ageless in his rumpled, three-piece suit, a pipe hanging from his lips, his glasses slipping to the end of his nose as he talked, rapidly as ever, in his deep baritone voice. Although he has lived in Britain most of his adult life, there is still a trace of the eastern European in his voice—a residue of his boyhood in the Latvian city of Riga, where his father was a wealthy timber merchant. Well into his eighties by now, Berlin had lost none of his intellectual edge. As before, he did not make small talk.

Indeed, we plunged straight into a discussion of Tolstoy's philosophy of history—prompted by the fact that I had recently published a novel about the last year of Tolstoy's life. The conversation ranged broadly, reaching back to the Greek historians, Herodotus and Thucydides. I told him how much his essay on Tolstoy ("The Hedgehog and the Fox") had meant to me over the years; he, of course, would not just take a compliment sitting down. He wanted to know *exactly* what I found useful in it. I felt uncomfortably put on the spot, like a graduate student in an oral exam; it was terrifying. Whatever I said seemed to interest him, however, and the conversation went tumbling forward, head over heels.

It was the first of many such conversations, held either at his college or mine. I used to love going to see him in All Souls, though: his study is a massive, dark room on the second floor of a medieval building; books of history, philosophy, and literature are stacked floor-to-ceiling. The air in that room has the faint smell of tobacco—the product of his pipe, which seems always on the brink of going out. A huge table at one side of the room is loaded with open books, manuscripts, offprints, letters. Berlin is utterly at home here, in this room he has occupied for decades.

I wrote the poem "A Conversation in Oxford" quickly one afternoon, late in the day, after a visit with Berlin. Much of the conversation took place in his study, after lunch. Berlin was in a particularly meditative mood that day, and he asked me point blank if I believed in God, and if not, what did I think would happen to me after I died. I found myself hemming and hawing, and finally admitted I had no pat answers to these questions. I said I was much moved by Emerson's optimism, however, and regarded his notion of the Oversoul as something vaguely akin to what, in my heart of hearts, I believed.

Berlin is no Emersonian, but he seemed quite happy with my response. He said he didn't like firm answers, which were almost always bluff. He said he mistrusted people with Big Ideas that they put forward as if they were unassailable. He preferred "fine gradations" of thought, believing these were more useful in the end. This brought us back to the idea of the hedgehog and the fox; we both admitted to being foxes, attracted to many different ideas, even contradictory ones. (I confessed a secret admiration for hedgehogs—I'm always dazzled by people who have "one big idea" which they hold onto resolutely.) I told him I was horribly inconsistent: a perfect Theist one day, an atheist the next; mostly, I said, I let other people worry about labels. My spiritual life was deeply connected to language—to the vision of reality contained in poems and novels.

The conversation ended as the afternoon light began to dwindle in the High Street, and Oxford assumed its familiar, dusky tones. In the poem, I (or the speaker of the poem, who is—as in all lyrics—a fiction) say to Berlin: "We find ourselves / alive without a reason, inarticulate / but always trying to re-form a thought / in words that never seem quite right." Berlin replies, "The world is what it is." It's a very British answer, of course, with a somewhat Wittgensteinian ring (echoing the *Tractatus*). I know that I have simplified Berlin's position, which in his style of conversation was elaborately subordinated, with endless qualifying clauses. But a poem is not a direct transcription of reality. It is, ideally, a transformation that nevertheless encodes within its many layers something of the reality that was there in the first place.

My poem is obviously much shorter than the actual conversation upon which it was based. I made the (perhaps) arrogant decision to try to reformulate Berlin's casual talk of that particular day in this brief format, and it doesn't really sound like him. The "Berlin" of the poem is (like the "I") a fiction, tangentially related to the Isaiah Berlin of "real life." But I think this a necessary fiction, and that the poem gets across something of what it means to live a life of the mind in the way Berlin has managed to do it. In many ways, the poem represents an homage to a way of being in the world, a form of life embodied by Isaiah Berlin.

In the last stanza, I move rather brazenly outward, attempting to frame my own belief that the reality of language is ultimately what matters, and that the "real world" is something of a dream:

> I claim this hour, a plum-deep dusk,
> the need to pose so many questions,
> late, so late—an Oxford afternoon
> when everything but language falls away
> and words seem all the world we need.

That stanza captures, as best I could, the sensations I felt walking home that afternoon from All Souls to Christ Church, with the sense of having inherited a piece of reality peopled by a thousand ghosts, and by many contradictory ideas. It evokes that sense of "reality" fading away as I spoke with Berlin, as the reality of language, in our conversation, took on an almost luminous immediacy. I was quite happy to live in that reality while it lasted: the feeling of a perpetual present in which the vicissitudes of everyday life pale, even fade away. The poem itself becomes, for me, a kind of simulacrum in which I can reexperience that moment—at least partially.

ROBERT PINSKY

Desecration of the Gravestone of Rose P. (1897-1924)

(Antiphony with "Church Monuments" by George Herbert)

A cautionless flagon threw the heart unphrased,
The devil's tongue. We thought ourselves evil, and
To prove it in our own eyes we four striplings
Ventured long off to the boneyard October night.

Drives all at last with lights, brews, hammers, crowbars,
Long-handled shovel. Exhalation, male
Exhilaration, primates packing out
Under clear autumn Zodiac with dead

To desecrate. Dry cells, sixpacks, work gloves,
Rocking a headstone downright unison chanting,
Sad granite bromides rocking in a widening socket,
Earthsmelling, smooth. Appliance of iron crow

Into the space, team curses and giggling, shoves,
Shovelblade under a graven toppling. These laugh
At jet and marble put for signs, To sever
The good fellowship of dust, And spoil the meeting.

And what shall point out them, When they shall bow,
And kneel, and fall down flat To kiss those heaps,
Which now they have in trust? A coffin dragonworm
Incaution through the packing. Devlin's bung.

Farts of demons. Cold sweat, cold beers, a fatal must.
Cackles and whispers and the pissing-on
Of headstone soilbeds. Spatter and mist of pisses
And badder yet, the striking of oval portraits,

Photographs from the nineteenteens and so on
Well sealed in domes of thick defiant glass
Banged with a hammer. Glancing off cheekbone and gaze,
Cracked glaze, glance clouding white time's bleach. Crazed glass,

That when thou shalt grow fat And wanton in
Thy cravings, thou mayst know, That flesh is but
The glass, which holds the dust That measures all
Our time; which also shall Be crumbled into

Dust, prancing like Shiva, glancing off cheekbone, one stone
Barked trunklike, with truncated limbs stiff symbolizing
A life cut off too early, set in the awful
Stone bark in her calm oval an oval faced

Young woman, dark, How free from lust, Dear Flesh,
Eaten by Kali, smashed by Shiva, partially
Effaced, deathfashion. Harsh breath panted in dispassion,
Drunk flagging. Unchristian, Sir. Joosh moluments,

Flame's phlegmshaped characters. Take a letter: Dear Flesh,
That when thou shalt grow fat And wanton in
Thy cravings, thou mayst know. Flesh: Dung-de-*dung-dung*!
If the dung-carrier labors all a life

In enlightenment and the priest or poet labors
In error, the dung-carrier attains a higher level
And returns at a higher level. Therefore I gladly
Trust my body to this school. In Gad we trust.

A hearthworn potion, contrition thrust between
The stirrup and the cup. A heartshorn passage,
How free from lust these ashes: Comparing earth
With earth in dusty heraldry and lines.

Notes on a Poem: "Desecration

at the Gravestone of Rose P.

(1897–1924)"

Three of my four grandparents are buried in Long Branch, New Jersey, in the pretty Jewish cemetery on Long Branch Avenue, where some of my aunts, uncles, and cousins also lie. The most mysterious and spectacular of these graves belongs to my father's mother, Rose Schacter Pinsky, who died in childbirth when she was twenty-six years old.

Rose's headstone is in the shape of a tree with truncated limbs, symbolizing a life cut off abruptly in youth. Vulgar, operatic, always moving to me, it was paid for by her husband, my Grandfather Dave, a successful young bootlegger and gangster at the time of his wife's death. I knew him as the gruff, patriarchal owner of the Broadway Tavern, prominent among Long Branch's many downtown bars.

In the center of the granite carved to resemble bark is an oval portrait of Rose. I have seen these portraits on gentile graves in Poland, too. Apparently an Eastern European fashion, the process must use something like a tintype sealed under thick glass. It works amazingly well; the last time I saw my grandmother's charming, animated face, a few years ago, the photograph was as clear and sharp as it was all through my childhood when, as the custom is, I would leave a pebble on the grave to show I had been there.

Several years ago, I heard that someone had vandalized the cemetery —tipping over stones, spray-painting obscenities on some, and banging at others with a tire iron or a hammer. They had hit my grandmother's portrait, and had damaged it, it wasn't clear how badly. Not long afterward, I was back in Long Branch for a funeral. After the service, I checked the family graves, carrying my handful of pebbles, making my way fearfully toward Rose's amputated tree.

The picture on the stone looked more contemporary to me, seemed less cloaked in the mystery of the past, than when I was a child. The young woman I studied was much younger than me now. A pretty face, delicate and mischievous, with an amused poise in the girl's shoulders and straight posture, and just one streak of white erasure across her rib cage where the hammerblow glanced away.

Carrying that image around with me for a few years now, I have found myself thinking about the desecrators. They were male, more than likely, and young, most likely between thirteen and their early twenties: the age and gender that more or less monopolize certain kinds of irrational, profitless, violent crime. In fact, I could not claim to find the vandalism inconceivable. On the contrary, it was the sort of thing I might have found exciting, at their age: thrilling, the danger of getting caught, the irreverent release, the required competence and daring, the conspirational laughter of the male pack.

The thought of that laughter brought to mind a line from George Herbert's great poem "Church Monuments": *These laugh at jet and marble put for signs / To sever the good fellowship of dust*. The desecration was in some sense perfectly in accord with what Herbert thinks as, about to go inside the church to pray, he pauses for a moment outside to regard the monuments in the churchyard, reminders for him of the futility of the flesh. I have had the poem by heart for years. In the days when I was afraid of air travel, I used to recite it to myself during take-off and landing, while imagining the faces of my wife and children—choosing what to have in my brain at the moment of death:

Church Monuments

While that my soul repairs to her devotion,
Here I entomb my flesh, that it betimes
May take acquaintance of this heap of dust;
To which the blast of death's incessant motion,
Fed with the exhalation of our crimes,
Drives all at last. Therefore I gladly trust

My body to this school, that it may learn
To spell his elements, and find his birth
Written in dusty heraldry and lines;
Which dissolution sure doth best discern,
Comparing dust with dust and earth with earth.
These laugh at jet and marble put for signs,

To sever the good fellowship of dust,
And spoil the meeting. What shall point out them,
qWhen they shall bow, and kneel, and fall down flat
To kiss those heaps, which now they have in trust?

Dear flesh, while I do pray, learn here thy stem
And true descent, that when thou shalt grow fat

And wanton in thy cravings, thou mayst know,
That flesh is but the glass, which holds the dust
That measures all our time; which also shall
Be crumbled into dust. Mark here below
How tame these ashes are, how free from lust,
That thou mayst fit thyself against thy fall.

Dust and earth laugh at the stones of marble and jet which must over the years bow and kneel and fall down flat—prolonging over a century or two the actions of frenzied mourners driven by grief to fall down on a grave, kissing the earth above it.

I found myself imagining myself as one of the vandals—as in effect I was, at their age—or even as Rose herself, somehow knowing Herbert's poem and marshaling it as evidence against grief. A spirit of anarchic truth, almost joyful, seemed to unite the hooligans and the Anglican poet and my grandmother and me in the insight that grief for the dead, though ineluctable, is foolish: grief for the body, or for the body's representation in a photograph or by a symbolic stone tree.

In a way, I think of the poem I wrote as art's babble against attachment to matter—a babble or rant accomplished in matter, in the human body that breathes these words. The vandal whose mind I interfuse— preposterously, I must admit—with Herbert's phrases would not think in any such way, I know. That is a fiction. But there is something vital and attractive about the preposterousness—of the mind that rails against its own body, of the headstone that apes a wounded tree, of Herbert's gorgeous rhymes and cadences that makes us grieve for the flesh he spurns, of the little pebbles a child solemnly, carefully places on the curbing of a grave, lifeless stone resting on stone.

STANLEY PLUMLY

Nobody Sleeps

One theory is that acid wastes in the blood
accumulate and depress the brain so much
it wants to lie down at the mouth of a cave
on a high hard ledge shelving over nothing.
It wants to think of nothing, be nothing,
and wake up empty with sleep in its eyes.
Another is that during waking the brain
uses up its oxygen faster than the body
can replace and is so starved by the end
of the day it seeks a bed of branching
in order to lay its head on laurel green.
And a third says that because the afferent
impulses of the neurons are contractile
with the dendritic process of the cells
any interruption over time isolates
the cortex from external stimuli and
as interruptions peak in sync with dark
the brain wants to lie all night by fire.
The theory of anaemia, involving the loss
of tone in the vascular heart of the medulla,
is too particular, especially since,
except in fits and starts, nobody sleeps—
though there are children who sleep through
anything, even memory and waking, and adults
who work the nightshift or the street
who only pretend by closing their eyes,
even in daylight. But the vertical brain
wants to lie down, beside water if it can
or under wind topping the tall pale grasses.
It wants to alter its relation to the bed
to give up gravity to the ground, to let
the mind float out in spirit-buoyant air,
to feel, at the foliate edge, the mind
relieved. And because it cannot sleep
it wants to dream the sexual narrative
of longing and connection, the journey

of the body in light continually dying,
the cold wet morning air silvering down
on the night earth warming toward the sun,
and then to hear the first bell-clarity of song,
which, if you were dreaming, would wake you.

Sleeps

There was a period in the summers I spent at my maternal grand-mother's that marked the best sleep I have ever had. Not that I could always fall asleep or sleep the night through—both of which were rari-ties—but that when I did sleep I slept well. I would have been six or seven and my first or second year of school just completed. And these would have been late June nights when the heat was stoking up. There was a large lime tree outside my bedroom window close enough that if I climbed out I could easily work my way along one of the big thick branches to the thickness of the trunk, where, at the joining, I would perch at twenty-five feet or so. In the dark the tree took on a primor-dial presence and otherness that seemed to trivialize the compulsions of the house. The tree was my station between not being able to fall or stay asleep and the need to find sleep, regardless of the hour.

What I liked about the tree was its size and density and the invisi-bility it gave me. It rose tens of feet above me, while I sat high above the weight and mass of the ground. I felt suspended, secret, buoyed among the heart-shaped leaves. Within its immensity was a cave world of night sounds and shadows and soft cool temperatures. You could climb around in it or sit still and drift. If you were careful you could look straight up through its canopy and watch what seemed the turning of the night sky, cloud or star. If you got dizzy you had something to hold on to.

Hiding in a tree in the dark was doubtless an escape, but less an es-cape from sleep than from sleeplessness, which was a condition of con-fusion, oppression, and sometimes claustrophobia, the iron railings of the bed like a jail. Climbing into the tree—or on rainy nights sitting in a rocker at the window—offered me a margin of difference between in-somnia and the moment, inevitably, when I would have to try to find sleep. Changing venue, so to speak, meant that in the middle of the night I could daydream, and could ease myself, in my own time, back to the rest I needed. Sitting in the lime tree or the cradle rocker I could travel or be so still I could see what I could not see in daylight; or I could memorize the day and try to think it through.

Children are notorious for hating to go to sleep, then hating, in the same cycle, to wake up. The child in the adult shares this hatred. This may be because, to the subterranean mind, the archetypal womb-tomb narrative of our extended lives, feels, in the small compass of a day, metaphorically reversed. To sleep is to die, to wake is to be reborn. Yet emotionally we resist falling in sleep to our deaths just as we are reluctant to replace the warm curl of the womb with the cold morning of our rebirth. It feels safer to stay conscious or if we must fall off to sleep to interrupt it as soon as possible. Insomnia is the death of sleep. And it is a distortion of the natural rhythm of daylight turning into nighttime and returning—no less so than when seasonal change is corrupted by a run of off weather.

Like most behavior, insomnia—the inability to go to sleep—and terminal insomnia—the inability to sustain sleep—are learned. I learned them young. Part of the innocence of childhood is that dealing with problems eccentrically is expected. The trouble with sleepless adulthood is that sitting high up in trees in the dark night of the soul is considered strange. A theme in my poem is that insomnia of all stripes is more general than we might wish to think; indeed, it is, in my estimation, universal—and in our time, chronic. Childhood-learned or not, just about every adult I know is or has been a sleep procrastinator or waker, or will be, all of which is a far cry from being an early riser. If we lived among more holy orders, eight hours of work, eight hours of prayer and play, and eight whole hours of sleep might be possible. That may be why most people join monasteries and nunneries: peace of mind.

But not even sleep promises peace of mind. When Gregor Samsa wakes from a night of uneasy dreams, he finds himself transformed inside out; and that the slow nightmare he has been living has turned from spiritual to carnal—he is now, truly, a dung-beetle. When Emily Dickinson, in #1670, finds a worm "ringed with power" in her bedroom ("He fathomed me—"), she runs, and since it is a dream she flies:

> That time I flew
> Both eyes his way
> Lest he pursue
> Nor ever ceased to run
> Till in a distant Town
> Towns on from mine
> I set me down
> This was a dream.

And when Walt Whitman, in his great surreal poem, "The Sleepers," wakes within his sleep he finds he must "wander all night in my vision" before he can return to sleep "and rise betimes." It is fascinating that in his night-journey dream he is compelled to visit those—by the hundreds—who *are* asleep or whose own dream-life he has become part of. His visitations, typically, cover a spectrum of humanity—from lovers to onanists, exiles to homebodies, lost swimmers to sailors, and memories, real and imagined, of his mother and, oddly and movingly, Washington's farewell to his soldiers. In so many ways, this is Whitman's most intimate poem; it takes us, without misstep, to an interior, more personal place, to the heart of the silence in his work, where, in the vulnerability of his restless sleep, he is responsible—both as a witness and an omniscience—for who lives and dies, is remembered and forgotten, redeemed and lost, and "averaged and restored." It takes us inside the sleeping-room, the unconscious, where "I turn but do not extricate myself / Confused, a past-reading, another, but with darkness yet."

But with darkness yet is the ontological condition of insomnia, even dream-insomnia. We all have a night visitor, interrupter, or postponer of our sleep. And its presence is not limited to the demons of technology and the cities. I am sure that the pastoralist also anticipates the hour-of-the-wolf warning of the shepherd's bell. I think there is something in our imaginative makeup, in the nightly interrogation of our hearts and minds, that makes us, like Whitman, vulnerable to memory, and so we are put into the position of having to mediate, as well as meditate, with the angels of sleep. It may be bad for our bodies but it resonates with our souls: in the middle of the night we are in touch with ourselves in a way we can never be in daylight. Our insomnia brings our night to life and the night inside us.

I am suggesting, of course, that insomnia is not necessarily a sickness to be treated and cured. What if your insomnia were *not* caused by caffeine, noise, irregular hours, job stress, money worries, physical pain, depression, alcohol, or medications, and any one of a number of other reductive sources: but was instead caused by nightingales (Coleridge's complaint) or the inability to distinguish between waking and sleeping (Keats's complaint) or the ice cracking on Derwent Water (Wordsworth's complaint)? What if the source of the trouble was the imagination itself, the mind whittling the wood of a possibility? What if the mind dreamed you awake or you woke in a dream demanding that you escape, by any means necessary, this prison-house? What if the night were so beautiful and variable that night after night, in some way, at some hour, you had to take notice? What if you were waiting for some sign or signal that could arrive only in stillness and darkness, when you were most ready to receive it?

In my poem I try to play the language of the science of sleep on the same lyric instrument as the language of sleep's poetry—I try to weave the narrative of the one into the story of the other. Both languages represent an allegory of longing, of lying down with ghosts and oracles and rising the wiser. I try to place the bed where it might best serve, simultaneously, the pastoral needs of sleep and the myth-making—dreaming or waking—desires of the mind. I put the bed outside on new earth, at the foliate edge, stars among the leaves. I put the bed there because in folktales the drunken father is always coming home late and breaking into the house, like a hard wind blowing open the door. The whole shakes and forms around his awkwardness. The mother has lain awake anticipating that with his arrival there will be an argument that will live in the walls. But I will have taken my bed, and my lament, into the fields.

WYATT PRUNTY

The Ferris Wheel

The rounding steeps and jostles were one thing;
And he held tight with so much circling.
The pancaked earth came magnifying up,
Then shrank, as climbing backward to the top
He looked ahead for something in the fields
To stabilize the wheel.

Sometimes it stopped. The chairs rocked back and forth,
As couples holding hands got off
And others climbed into the empty chairs;
Then they were turning, singles, pairs,
Rising, falling, through everything they saw,
Whatever thing they saw.

Below—the crowd, a holiday of shirts,
Straw hats, balloons, and brightly colored skirts,
So beautiful, he thought, looking down now,
While the stubborn wheel ground on, as to allow
Some stark monotony within,
For those festooned along the rim.

The engine, axle, spokes, and gears were rigged
So at the top the chairs danced tipsy jigs,
A teetering both balanced and extreme,
"Oh no," the couples cried, laughing, "Stop!" they screamed
Over the rounding down they rode along,
Centrifugal and holding on.

And he held too, thinking maybe happiness
Was simply going on, kept up unless
The wheel slowed or stopped for good. Otherwise,
There were the voices, expectant of surprise;
Funny to hear, he thought, their cries, always late,
Each time the wheel would hesitate,

Since the genius of the wheel was accident,
The always-almost that hadn't,

A minor agony rehearsed as fun
While the lights came up and dark replaced the sun,
Seeming to complete their going round all day,
Paying to be turned that way.

Later, standing off, he felt the wheel's mild dread,
Going as though it lapped the miles ahead
And rolled them up into the cloudless black,
While those who rode accelerated back
And up into the night's steep zero-G
That proved them free.

Perspectives

I find it difficult to look at a Ferris wheel without thinking of rail-roads, bridges, steamships, and other mechanical triumphs of the nine-teenth century, and it is difficult to think about that century's pre-occupations without wondering about today's, whether they are found woven among electronic bits and hits or observed in an amusement park. We love equipment that articulates the will. We are an equipmen-tal bunch, for whom the question seems to be will versus worth.

An early name for the Ferris wheel was "pleasure wheel." Other names were "Eli wheel," which translates high wheel, and "big wheel." All three make good names as far as the will is concerned. Of course, long before it had a specific name the wheel was one of the six simple machines invented in the ancient world, a time when, we like to think, will and worth did fit. But what worries the modern man described in "The Ferris Wheel" is the uneasy sense that a powerful vehicle, here used for amusement, is characterized by disproportion—its force versus human force, its mechanical heft versus the physical vulnerabilities of those who ride it. Never mind that someone just like the wheel's passen-gers designed and built it, this mechanical wonder dwarfs the weight, strength, and endurance of anyone who confronts it.

The mechanical engineer George W. Gale Ferris built his wheel, the largest yet, for the World's Columbian Exposition in Chicago in 1893. After that, contemporaries allowed his name to replace the word "plea-sure." Quite a compliment. Ferris's wheel was a tall affair, standing 250 feet in diameter, with thirty-six cabs holding sixty people each. That converts to 2,160 people going round the same way at the same time, which converts again into a lot of pleasure, or vertigo.

Physical giant that it is, though, the Ferris wheel exists in small terms, as an amusement. And this, pitted against the force it possesses, is one of its dangers. Making a sequence of the last lines of the poem's stanzas provides a summary. With one line altered slightly, they read,

> To stabilize the wheel.
> Whatever thing they saw.
> For those festooned along the rim.
> Centrifugal and holding on.
> crying Each time the wheel would hesitate,
> Paying to be turned that way.
> That proved them free.

The contrast between the innocent associations of an amusement ride and the angular experience aggregated here introduces a larger problem: the man searches "ahead for something in the fields" to "stabilize the wheel." And, speaking of the others looking out from the wheel, he says, "whatever thing they saw," suggesting one view equals many, that there is no field, spatial or gravitational, no one prospect by which to "stabilize" understanding.

The Chicago example of the Ferris wheel had a second life when it was transported to St. Louis and used there for the Louisiana Purchase Exposition in 1904. After that, Ferris's project went for scrap, as of course the railroads, bridges, and steamships of the same era have long since gone. Unlike these last three constructions, however, which played their utilitarian roles before adding to the heap, from the start the Ferris wheel had more look than last, more whoop than work.

No locomotive or steamship could match the Ferris wheel at joining ergs with idleness. Imagine all that steel bolted together and going round and round to nowhere. Small idlers are scolded in school, fired from work, court-martialed in war, demoted in heaven, and cursed in hell, but the big guys, the really big idlers come off great. They're bon vivants, good-time-Joes. That is the billing the Ferris wheel enjoys; it is spectacularly useless, therefore fun, and we must admire it for this, with only one possible exception: there *is* one real service the Ferris wheel performs, and that's anxiety.

The poem's title suggests that we are going to hear about a familiar amusement park ride. But then the wheel turns, people show fright, and another fact appears: no amount of human crying retards the wheel's movement. And for those riding, this seems to add both anxiety and pleasure. Or is it just vertigo? Passengers have no choice but to hold on, as what they grip for safety keeps driving them round. Their origin, "the pancaked earth," comes "magnifying up," as they sweep backward through the circle's base heading for the ride's high stomachless top.

Ferris's wheel was used for Expositions in industrialized Chicago and St. Louis, but in the poem the man who rides alone appears to be an unlikely candidate for anybody's exposition. He's a spoilsport, a drag, a retarded yea, a long sigh in the fun. Promotions are wasted on him, along with boosterism, optimism, and any other *ism*. Whatever's selling, he's not buying; he's out of the market. For him, the wheel is more complex than anything an exposition can present. He sees a kind of mechanistic will in action, plus our mysterious capacity for imagination and substitution.

The mystery for the man riding lies in why people derive pleasure from anxiety. We are told that "the genius of the wheel [is] accident, / The always-almost that hadn't." For those who choose to ride, danger seems to cause desire as much as it does fear. Physically, the tug of gravity and the wheel's centrifugal force compete, but those experiencing this make more of it than physics. They are the ones who, accelerating back "And up into the night's steep zero-G," experience a starker sense of freedom than they wanted.

The wheel's "going round" repeats an imbalance that those riding find even on the "pancaked earth." Stopped, the wheel does this all over again, as the chairs at the top "dance tipsy jigs," causing "A teetering both balanced and extreme." Or so the man who rides alone decides, as he watches the couples below climbing on and off, until reloaded the wheel lurches again, and those riding cry, " 'Oh no' " and scream " 'Stop!' " However strange, he knows that for others this adds up to a good time, or, more accurately, what he calls a "minor agony rehearsed as fun."

Agony has its etymological origins as the word for contest or struggle for victory, but here the contest is small, and there is no victory. People merely clutch what's nearest to hand, until the man who rides decides, "maybe happiness" is "simply going on," simply weathering "the wheel's mild dread." "Later, standing off" and looking back, he studies things in terms of "the night's steep zero-G," no Fortune's wheel here, just blind mechanics, with people holding on so's not to be trajectories.

The man sees that the wheel turns "as though it lapped the miles ahead/And rolled them up into the cloudless black," and there seems no end to this, only mindless going, with the alternating sense of weightlessness at the top and increased weight below. The wheel's circular motion carries its riders so they pass continuously into and out of place. In fact, there *is* no place, just motion, for passengers who feel freed of limit and fearful of loss.

When he rode, the man tried to control his uneasiness by looking "ahead" and "Below": "ahead" to discover "something in the fields/To stabilize the wheel" and "Below" because he found "the crowd" milling about beneath "so beautiful." But perspective and beauty inspire only willed endurance. At the end of the poem, when the same man reverses his position by standing in the fields he looked to before, what he sees from that vantage stabilizing the wheel is the illusion of freedom, experienced as "The night's steep zero-G," its zero gravity and the general emptiness those riding find. There is no power at the dark top or anywhere else along the wheel's path, only force.

For those "festooned along the rim," fear and anxiety, and the thrill in which these two combine, almost displace the wheel's "stark monotony within." Monotony, what you expect when standing on a "pancaked earth," is where the problem lies, especially for those placed just above, along a curve that going nowhere lets them see it over and over. Any pleasure here is tautological, as the wheel's going up and going down have become tautological. Those who ride the wheel find pleasure in the anxiety created by its opposing forces and their "holding on," but anxiety for what, change or distraction? Only distraction it seems. Change would be worth the hard ride, but why this is so, the will and worth of it, requires a larger perspective than either those who build and operate the wheel or those who ride it possess.

LAWRENCE RAAB

Years Later

Sometimes my father returns
in a dream, backlit
in a room that belongs
to none of our houses. Although
we do not speak, I know
he hasn't died. That was
a mistake, my error. And always
I'm grateful to understand this.

Now I can start over.
Now I can begin imagining you.
In those beautiful black-and-white photographs
you're young and handsome, posing
beside some monument, or proudly
holding up a string of fish.
Here is the lake in New Hampshire,
early morning with the mist in place.
Here's your rusty tackle box
and that old wooden rowboat.
You slide it into the water, adjust the oars.
When you reach the place
in the cove among the waterlilies,
you cast into the fog, watch it rising
around you until all the cottages
emerge in bright duplicates,
still guarding their sleepers.
Then the first breeze begins
rearranging those reflections, and your boat,
unanchored, drifts through them.
You open the thermos of coffee.
It's Saturday. This is happiness, you think.

If we could never speak to each other
whose fault was that? In every family
someone is more silent, and the conversation
circles around him, the jokes

turn against him, which he permits.
I always thought you knew
what you wanted your life to be.
And when you got it, you couldn't
imagine anything else you might need,
anything you should have needed.
Or you kept it to yourself.

It's Saturday, and you
haven't caught a single fish,
but that doesn't matter.
You give yourself another hour.
Even then it won't really matter.
Your wife is still asleep. Perhaps
I'm back there also, still asleep.
But no—this should be earlier.
Now you can see the cornfields
behind the cottage. You can hear the crows.
A screen door opens, and she steps out
onto the porch in her bathrobe.
She waves, but not to call you in.
Everything looks so clear.
I should let you go.

In another dream
soon after my father's death,
I found myself walking through a town
I'd never known, down a worn cobbled street,
and I saw him in the back of a wooden cart.
We noticed each other without astonishment.
How are you? I asked. Meaning:
How does it feel to be dead?
I'm fine, he answered quietly.
But I could see this was awkward for him,
and I thought perhaps he wasn't
permitted to speak of his new life.
He was almost gone when I asked,
And is she there with you?
How is she? Fine, he replied.
She's fine too. How strange, I thought
as I began to wake—
that he would say so little, that I
could give him so little to say.

Elegiac Problems

Beginning a poem drawn from personal experience, the writer might ask: Why should anyone care about this? Then a more useful question follows: How can I make a reader care about this? Commonality of experience is no help, is in fact a difficulty, since it can so easily lead to assumptions that will remain unchallenged or insufficiently worried about within the poem itself. Personal subjects that appear universal will always be invitations to self-indulgence. A poem that is only a recounting of experience cannot survive its occasion.

All of us have suffered the deaths of parents, or will, if we live long enough. If grief can reduce us to tears, the poem about grief should not try to solicit a similar response. However foolish it may seem to say that a real death is different from a death depicted within a work of art, such a confusion—between the power of experience and the very different power of its representation—accounts for a great deal of bad art. The poet's endeavor, in an elegy, is not the same as the job of grieving, although they may seem to intersect.

Tone, perhaps, is the key—the way the material is handled, which means the acknowledgment that it is being handled, not merely transcribed. Tone is the medium—to speak for oneself but not only for oneself, to remain aware that each phrase is directed toward a stranger who is the reader. It's easy enough, gripped by the aggressive force of grief, to cause those inclined to share such feelings to respond. It's harder to say something significant to that stranger who, we must assume, is not eager to be so burdened.

Any elegy presents these problems, as my poem, "Years Later," does. Death is the occasion for thought, for invention, for inconclusiveness. The poem was hard to write, but the specific difficulties were primarily organizational rather than personal. A substantial first draft was assembled from various pieces of previous poems, some written before my father's death. And when the poem started to come together, and to generate new, seemingly necessary material, the experience was exhilarating. Sometimes, of course, the distance between a poem's emotional climate and the way the poet feels at the moment of composition is narrower. Nevertheless, the demands of revision eventually assert themselves, and the poet must begin to imagine himself as his reader. Almost two years after "Years Later" seemed finished, I dropped a section when a friend convinced me that those lines weakened the ending by anticipating its focus. Such errors, I find, are the hardest to identify. At one point that section appeared crucial, and for a while it probably was — a way of articulating for myself concerns that, once known, could be located more persuasively elsewhere.

In making this poem out of earlier, failed poems that often expressed the anger of frustrated communication, I was most pleased to devise for my father a specific moment of happiness. It seemed true to me, perhaps because the moment asserts itself as imagined rather than remembered, and because it allows my father his solitude. My father's self-protective nature was matched by my own. In that regard, in real life, I was clearly his son. And in the poem I wanted to maintain that uneasy rubbing of one worrisome self against another. The temptation toward any larger drama was defeated primarily by lack of incident. Whenever I got impatient with or angry at my father, he retreated, pretending to consent. Then he forgot about it. Or pretended to forget. So the poem, in part, seems to me to be about the desire for a certain kind of intimacy I never felt but that, in an imagined form, may now exist within the poem.

A poem is a way of ordering memory, of revising it, even of inventing it. Memory, after all, is itself a process of revision, although we may feel it's how we reclaim the truth. Of course it's both — simultaneously, indistinguishably. The truth of memory appears from the perspective of the unstable present, in which our needs and demands are always changing — our willingness to forgive, for example, or our desire to think better of our former selves. The pressure to remember, being selective, is also a mechanism for forgetting, or repressing, or otherwise canceling out that much larger and more burdensome part of the past that doesn't fit. And then, in dreams, memory returns disguised as images that may feel both mysterious and significant, the way they sometimes feel in poems.

In important ways poems are like dreams. And for a while, during the initial stages of composition, the poet may usefully claim some of the privileges of the dreamer. Any appearance may seem to precede the reason for its existence. Images need not immediately justify themselves. The surreal and the extravagant can look like their own rewards. But the allure of dreams resides in the possibility of interpretation, the uncovering of hidden significance. To be interesting, what happens must appear potentially revelatory. A poem works similarly. As readers, we can enjoy what we don't at first fully understand because we trust we're being led somewhere—the poem's design will appear, and all of its disparate moments will prove to be related, necessary, and consequential. And for the writer the process is the same—he tries to establish those connections and make them work. "A thing in a dream," Freud writes, "means what it recalls to the mind." And a thing in a poem means what it has been designed to recall to the reader's mind. Both dream and poem are completed by acts of sympathetic understanding.

The dreams in "Years Later" happen to be real. The first was repeated after the deaths of both my father and my mother—that wrenching sense (quickly transformed into relief, then back again into loss) of having been mistaken. The dream in the final part occurred only once. I like to think I could have invented those dreams or, if the poem had insisted, made up different ones. I felt, in that regard, no obligation toward the real. But probably I wouldn't have started the poem without the actual dreams to guide and locate me, to assert their insinuating and challenging presences.

I still remember waking up from that last dream, my awareness shifting from being a figure in a dream to the knowledge that I was the dreamer—as if I'd been in control until I realized that fact, and so lost the power. But I wasn't distressed, or even surprised, by my father's reticence. Had he provided a more dramatic revelation, I might well have distrusted it. The disconcerting strangeness of the moment applied equally to us both. It was the ordinary truth of our lives.

Sad Stories

He was born in a basket, he carried his own bones
in a bag. A man prone to purity, he was a ghost.
Such a sad story, why do you listen?

You see that saying is believing, piety the easiest
delusion. Isn't it a kind of failure, all these words
like the Bible says? Oh that my head were waters

and mine eyes a fountain of tears, Jeremiah wrote,
that I might weep night and day. And they bend
their tongues like their bow for lies. I like that one.

So it is a small story which has a moral, and a hero
who loves children and there is clarity and precision
throughout the land. No more hunger. Or

only hunger, there is nothing but hunger, appetite
survives and that is the moral of the story. Writing
about the need of the people, and turning

the story into anything, dance & music for instance,
and then we are happy as anything living the life
of leisure, the pen in her hand, her very hand a ballet.

Tell me your terrors, she said to me that first night,
that woman of will and wisdom, for a hundred dollars
per hour, more or less. We spoke of terror

and tenderly shivered together as if no one before
had ever known. It's allowed, she said, there's
a war on. And we wept together like Jeremiah.

Homage

Some time ago it occurred to me that I wanted to write like scripture: to make with language something like the Bible, like my own personal and peculiar memory of and relationship to the Bible; to reproduce in language my recollected experience of hearing Biblical texts when I was a child. One implication of such a gesture is that I want to sound anony-mous. I love the ambiguity of the text, and the little frisson I feel when I hear, for instance, "the hand writing on the wall," as opposed to what most people hear, "the handwriting on the wall." As a child at Mass, I liked it when the priest announced the "text" for his sermon. I have a curious sense of sermon these days, but the usefulness of such texts re-mains for me.

I try to precipitate poems. I will make up, or find (for instance, from discarded poems of my own) phrases whose "meanings" are ambigu-ous but whose sounds and appearance are interesting. The line-and-a-quarter that begins the poem under consideration, "He was born in a basket, he carried his own bones in a bag," was the precipitating element of this poem, and I have no idea where it came from. It rattled around my head, and sometimes it was funny, and sometimes tragic, and some-times I thought there must be something wrong with the sort of person who would recite (even in the privacy of his own skull) such foolishness for weeks at a time, to no purpose. Of course I realized that it was in part simply a topological image of the body, a skin bag. I am sure I heard someone say, for instance of me, that he was merely a bag of bones. Per-haps playing with such alliteration was the origin of the poem.

But nothing is more beautiful than the language of Jeremiah, except that of any of those angry ancient voices. I gave up trying to equal them, or to compete with them, long ago. I just use them, like any minister selecting a text and letting the inspiration take over.

I have nothing to say except the poem.

I will say my nothing anyway.

I want to be anonymous; the purity and the precision of the fairy tale, for instance, result from the scraping off of the individual touch, the mingling over time of many touchings that depletes the taint of ego. Yet the household tale, the folk tale is fully contaminated (happily) by the prejudices and failing of the cultures that produce them. (But no one can aspire to *folk* status).

The way to become a prophet is to keep the best secrets.

The way to prophecy is secrecy.

A hint counts strongest. Ambiguity is the path to God, or to some sense of godliness, or at least to his house—his hovel or cave or den or palace, all the same I suppose. His or her. Which suggests the issue of sex.

My fear of the body—no, my embarrassment at having one—is here, in this poem. By "the body" I probably mean sex, but all those messinesses are part of the same problem. While capitalism suggests everything of value is for sale, the body's official value must be as a site for erasure: the sale of apparel, implements, potions and salves to decrease, denigrate, subvert, de- or re-odorize, sanitize, and re-size the body dominates the popular media (i.e., weight machines, soaps and deodorants, the fashion industry, and the Internet), while everything that deals directly in heightened physical sensation (drugs and prostitution, and alcohol) is suspect or downright illegal. Thank goodness.

I suspect this poem, among others, pays a kind of homage to repression. Much art is the result of clever maneuvering around the regulations, the superego. Hiding the body, and hiding the rapture, produces monsters of loveliness, as well as institutions, such as The Family (including the Holy).

HILDA RAZ

Sarah Fledging

Soft feather heart
bluejay and thrasher
and eagle's down she has gathered,
each nail smoothing each barbed shaft
oiled so her fingers shine.

Meadowlark and finch, cardinal,
the junco, right-upside-up nuthatch,
feather skim on teak where she dips
from a bowl to chamois
against afternoon chill,
pulls her needle through
blood spots dried mahogany.

Flutter heart of feather bowl
as she shakes loose another
amber and dove wet pebble
from the patch by her elbow,
reaches, gathers each shaft for a linen loop,
and waxes and ties off.

Whirl, circle, and wave of feather
jackdaw, hawk, the golden swift
scooping mosquitoes from the backyard lathehouse,
her hands reach to steady the softening cloak—it quivers,
air from the floor vent—she turns.
And now she reaches for the lamp and rises.

A Vision

"Sarah Fledging" began as a vision.

My biologist child Sarah had been working at the Wild Animal Park at the San Diego Zoo when she required emergency abdominal surgery, twelve hours worth, and subsequently developed a set of blood clots in her leg and groin that almost killed her. During her recovery, I was aware of her strong desire to live, but also to transform her energies into art. Sarah had long been a writer of gaming books, a visual artist—jewelry maker, mask and paper vessel maker—a maker, in fact, in the old way of Icarus's father Daedalus, the maker of the labyrinth; she was a maker: a poet, a fabricator, a collector of old texts. On her hospital bed, in pain, attached to tubes and monitors, she lay reading Darwin's account of his voyages on the Beagle. One especially hard night she told me about Darwin on deck watching women standing on shore, naked in the rain, nursing their infants, watching the man lying on the deck, deathly ill from seasickness, watching him watch them. I think what Sarah took from the *Voyage of the Beagle* was a vision of courage—Darwin's, in sailing so far, always sick, to find news of the natural world, and the women's, standing naked in cold rain, holding their children, to watch him—though she wouldn't have said so. Maybe something about growing impervious to the messages of the body when the external world calls out loud? I don't know.

Well. I won't forget Sarah. Who could, who knew her? From birth she was both fierce and patient. Once, between her eighteenth and twenty-sixth months, when we lived in London and often rode the Underground, she rolled off her seat, removed her coat, cherry-red shoes, peeled off white tights and her flowered corduroy dress, put back her warm coat and never again in her life wore a dress. At six, her second year in school, she was always late. To discover why, I followed some distance behind, watching her linger to pick up and open each leaf and worm, each chrysalis, each feather she could find by looking and poking with a popsicle stick from her pocket. Sarah was learned in the old ways—and showed joy as well as the knowledge that careful observation brings. She was a naturalist in the way of Alfred Russel Wallace, as the poet Diane Ackerman is, or Sue Hubbell, or Barry Lopez—steady observers of the natural world.

So my vision of Sarah was Sarah transforming. During her illness, I thought she might die. But when "Sarah Fledging" was written, I knew she would live—was well, in fact, and thriving. But still, that steady urge to undergo metamorphosis, to understand and recreate a transformation was so strong in my child that I perceived it and, as poets do, I wrote it down—as a figure for art, maybe? As an explanation for her passionate interest in and study of the creatures of the world? Naming, Adam's task, didn't seem to be hers.

So this poem documents my sense of Sarah gathering feathers, "soft feather heart/blue jay and thrasher/and eagle's down" into a huge shallow bowl, maybe of gold (though that detail fell away). I see each of her strange fingernails, warped from the strains of manipulating silver and gold, clay and papier maché, and paper clips and teeth (once she'd brought home from the dentist's office her wisdom teeth and her brother's, all removed the same hour so the children could recover together, and set them into a sculpture, his tooth drilled through and set with an old quartz), smoothing each feather's barbs so carefully that her fingers must be covered with the natural oils of the feathers. Each detail seemed to fit: the feathers from so many birds, "meadowlark, and finch, cardinal,/the junco, right-upside-up nuthatch," the birds she would watch and catalogue for me when she was tiny—each feather smoothed and sewed into a length of chamois, a cape perhaps, "against afternoon chill"—and each feather drawn through at the base by her needle and surprisingly attached to "blood spots dried mahogany" on the chamois.

I suppose, when the blood spots appeared on the chamois in my vision, that the bowl of feathers began to flutter, to animate, at her touch, so skilled is she with her nimble fingers, so carefully she "shakes loose another" feather, each one a different shade, one the color of amber, or dove, the color of wet pebble. And then, I suppose, I knew she would begin to reach for the linen thread, linen like a shroud, to make for each one "a linen loop" to wax and tie off.

By now, I suppose the chamois is covered with feathers, the blood spots covered over by so many different feathers, and the chamois a shape to cover and whirl now around my Sarah, a chamois so light and covered by feathers—"jackdaw, hawk, the golden swift/scooping mosquitoes from the backyard lathehouse"—that her hands would have to "reach to steady the softening cloak" that "quivers" now—"air from the floor vent"?—to steady it. But no, instead she turns.

"And now she reaches for the lamp and rises."

Sarah transformed. Certainly the poem documents my vision.

Some months later, Sarah wrote me a letter to say she would be changing soon, she hoped I'd understand. Through the next months she and I talked often, through the distance that separated us, and then she came home and we walked each morning to the lake to watch geese rise and land and rise again. I came to understand, as well as I am able to understand, a mother who loves her child, that Sarah is my own only on the page. I am the parent of a transsexual child, now named after my papa Aaron, my mother's father, as she would have been had she been born male. After the surgery, I nursed him as I had Sarah—preparing food, holding and swabbing, and steadying him for his debut. And now Aaron is here, fully here, and I am telling you the story of my poem, which must have anticipated—in the ways art can anticipate, and only art can—the extraordinary stories of our kind.

IRA SADOFF

Solitude Étude

I spent years on my knees while she
got off before me, her eyes fluttering closed,
her mind several men away, their cocks
glistening spit and then, when twitching
turned to tedium (every night the same position)
she deigned to let me in, and waited patiently
for me to finish up. Shut up, I'm talking now.

And as I speak, some psycho with tattoos
drills MacDonald's with his M-16. Killing children,
yes, and priests and Digital execs. Mothers, wives
and daughters. Serial killers, mass murderers,
they're the latest chattel on the avenue. Curious:
we like them with one leg, eating gruel
from garbage cans—half-savage, pornographic beasts—

or else well-dressed boys with A's.
The neighbors said, We *fed him milk and cookies*,
I stood before that counter, waiting for my meal,
or used to stray behind my house in the flats, picking up
old toys soaked with mud. I longed for one small gem,
ruby or amethyst, a gift for her, to prove
I was more than a standing pond, the slick

wet granite of a shallow ditch. The night my wife
bedded down Nick Gonzales (why spare his name?)
I found the proof I needed playing pinball
at a truck stop in Wyoming: I'd never felt more lost,
more ashamed, more myself. A man my age
was on the next machine, praying
to bells and lights named for women's breasts.

Dry mouthed and needle-pocked, half-hypnotized,
teary-eyed, swooning with a moan, he sang,
Oh mama, please don't bring me down,
Who's to blame? The Reverend Moon,
Sigmund Freud, Phil Donahue? Her brute

of a father, fucking his way through her mother
in his lover's voice (did I really lick her wrist)?

Movie sex, where a healthy buck will raise
his partner to the counter, and stuff her
full of ammunition? Now they retrieve
the carcass of a child, his ninety-nine cent meal
pressed to his chest. The killer's beside him,
handcuffed, arms behind his back,
overweight, expressionless, his face gone slack:

he brings me back to *Little America*,
that dank pisshole near Laramie, where I'd shake
the sleepless man whose fists are curled, who's snagged
on rage and blame, and in the morning, dress
and raise him up before the hotel mirror,
open the door on that mesmerizing, snow-capped,
mountain-range: jagged, treacherous, too slick to climb.

On the Composition of
"Solitude Étude"

Few poets I know consciously alter their writing strategies; rather they let each individual poem emerge from their "unconscious" and "the language itself." This approach, almost automatic in our psychoanalytic age, often helps defeat willfulness and artifice. When my work is going well I too start with a piece of language, an image, a rhythm or a sound, a phrase, and then begin the associative work of the imagination, asking *What's next?* But just as self-consciousness often constricts a poet, a lack of self-consciousness can lead to writing ritually, repetitively, recycling the same images, rhythms, and concerns. Many times I've picked up books by writers whose previous work I've admired and have been disappointed by how they've repeated themselves, sometimes diminishing their work to caricature, occasionally diminishing my pleasure in their earlier work. Whether a poet is motivated by a desire to please, or by the romantic view that the direction of the work is "out of his or her control," I have often sensed a relaxation or laziness in a writer who comes to repeat earlier successes. It also happens, of course, that poets suffer from stasis in their work or lives and simply don't have the resources at a given moment to direct either. That's how I felt in 1991, although at the time I might have expressed those feelings—to be generous with myself—more obliquely, using the discourse that middle-age was a time to come to term with "limits."

Before writing "Solitude Étude," one of the first poems I composed for *Delirious: New and Selected Poems*, I'd been gravitating more toward an intensifying lyric and away from the meditative voice that seemed the dominant mode of *Palm Reading in Winter* and much of *Emotional Traffic*. I *am* self-conscious, a tough critic of my own work as well as the work of others, and I do from time to time appraise the direction of my work, particularly after reading work by other writers that moves and surprises me. And I had been trying for some time to bridge more intimate poems (which offered immediate emotional connection for the reader) and more public poems (which would contextualize those feelings, give them scope, breadth, and ambition). I'd been frustrated by how feelings are always privatized in this country, as if they only originated in an interior which was insulated from culture, when in fact those attitudes toward feelings are very much a product of American culture. I've always felt the greatest poets make the greatest connections, which is why we call them "visionaries." It was impossible, of course, to bring such lofty ideas into practice in my poetry. They were only ideas about feelings. The change that brought me to "Solitude Étude" and a half dozen other poems in my new collection was some fusion of a change of character, a different way of seeing and living my life, and finding in the poetry a heightened diction, rhythm, and a wildness of association. Without dwelling on the confessional (although in this case it's impossible to ignore), I was going through a long and painful end to a two-decade marriage; it became impossible to avoid facing my own desire to please (women especially) or my own self-hatred; I mistrusted and was ashamed of my own powers, in fact, of any power at all. In my earlier poems I had often valued the modest, rigorously controlled, highly structured poems that showed classical restraint; I avoided and sometimes disdained expansive egotism, but also, in some ways, edited out the imbalances passions often provide. Just beneath the surface of the modesty in the poems was shame and paralysis, and my more recent poems had seemed ghostly, drained of vitality, recirculating many versions of the same intimate struggles. I was very unhappy, and an inward turn, resulting in melancholy and nostalgia, scarred the work.

I eventually lost patience with the stance in my work and in my life, and was in the process of making changes: I wanted to live my life more fully, and I began to believe I had a right to ask for more from those I loved and from myself. I wanted to recover a sense of play and joy I remembered vividly from my twenties and early thirties. Almost simultaneously I began to ask for more from the poems I was writing: more open-endedness, expression of expansive emotions like rage and the ecstatic, emotions that had often made me and others uncomfortable; I knew early on I'd risk losing whatever audience my earlier poems had gathered. I hate the term "political correctness" (it's often a conservative's disguised excuse to affirm bigotry or prejudice), but I also discovered quickly that an angry middle-aged white man, which is what I was, was likely to offend those with whom I shared political convictions. But I ultimately felt that I had little to lose, that my way of being, as an artist and a person, had failed me. To continue writing and living the way I had would have, at least metaphorically, killed me and the work.

A few other convergences: I was on sabbatical, reading Whitman's long and expansive public lines closely for the first time in years, preparing to teach a class on his work and Dickinson's; I was living in Berkeley, away from close friends, but near bookstores filled with the adventurous but often emotionally distant books of Language Poets. I read them with as open a mind as I could, and though I was often more convinced by their treatises than their work, their belief in disjuncture and syntactical movement made an impression on me. Berkeley, too, because of its climate and its liberal politics, had more than its share of homeless people who roamed the streets; many of the men were Viet Nam vets who required wheelchairs for transportation. Many of the homeless, though, were seriously mentally ill, released from hospitals during the Reagan era. A number of the males were angry, violently out of control. In my own domestic unhappiness I went for long walks at night. It was not uncommon to see knife and bottle fights among these men; approached by them for change and food, I sometimes feared for my safety, I walked with my fists curled, and I felt deeply ashamed that I could be so inured to their humiliated pain. I remember coming home one night and turning on the TV to find that a mentally ill man had gunned down two dozen people at a McDonald's in San Diego. This odd conflation of the public and private stirred me to begin writing "Solitude Étude."

The first stanza, which was kind of a tour de force, came to me early, though it had been preceded in earlier drafts by warmup writing, getting there. But then I was stuck. I began to hear some critical voice, some shadow version of my mother telling me I couldn't talk that way, it was "unfair" and "melodramatic," it was too "intimate." I sat at the typewriter for hours at a time trying to make those feelings go away, to modify them, but the language was flat, it was all in my head. Out of frustration I wrote the lines "Shut up, I'm talking now," the kind of diction I'd never used in a poem before. So fearful a person, I felt as if that kind of talk was nearly pathological, which is what brought me to the killer at McDonald's and to the innocent children he killed. Two ends of the same rope, as Melville would say. And then I just improvised. I noticed along the way that my rhythms, usually some variation of the anapestic and iambic, had become much more heightened and fractured, containing many more spondees and trochees. Much more consonance and internal rhyme and slant rhyme, set off against a much more irregular pattern of speech, adding to the poem's jaggedness and surprise. Eventually I was brought to a fourth memory: the muddy backyard of one of my many childhood homes, where I was trying to dig up something (it became a jewel in the poem) to give to my mother, whose response was (probably quite appropriately) disgust at my dirtiness. I felt it then, those same feelings in the present while writing the poem, and all of a

sudden that memory opened up what became the spine of the poem—
an incessant desire to please, to efface my own feelings so as not to lose
the love and approval of my wife or my mother. And in the course of
the poem I cut off perceptions in mid-sentence, moved to different land-
scapes, used the heightened diction of the hurt and the enraged, gave the
poem shadow voices (parodying the originating impulse), gathered other
memories (a betrayal I never faced), and relentlessly stuck with the cam-
era and crossed out judgments. I took in more of the world, confronted
it without mediating it, and used my knowledge of jazz improvisation
to listen only to the chord (line and stanza) that preceded the present
tense and responded to it with another association, a counter. In other
words I interrogated the poem, I disagreed with myself, I intensified and
amplified, attending to questions of vividness and vitality, the clash and
clang of consonance set against assonance, before trying to make those
voices come together—not intellectually but emotionally. I did this not
to make the poem cohere, but to make the poem live fully in its conflict.
It took months to get the ending right, moving away from statement to
scene and image, finding in another figure in the poem all the violence
and defeat I'd so long turned away from.

I'd never had so much fun writing a poem. The process was full of
permission giving and play, it was as much musical as linguistic. Even
while I was writing the poem I felt as if I'd written something unlike
anything I'd ever written: that kind of thrill comes so rarely when you
write poetry for a life's work, I took it in and treasured it. A short time
later—and I don't think this is an accident—I fell in love. And for a
while afterward, nearly two years, I was on a roll, refining and expand-
ing the strategies that gave me "Solitude Étude" (it allowed me, for one,
to fuse public and private concerns in a direct and authentic manner,
without moralizing or turning myself into a morally superior hero as
so many poems about injustice do). I had allowed myself to be silenced
for a long time, and thanks to many factors named here (and some I
can't yet identify) I'd found a wider range in my voice, I was, oddly—
though I thought I'd been doing so all along—writing more for myself
than ever, and felt I'd represented myself more fully than I'd ever done
before. Gradually, of course, as I was changing, my voice was changing, I
began to feel that I was pumping new poems up (rhythmically and visu-
ally) to energize them, and now I'm back to wrestling with the same old
question, What's Next? I'm reading new writers, I'm listening and look-
ing for something to seize on, working toward that passionate feeling of
intense discovery and development that makes writing so consistently
challenging and rewarding. But now I do it with much more hope.

ROBERT SIEGEL

Silverfish

It lives in the damps of rejection,
  in the dark drain, feeding upon the effluvia
    of what we are, of what we've already been.

Everything comes down to this: we are its living—
  the fallen hair, the fingernail, the grease from a pore,
    used toothpaste, a detritus of whiskers and dead skin.

All this comes down and worries it into life,
  its body soft as lymph, a living expectoration,
    a glorified rheum. In the silent morning

when we least expect it, it is there
  on the gleaming white porcelain: the silver scales,
    the many feelers *busy busy*, so fast, it is

unnerving, causing a certain panic in us,
  a galvanic revulsion (*Will it reach us
    before we reach it?*), its body

translucent, indefinable, an electric jelly
  moving with beautiful sweeps of the feet
    like a sinuous trireme, delicate and indecent,

sexual and cleopatric. It moves for a moment
  in the light, while its silver flashes and slides,
    and part of us notices an elusive beauty,

an ingenious grace in what has been cast off.
  As if tears and the invisibly falling dandruff,
    skin cells and eyelashes

returned with an alien and silken intelligence,
  as if chaos were always disintegrating into order,
    elastic and surprising,

as if every cell had a second chance
  to link and glitter and climb toward the light,
    feeling everything as if for the first time—

pausing stunned, stupefied with light.
  Before we, frightened by such possibilities,
    with a large wad of tissue come down on it,

and crush it until it is nothing
  but dampness and legs, an oily smear
    writing a broken Sanskrit on the paper,

a message we choose not to read
  before committing it to the water
    swirling blankly at our touch,

hoping that will take care of it,
  trying not to think of it—the dark
    from which it will rise again.

An Alien and Silken Intelligence

Before writing "Silverfish," I had repeated encounters with *Lepisma saccharina*, denizen of bathroom drains and other damp and shadowy places. Invariably the encounter began with a shriek from one of my three daughters who had discovered its presence just before (or worse, while) bathing. I was instructed to catch and destroy the offending insect, usually with a wad of bathroom tissue, and flush the remains. Left alone in the room with the victim, I had ample time to reflect on this act of extermination. After a time or two, the destruction of something so quick, lithe, and harmless felt wrong, and I released the creatures outside or allowed them to escape down the drain while pretending to remove them. These small acts of deceit and mercy made the silverfish more attractive to me and I soon grew to be an enthusiastic conspirator in its escape. The effort moved me to think about the uncompromising rejection most people show toward many-legged and quick-moving insects (or small rodents, for that matter).

So I was not surprised when this poem came along demanding to be written. For me, as for authors of medieval bestiaries, animals often serve as symbols or totems—in my case, foci of remote meanings of which I'm only partially aware. When a poem comes that touches upon the mystery underlying the self and the world, it's likely to contain an animal. It may, like this one, say things I only begin to understand afterward, if ever.

The thought that initially sparked the poem was the economy of the silverfish's existence: it is made of our detritus, the parts of us that disappear down a drain: the fallen hair, fingernail, whiskers, and dead skin. The body changes its cells every seven years (except for brain cells) and the silverfish "recycles" the old cells we cast off. What dies of us is reborn in it. It becomes our opposite, our complicit Other, our double. As with other doubles, we may not at first recognize it; in fact, we may re-coil from it in fear and disgust.

With the double, the Other, comes a rich trove of implications famil-iar to us from literature, such as Conrad's *The Secret Sharer*, or from psychology, the Jungian shadow self. We know the shadow self consists of those parts of ourselves, positive and negative, of which we are un-conscious. Jung observed that if we do not integrate these parts with our conscious self, the shadow will manifest itself, willy-nilly, in our ex-ternal lives. Our reaction to the silverfish (and other hapless creatures) suggests to me our resistance to know, and integrate with, the shadow self, or double.

The detritus of our bodies, hair, dandruff, mucus, et cetera, is poten-tially shaming or embarrassing. The lively physicality of the insect may therefore alarm us, as if our unwashed, animal body came back to haunt us ("electric jelly . . . delicate and indecent"). Yet the excreta we wash away are also dead or dying. The silverfish grows from our decay; the insect and the darkness it dwells in may embody the ultimate Other, death, as opposed to life. Yet in this case the darkness possesses a strange and alarming vitality. We have ambivalent feelings toward this kind (per-haps any kind) of resurrection or reincarnation.

The ecology of the silverfish also suggested to me a parallel to Chaos Theory, the mathematical theory recently developed to explain appar-ently random, chaotic events, such as fluctuations in the weather, mos-quito populations, or the stock market. Thanks to the silverfish, our skin cells and eyelashes return

> with an alien and silken intelligence,
> as if chaos were always disintegrating into order
> elastic and surprising.

The theory reveals that chaos itself is not disorderly, but has its own order, expressed in equations such as the Lorenz Mask (named after the mask-like shape the equation makes on a graph). Fractal equations yield beautiful and symmetrical patterns. But this new and alien order may threaten our sense of control, because the unpredictable element of chaos (the theory tells us) is what threatens and changes any estab-lished order. Creativity and procreativity have an element of chaos in them and bring about unpredictable changes in the order.

This element in history is exemplified by Cleopatra, who unpredict-ably fled in her trireme at the Battle of Actium, causing Anthony to pursue her and lose the battle (and indirectly unify the Roman Empire under the victorious Augustus). The silverfish, with its legs and rows of oar-like cilia, resembles a "sinuous trireme." Like Cleopatra, it has a sensuous, unpredictable energy. Perhaps the prospect of this alien order is even more alarming to us than the thought of darkness and decay. It violates the death-wish, the desire for dissolution, and challenges us with rebirth,

>as if every cell had a second chance
>   to link and glitter and climb toward the light,
>   feeling everything as if for the first time—
>
>pausing stunned, stupefied with light.

For me, these lines are the heart of the poem. They suggest the rebirth of wonder, of seeing things freshly, "with the doors of perception cleansed," in Blake's phrase, or with the "enlightenment" of the Buddhist. The silverfish, which pauses in the porcelain-white room, as if blinded and stunned by the brilliance of light, embodies this wonder. To see the strangely beautiful silverfish, itself glittering with light, stunned with the wonder of light is an epiphany of the sort that converted me to saving this "delicate and indecent" creature. "Stupefied" also implies losing one's earlier knowledge, or preconceptions, becoming "stupid" or foolish in order to become wise. What was formerly homely and ordinary, even ugly and frightening, from a new point of view is graceful and beautiful.

The threat of death and rebirth, of abundant new life, of the Other, of an alien yet familiar order, may all help to explain—along with the plainly physical "galvanic revulsion"—our destruction of the silverfish. Most often we choose to come at it buffered with a large wad of tissue in which we crush it until only its legs are left, like a strange broken writing reminiscent of Sanskrit (one of the world's sacred languages) or the writing on the wall at Belshazzar's Feast. We choose not to read the writing, but commit the silverfish

>   to the waters
>   swirling blankly at our touch,
>
>   hoping that will take care of it,
>   trying not to think of it—the dark
>   from which it will rise again.

We blankly ignore the vision in the light, casting the silverfish back into the shadow of our willing forgetfulness, into the mystery of the Other, into the darkness from which we come and to which we all return—trying not to think of it. For out of that dark drain the silverfish (or its kin) will rise again, the rejected will return, the disturbing resurrection occur again, to trouble us—who are half in love with easeful death—with the possibility of life.

DAVE SMITH

Making a Statement

Thousands, lately, have asked me about my hair.
Why is it so long? Why haven't you cut it?
I think about Sampson, of course, and his woe.
His hair like thickets where I was born, swamps,
tall grasses bending with red-winged blackbirds
like a woman's nipples in the quick sun-gold.
I could tell about Sampson, about the girl,
but I say my head is cold. I need cover.
Playing tennis with a leggy blonde I love,
I admit I can't do anything about it, my youth.
She rolls her eyes into a smashing serve.
"You old guys," she sighs with her drop shot.
Back and forth all day, yellow balls, long gray hair.

"Making a Statement"

Richard Hugo once said to me that he thought he was at his best writing a poem of 50 lines or less. We had been speaking about love of play and physical games, Hugo once a baseball player and I once a football player. People who play games seriously have a deep feeling for the mysteries of *form*, by which I mean rules, moves, how things must be done. I wasn't surprised that our conversation shifted easily from games we had loved to writing poetry and the forms we sought to get it written.

* * *

William Heyen, an ex-soccer player of All-American caliber, wrote me—speaking about forms—that he much admired bodily grace. He said those poets he considered the finest were, consistently, athletes who transferred a love for physical movement into sinewy, athletic language. He offered an impressive list of athlete-poets that included Dickinson, Keats, and Edgar Allan Poe (a boxer of some distinction and a man who recorded a six-mile swim in the James River, against the tide). Perhaps the most unsurprising thing here is the poet's predilection for examining acts, making leaps and linkages, an observing intelligence that seeks clarity. The surprise is that so much dull poetry exists to chronicle somebody's day with a ball. Does this mean there is a huge appetite for grace that movies and novels do not satisfy?

* * *

Is grace a clumsy word for what poets want? With the athlete, it can be refined to advantage but not acquired whole. One has it or does not, like an identity. Athletes like Michael Jordan have superior power, balance, timing, and strength, but true greatness comes, as coaches say, from "playing within abilities." That requires awareness and discipline. Some years ago I saw that I wrote a certain kind of poem. Bill Heyen told me that he believed we all write a few poems that are distinctly our own. We write many others that "belong" to other poets. Usually, we know which are which, although readers often remain ignorant. The poems we collect into books are imitations—of poets we read and of ourselves. Few of us are close to original talents, but who wants to acknowledge a lack of identity? We write in a kind of disguise that is actually an "unclarity." But when we have written our own poem, and know we have done so, we are more than gratified. Only then do we earn the right to be called a poet.

*   *   *

The poem I wrote, my old form, fell between 75 and 150 lines, a long poem by contemporary standards. It presented an oblique, multi-layered tale seeking resolution of some "obligation" problem, but it assembled and worked through a weave of language touching upon various embedded mysteries. It was a closet of selves wanting air-time. "The Roundhouse Voices" is typical, a funeral elegy for my uncle who had been the foreman of a Baltimore & Ohio Railroad roundhouse; I worked on the poem eleven years. That poem's unclarity exists because, among other reasons, its subject was, I now see, *the language of presentation* more than a dramatic situation. Maybe I was writing poetry about poetry writing and its difficulties. I dislike poems that assume poetry is the measurement of reality. They make me feel I am trapped in a roomful of Twomblys and Mondrians. I am forced to watch yet another Broadway musical about Broadway musicals. Maybe I was less aware than I should have been.

*   *   *

So what was I doing? I wanted to find, beyond webs of self, a grace and a life. I knew the disadvantages to the poem I attempted. Who could comprehend it? One reviewer liked my "Goshawk, Antelope." He praised the goshawk that died crashing into my car's windshield. I don't consider why that pleased him, but my car does not move in the poem and no bird strikes a windshield. I thought that man dim and weird. But I was dim. I failed to provide transitions, clear scenes, nouns and verbs adequate to expression and intention.

To write ambitiously is necessary, but big ambition can easily become loud chatter. The confused poet, in a democratic community of aesthetics, finds ready access to good alibis: he is meditative, interior, lyrical; or is self-appointed with a message of polemical salvation, and so on. Confusion, however, is still confusion. One of its manifestations is the poem that speaks with the voice of another poet. No one chooses that who wants the clear, confident voice of a self. This is the poet's identity, and there is nothing harder to find. Unless it is keeping that voice, for it will waver and fade out, and sometimes return like radios on a country night.

*   *   *

Poets rarely stop writing rather than repeat what they have learned to do. They write the voice of the great Other. Some say we have to write to live. Many breathe who do not threaten the paper. When I assumed a journal editorship, I did not write sometimes for months, after years of a daily habit. Writing became making the machine work; the poems were no longer faintly mine. I knew the trash in my hands. My problem was a barrenness and, in part, a lack of time to loaf and invite my soul. The latter is a primary difference between what poets do and what fiction writers do, those whose work ethic would delight a Scottish plumber.

*   *   *

I had enough of that ethic to ask why I wasn't writing as I had done, enough to seek remedies. I knew my excuse about a lack of time was baloney. Being diligent was all I needed to get words on the page. Quality was, of course, another matter. I therefore gave myself an assignment. And a permission. The assignment was to write a short poem every day, stealing whatever minutes I could. And I would repeat the "form" until it bored me. Brevity meant I could do a full draft in a sitting. I might lose the looping orchestrations and long puzzling narratives, but I might make poems jump with mysteries, records of the world I lived in, snapshots of daily events connected to god knows what. I'd been a plodding reviser hoping for archeological discovery, a habit that needs stamina and trust there's treasure in the dig. For various reasons, my body no longer gave me what it did all those years. Should I stop writing?

If you stop writing, you do not fail. William Stafford told me he had never had writer's block because he was not afraid. He gave himself permission to fail every day. Writers learn from other others. Maybe ambition for "art" had become more important to me than pleasure in writing. I tried to think of the poem as a window suddenly open. I wrote about long-necked water pitchers used for flowers, about wrecked cars, pelicans, B. B. King, etc., and I tried to forget "poetry" while language might mumble or sing or flow, as I pleased. Oh, that's not exactly true. I wanted language to seem true to what I felt. I wanted the inevitable and compelling, but I renegotiated what compelling meant. I gave myself permissions.

I thought the first poem I wrote was a sonnet. I did not come back the next day, as intended, but later, and found I had written a thirteen-line poem. It had no sonnet's internal logic. But fate gave me that template, so I wrote what I called "shorties" and proceeded to invent rules. There must be progression, if not narrative, some dense pattern, and some surprise that grows from a poem's elements. My progression was a sort of jazz zigzagging that is emotional rather than rational. It seems to me now that in trusting what language kept hidden from me, I was seeking both grace and clarity.

My line length was irregular, though short when I started; I don't know why. With repetition, the lines took on consistently a hendecasyllabic shape, the final foot often feminine, or weak. I wasn't comfortable with this and tried to resist the falling rhythm by "jamming" multiple stresses in the line. I wanted lines to end with a flourish and firm sharpness, perhaps because I favor the muscular character of Anglo-Saxon language. But I hoped to balance this with the sprawling, plain idiom of the human voice that lives outside of books.

I read, in this period, many small poems. I thought some design of narrative might be valuable if a book could be teased from this work. Books seek and depend on unity. When I had more than seventy poems I started thinking about transitions, links, and orchestrations. I wanted variety, too, so the effects of sonic juxtaposition and interplay increasingly attracted me. I indulged an old affection for rhyme, despite my distaste for the manifestos of the neo-verse writers, and soon I was deep into envelope rhymes and mid-line rhymes, and final couplets. Compressions of various kinds, which are discipline and grace, made new possibilities for me where habit had thickened like old waistlines. The thirteen-line poem led me to my book *Fate's Kite: Poems 1991-1995* because it permitted me a field of play with important consequences, or statements.

W. D. SNODGRASS

Lifelong

—for the marriage of Charles and Lucina, Candelaria Day,
    February 2, 1995

So long as you both shall lift
    An echo in night's tunnel, lift
    A child from numbing pavements, lift
    A hand to hold back, set loose, to enfold;

So long as you both shall leave
    Proud pursuits go their own gait, leave
    The trampling and bright trophies, leave
    Your tidemark on the mind's strand;

So long as you both shall laugh
    At sworn lies and their catch tunes, laugh
    At all contrived, all forced growth, laugh
    From peaks of occult, calm passion;

So long as you both shall leaf
    Through sanctimonious parchments, leaf
    Gold on a new daybook's edges, leaf
    Out, then blossom the nerves' branchings;

So long as you both shall listen
    To the song latched in the ribs' cage, listen
    To breath, soft, in the next room, listen
    To surfsound down the blood's ways;

So long as you both shall love,
    So long last; none lasts longer.

"Lifelong"

In the mid-'80s, when I first visited San Miguel de Allende, I met Charles Kuschinski, an American living there. I can't say that at that time I liked him very much—though intelligent and well-informed, he seemed brash and opinionated. But since he, too, was a writer and translator, we ran into each other from time to time. At the intermission of a concert, he told my wife and me we should leave our expensive first-floor seats and move into the top balcony among the poorest Mexicans—the sound was much better there; he was right. Again, I met him walking in the street carrying a patio table over his head—taking it home to the young woman who lived nearby. I soon discovered that one could call him only through *her* phone; in time, if I encountered him in the Jardin, he was carrying not a table, but a child—a boy he obviously doted upon and with whose rearing he was much involved.

No doubt their mother had as much effect on him. She was Lucina Kathmann, a lively and independent person, also a writer and translator, involved with dance and theatre (which often took her back to Chicago) and with humanitarian causes. Soon the two became active in San Miguel's chapter of PEN; later, willing to do the drudge work, they came to be in charge of it. They turned its direction resolutely toward programs for writers in prison—at meetings or readings (which my wife and I sometimes gave, sometimes attended) we would find half a dozen petitions addressed to far-flung governments, asking that some persecuted writer be treated with mercy and/or justice.

So far, I confess, their concern seemed to me somewhat programmatic and impersonal. Then Lucina became pregnant again. So did her next-door neighbor and friend, a Mexican woman who had five children and who sometimes babysat for her. By this time, Charlie and Lucina had not only consolidated their households; in a sense, the two families tended to share each other's spaces and the adults shared their child-raising duties.

The two women delivered within weeks of each other. Their Mexican friend died in childbirth; Lucina nursed both babies. The five other Mexican children (some, of course, fairly grown) stayed in their own home next door but were cared for, fed, and clothed by Charlie and Lucina.

I might comment here that my wife and I were much surprised at how well many Americans in San Miguel behaved toward the Mexicans. There were exceptions: we had known Americans who actually scolded compatriots for being "too generous" to Mexican servants or workmen, fearing it might "spoil them" or that other servants (e.g., their own maids or gardener) might demand the same pay. But those *were* exceptions. American groups had funded hospitals, programs for handicapped children, established a large bilingual library for Mexican students, were building a home for the destitute aged. They certainly had done better than those rich Mexicans who took holidays in San Miguel and seemed to show no concern for their poorer countrymen. We had known no one, either Mexican or American, who put their lives so firmly behind their stated ideals as had Charlie and Lucina.

We've all said that sorrows never come as single spies and that no good deed shall go unpunished; rediscovering that is always a shock. Charlie's cancer, which we had almost forgotten after his operation, came back, spreading through the lymph system. At the cancer center in Houston, he was treated coldly, told that since he had no insurance program he would be eligible for a marrow transplant only if he could put $20,000 cash up front. He was given six months to live, but they tried to keep him in the hospital there for that period. In Mexico City he found a woman doctor who at least made a serious and humane attempt, though he began to grow weaker, unsteady on his feet, more often nauseated.

It was this that led to their civil wedding in the private quarters of one of the local judges: to insure that Lucina would inherit their properties—problematic under Mexican law. My wife and I were honored that Charlie asked us to stand as his witnesses; Lucina's witnesses were a lesbian couple, one of whom edited the town's weekly English newspaper. The day was bright and cheerful; Charlie seemed as proud and jovially energetic as if they did all this by choice. One of Lucina's witnesses said, "I just think it's wonderful that you're having a pair of dykes for bridesmaids!" We all laughed quite a lot.

I was glad I could give Charlie and Lucina a copy of this poem that day. It seems to me somewhat different from most of my poems. For one thing, it attributes certain admirable qualities to this couple that I might have felt had to be demonstrated or otherwise corroborated in another poem. Since this poem was specifically for their eyes, that seemed all right; they would know what qualities, what actions I meant. I am happy for the chance to open this to a wider audience.

Charles Kuchinski died at his home on January 31, 1996, two days before what would have been his first wedding anniversary.

KATHERINE SONIAT

The Captain's Advice to Those Heading for the Trees: 1609

> *Lastly remember that faction, pride*
> *and security produce confusion; so*
> *the contraries well-practiced will*
> *make you happy.*
>   —John Smith, *Travels and Works*

I. On Arrival

Come in off the tidal marsh, past the known
Sea of Virginia and you will see
a river curving to the northwest,
shimmery arc like our moving, setting sun.
A mineral heat, the very gold of day.
Sail into those headwaters,
mindful of a deep draw for your barge.
Chilled air signals an elevated earth,
hillsides where you can peer down
upon the *naturals*, either of a beastly
or human kind. Responding to such
loftiness, they will look up to you
with that certain fear of the smaller
for the larger, be it of true measure, or not.

II. On Guardedness

When you spot blue shadows
on the river, deep cove of spruce and pine,
you'll be in the foothills
of mountains called the *Apalatsi*.
Wading from cold waters,
do not be numb to the uneasy state
of your barge, tied surely to shore.
Closet its sails and anchors near,
bedfellows for the dark. They are the metal
stays and billows of your divining rod:
the ship, our most blessed tool.

There are those among you who would
steal her away, leaving the men stranded
as birds in thicket thorns.

III. On Novelty

Search for what most resembles a clearing,
that thinning in the woods
where mulberry and her low cousins
range beneath the grander oak.
A cleansing of twenty acres a year
will be no small task.
There you'll come to know the foliage
as that of childhood, a hideout,
but one alive with eyes
and arrows. Even tall grasses
offer refuge for the creeping spies,
each tree a watch tower full of malice
overlooking open space. For a time only
will you be a thing of study, of curiosity.

IV. On Exterior Expression

From their greenery they will watch you
sweat and harden, and chop
out a life of sorts. Take care
neither to show a face of sickness,
nor that more irksome one of fear.
Make your features like stiffened putty.
Those of looser visage should weep
or vomit peering steadily at the ground.
Offer an iron mask
to those figuring you from the trees,
and when need be, allow only the best
marksman to pull his trigger. That bullet
must not be a wobbly spear,
but a sudden stopper to the heart.

V. On Natural Connection

Those you meet who are akin to the forest
should receive keen regard.
And when the land you walk upon
is of proper tint and texture,

look then to each man and woman;
they bear evidence of their world
in the flesh. What is boggy,
slick to the foot, breeds a country folk
of puffed belly. As the high elm
and firm dirt appear,
you may discover the tall tribe
of Susquehanna—clan and tree
sprouted from earth
as if watered on a summer day.

VI. On a Vast Darkness

Beyond your hard-won clearing,
the forest rises which for the newcomer
holds no paths with chartlike meaning. Perhaps
you'll want a guide other than our compass.
Some Venus walking under the leaves,
like that star we looked to at sea?
But do not trust those *naturals* who bow
by day and lead you dancingly through the sun.
They will spring treachery
on you at night—and probably not far
from the encampment called home.
Now who of you was it that advised
an unwalled fort for fear of hurting
these crafty ones' feelings?

VII. On Priorities

Once the trees are hacked back
to blue sky, turn your ax
toward building—the storehouse
first to rise, a graceplace
for summer's plenty. Then see
public structures go up before a single
private house, keeping the Company as a whole
at the center of desires. Select order
over confusion; it is almost as easily done,
the houses set in a straight line,
streets planted with wide berth.
As men feel this welcoming beckon,
they'll excuse themselves from the inward,
each step carrying them closer to town square.

VIII. On Taking Advice

Lastly, and this image should dance
and shake in your sleep. You are
being meticulously observed.
Those eyes that feed upon you
will wish only to send you
packing from their land, or to remain perhaps
and play a cunning game of torture.
They take you as the slow dumb tinkerer
knowing each beginning like the first.
Who of us would write home of our discouragements
after crafting a fortress upriver,
uphill for hope? Better this clearing
send up smoke rings of fortune
from men marrying survival.

On Reading Histories:
"The Captain's Advice to Those
Headed for the Trees: 1609"

Receiving an unexpected grant a few years ago, I found myself headed toward the Chesapeake Bay to begin a group of poems that might focus on place. I had no other formal plans. The day before leaving, I came across John Smith's *Travels and Works* in the library and threw that into my bag. A friend arranged a three-week stay for me in a house on the Choptank River near Easton, Maryland, where I arrived in late May, amidst black flies and folks pushing lawn mowers with paper sacks on their heads, clothed from head to toe. I would try to settle down and write beside this river leading into the Bay.

The tale of writing this poem, "The Sea Captain's Advice to Those Headed for the Trees: 1609," is finally the story of a collection's inception, a book of poems now entitled *The Landing*. That late spring, five years ago, as I began reading Smith's journals, looking out at a river landing, I was struck by the surprisingly lyric voice of this mercenary soldier and explorer. I read his finely recorded details of the Bay's flora and fauna, the journals' narrative suspense accumulating as Smith told of what seemed extraordinary occurring day to day. I was also becoming aware that if I read too closely, if I took notes as conclusive blocks of information, this poetic endeavor was doomed to the coldly encyclopedic, and nothing more. Smith's perceptions of the Bay had a pristine, almost childlike awe about them, as if these elements of nature had never been encountered. I wanted to translate and reinvent this vision, without using the source verbatim. So I scribbled notes, phrases, an impressionistic pastiche, as I turned through his diary, ending up with perhaps five or six pages of material.

All morning I would read *Travels and Works*, and since I was in an isolated circumstance, not often speaking to others during those three weeks, I learned to hear and think in that seventeenth-century voice.

Sitting by a window watching the slow Choptank or the landing of an eagle in her high nest, I visualized his initial Bay elaborated upon in the journals, where fish were so thick they were scooped up in frying pans. When my first set of notes was completed, I then read Smith's revised and edited journal from 1621. Certain information was deleted, such as the more specified details of the Englishmen's involvement with native women. When reading certain sections of the 1621 account, I sensed that what I had read previously was presented in a different way. On checking, indeed, the facts had changed, though subtly. What is peculiar about this detective work was that, as I mentioned, I had made a deliberate effort not to read with scholarly care. Apparently, the dramatic particulars of the narrative had formed a vivid enough scenario within my imagination that when one of the original props was removed by Smith some twelve years later, my mind took note. At any rate, I now had several takes on these "histories," Smith's original account, his revised 1621 diary, and my own interpretations.

What would be the style of delivery for these collected impressions? Looking over my notes, I circled what I thought thematic divisions, then created rather abstract and encompassing subtitles for sections, the nine headings which are presently within the poem. After a few drafts of the first two sections, *On Setting Out* and *On Guardedness*, I noticed that these topical renderings were falling roughly into twelve- to twenty-line composites. The pitfalls in writing this poem were going to be overelaboration, the inclusion of too much "information." Thus, fairly early in the process, I decided on a 14-line or a loose sonnet form for each piece. Such a formal approach seemed true to early seventeenth-century poetics also. Once I was working within the linear constraint of the sonnet, the poems came forth rather willingly—as if my mind had been told to take its place and was handed a set of rules. Top of the list: thou shall not ramble on.

What details to include? Should the contents be presented in John Smith's vocabulary, or mine? There are indeed certain exact words, such as the reference to the "naturals" (American Indian), which are Smith's. His use of the word "natural" strikes me as both literal and highly figurative at once. In other words, his term for the animals and the native is literally or common-sensically correct: these creatures were as vital coordinates to a place as geography and season are; they are a part of the same fabric, and thus, quite literally "natural." On the other hand, figuratively, one speaks of a good swimmer as a *natural*, meaning she was born with the gift of moving through water like a fish. So too, these indigenous folk had an affinity to a region, were as at ease in and knowledgeable about their region as a fishlike swimmer is to water. Of course, if this logic is accepted, then one could assume that the Europeans, their claim on the land and very presence, were secondary, or "unnatural."

A few other details were fully attributal to history: the *Apalatsi* was a native term for the Appalachian Mountains; the Sea of Virginia was the English name for the Chesapeake Bay. Most of this poem's phrasing though derives from my imaginative engagement with Smith's narration. I have not returned to check these diaries for authorial "real estate," for who owns which phrase. For me, these poems are a seamless incorporation of imaginations threaded across the centuries.

This poem is more than commentary on the seventeenth-century environment of the Chesapeake Bay; each section also reflects what I interpreted as specific warnings given the coddled English of that initial landing party. If there was a single sense of foreboding recurring in *Travels and Works*, it was that constant instruction and reinforcement of rules were of utmost importance; how quickly these men seemed to forget all that they had learned. Smith saw his fellow countrymen as unprepared, indeed, uneducated for the practical and hazardous tasks of exploration and settlement that lay ahead. I want to emphasize that these cautionary pieces of advice are concluded from what I conceived after reading the diaries. Such declarations, of course, were not forthrightly recorded in the diaries.

In each section of this poem I focused on an instruction that seemed necessary for survival, advice ranging from where to land in Virginia to, finally, the proper information to include in letters home. Other sections address the dangers of mutiny; the dangers of constant observation by the natives so that the outward expression of the English was of final and great import; the need to recognize that the health and topography of the land were reflected in the physical constitution of the natives; the warning never to forget the vastness and danger ever-present at the forest's edge. There are also directives on how to construct a patterned, orderly town, to buttress those dark trees. Finally, pride is encouraged in accomplishments hard won, but always with an alert eye turned toward the "naturals" and their forest. Each piece of advice seems conceptually applicable beyond this prescribed historic setting. Using a little extrapolation and imagination, could we not benefit from such cautionary tales as we enter our new century and ventures?

That summer as I whittled away at the poem, I wondered what more might arise from sitting by the Choptank reading *Travels and Works*. John Smith's records would only go so far. And "so the rest of the story," in brief: After mornings immersed in the diaries, I drove the back roads of the Eastern Shore. One day I came upon the now-defunct ferry landing from Annapolis, the tiny village of Claiborne, Maryland, and there at its center lay Miracle House Road. How could a poet pass up such a bait? Indeed, Miracle House Road led to Miracle House, a piece of property that, I soon discovered, had served as a tubercular "preventorium" for children from Baltimore whose parents had TB. From the early to mid part of this century, these children were sent to Miracle House for the summer to be nourished into a healthy resistance. As I peered over the fence that first afternoon, I spotted a one-room schoolhouse, beautifully preserved, then saw the present-day owners' house, which I later found used to be the chapel on the original facility. Mindelle Moon, the owner, was soon at that fence, full of Miracle House stories, and eager to rent me the schoolhouse the next summer for a nominal fee.

Even stranger were the other connections that unfolded: I had spent the summer before this one finishing a collection of poems about my mother's early life in Louisiana. Orphaned at birth, she was raised by her grandmother, whose last name was Claiborne; my stepfather was also Claiborne, just as this village along the Bay was named. Another serendipitous similarity that arose was that in the 1950s when my mother had had a long and dangerous bout with tuberculosis, I was sent away to live for a year. Mindelle Moon not only owned the Miracle House property, but as a teenager had worked there as a caretaker for these children of the tubercular in the late '40s and '50s. In 1970 she bought the land she'd grown so attached to during her summer work, and proceeded to devote her career to being head of the Maryland Easter Seal Society. Here at my elbow, and she virtually was for the next few summers, was a woman who knew fully both the disease and the sadness of the kids who had had to leave their homes. After an hour standing there chatting by the fence, I knew my John Smith poem was opening onto a new imaginative landscape; a sense of discovery came to me as Smith might have felt upon entering what he slowly surmised was an enormously wealthy bay. My work was moving onto a larger loom. One day I would weave John Smith's vital "Sea of Virginia" to this town of Claiborne, to Miracle House, and finally to a mother whose lungs were flecked with TB. *The Landing* is now the title of this collage of histories—his landing, and mine.

MARK STRAND

I Will Love the Twenty-First Century

Dinner was getting cold. The guests, hoping for quick,
Impersonal, random encounters of the usual sort, were sprawled
In the bedrooms. The potatoes were hard, the beans soft, the meat—
There was no meat. The winter sun had turned the elms and houses
    yellow;
Deer were moving down the road like refugees; and in the
    driveway, cats
Were warming themselves on the hood of a car. Then you turned
And said to me: "Although I love the past, the dark of it,
The weight of it teaching us nothing, the loss of it, the all
Of it asking for nothing, I will love the twenty-first century more,
For in it I see someone in bathrobe and slippers, brown-eyed and poor,
Walking through snow without leaving so much as a footprint
    behind."
        "Oh," I said, putting my hat on, "Oh."

Beginning to End

There are no secrets in this poem, no allusions to little-known texts. There is an allusion to Virgil's Fourth Eclogue, but that should be obvious. Attempts are made to be humorous throughout the poem, and I suppose this in itself casts a shadow over what we can expect from the twenty-first century despite the appearance of a divinity who seems either senile or on welfare. This, in some quarters, will be considered ironic. My reason for talking about/around this poem is its ending. I've never concluded a poem with such abruptness, nor with such a clear invitation to continue. An ending and a beginning at the same time strikes me as something to be grateful for. That is, the way is clear for me to write about the twenty-second century and to extend the rhythmical lunacy of the dialogue.

DABNEY STUART

The Tapawera Raspberry Festival

The open grasses braise
in the thick light.
None of the trout
in the Motueka
River rises
to the heat hovering
above the surface,
another river spreading
over the wide fields.
The sun disperses.
A would-be barker
calls the rare young
women together
to settle a queen.
They climb onto the strapping
shoulders of their men
and begin to grapple;
the droll-limbed creature
they compose
gradually unbuilds
as the maladroit and unsupple
dangle and fall.
This has taken long
enough for the light
to diminish, too, the midges
near the shallows to hatch,
the fry to gather
and the trout to stir
in their own stream
therefore, and the lamb
chops sizzling on the vendors'
grills to char at the edges.
The queen, her victorious
T-shirt torn
at the shoulder, a cheek
bruised, stretch-
es her arms to the ridges

westward where the sunlight chafes.
The crowd is a delta
of cheers for her; the losers
join in this good nature.
As the man who bears
her takes a last turn
in the dusk she opens
her hands, fingers fanned
into the light thinned
over the curling grasses.
A trout rises.
Another. The surface
of the river mottles
as if with rain, deepens
with the dark that settles
inward. A clutch
of gnats for an instant
writhes in a stray
pocket of afterlight, glints
in the glancing eye,
and stays.

Good Nature

My wife Sandra and I lived in New Zealand for nine months in 1987–88. After making the best of a tiny sublet in Auckland (the Queen City) for three months, we divided the rest of our time between two cities on the South Island. In Christchurch we planned to see New Zealand's premier bowler, Richard Hadlee, break the world's record for number of wickets in a career. He was likely to do this during the first or second day of a five-day test match against England. We checked out the pitch—Lancaster Park—the day before the match was to begin. Conditioned by such events in the States, we expected security everywhere, gates locked, access impossible. Instead, we walked in, toured the stands and the VIP lounge, strolled onto the pitch itself. No one seemed to notice us. As we walked through the tunnel from the pitch to the front gate, passing the players' entrance, Hadlee stepped out of a Honda Civic, collected his gear from the boot, walked past us close enough to touch, and disappeared into the locker room. We gawked, like schoolchildren awed by their current idol. But it was, at the same time, no more than another moment in the day's passing.

Christchurch was much to our liking, but I became (and remain) especially fond of Nelson. The town itself is open and flat (by New Zealand standards), inviting, modest, and genial. It's a center of crafts, especially pottery. Local farmers and vendors had stalls on the main road to Stoke and Richmond, selling fresh fruits and vegetables: nectarines, peaches, stone fruit, plump onions, squash (called pumpkin) of all sorts. They were magnificent; it was impossible not to eat well. An informal downtown tea shop—Chez Eelco—with tables out front, served customers from all over the world. Multicolored backpacks and rucksacks nestled against one another along the walls inside the glass front and against the rows of planters outside. It was a bright scene on days when the weather was fine—which was most days that summer—casually festive, amiable, a place people clearly liked to be.

This is the area, too, where the Nobel laureate Ernest Rutherford grew up. Signs and other reminders celebrated his eminence in the history of physics, but all that seemed integrated into the ongoing life of the place in much the same way that the cricket match fit into the daily routines of Christchurch, and the remarkable produce of this fecund land, though meticulously nurtured and tended, seemed a given, taken for granted. The exceptional and the everyday coexisted contentedly, acknowledging each other as if somehow they shared celebrity equally and enjoyed the resulting balance, stretched over time. It was not a leveling, however, but a mutual heightening.

Some of New Zealand's most beautiful rivers—icy, crystalline, glittering—flowed in the area inland from Nelson and its harbor: the Motueka, the Wangapeka, the Wairoa. We sometimes visited friends in this area, outside a settlement called Tapawera. It was here that, by accident and perhaps a wider charm, we attended the Tapawera Raspberry Festival.

It took place near the small village in open fields at the far edges of which, screened by rows of Lombardy poplars, the Motueka wound its unobtrusive course. On a number of "barbys" lamb chops grilled and smoked; an area about half the size of a football field was studded with old tires for the boot throw; people milled around, talking, neighbors all, their livelihoods rooted in the ground. There were three-legged and sack races, a pie-eating contest, and other like-spirited activities. Everything culminated in late afternoon in the contest for the title of Queen of the festival, who was selected through a game from my distant childhood that we called "chicken fighting." In this version the young women who were competing climbed on the shoulders of their young men (I want to say "swains," or "champions," for their connotations touch the essence of the event). They subsequently tangled. The person to stay aloft longest, won.

At the "bloody crossroads" of narrative and culture, Matthew Arnold believed, art occurs. My experience leads me to imagine that poetry arises from the mysterious conjunction of the unconscious (all the "meaning," according to Jonathan Lear, that we have stored up because we haven't known what to do with it, as well as Freud's notion of repressed contents) and silence. At such precious reprieves from the fray of distraction that is life for most of us, we have access to our sources, our beginnings, our concentrated selves, as Aladdin had access to the spirit in his lamp. If we are lucky, and practice incessantly, we learn to attend the spirits appropriate to what we might say, and are led by them, which we already embody, into music.

This way of imagining the inception of poetry—of the conditions of its access—presumes an interdependence among various energies, largely as unpredictable in themselves as in their coordination, so that making poems, with all its discipline and conscious finagling, becomes wonderfully accidental and miraculous. Those occasions when we hear what we can keep are rare, regardless of the time and labor we put into the pursuit. I find as well that, as rigorously as I resist it in most other ways, my perspective here approaches the Platonic. Though I speak of the personal unconscious, and of the accumulated self, I feel also that *something* precedes all that and stimulates and thrills it. I couldn't define that "something." It may be partly the emotional spindrift thrown off by associative surprises, but when I ruminate on it (as close as I come actually to thinking) I sometimes turn to St. Augustine's *The Trinity*. This passage from book 15 suggests why.

All knowledge in the mind of man . . . is preserved in the store chamber of memory, and from it is begotten a true word, when we speak what we know. But this word exists before any sound, before any imagining of a sound. For in that state the word has the closest likeness to the thing known, of which it is the offspring and image; from the vision which is knowledge arises a vision which is thought, a word of no language, a true word born of a true thing, having nothing of its own but all from that knowledge of which it is born.

I'm not inclined to comment on my own work, and feel sheepish doing so, but if I brought to bear on this poem the sort of reading I do by temperament and choice on poems not my own, I would draw certain of its aspects to attention. It interweaves two "scenes" as if they are contiguous enough for the speaker of the poem to see them both, though the river activities are largely imagined. What brings these two occasions together—the design that emerges when their woof and warp are combined—are the themes of celebration and predatoriness, itself a mesh. I like the complementary images "braise" and "sizzling" and the pun in "fry" suggest, for instance, as well as the kinship of the winners' fanned fingers and the clutch of gnats, each in the sunlight, a kind of exultation in both cases at the escape from relative dangers. The event occurs to celebrate a harvest, so the participants are beings of various natures. Though raspberries aren't mentioned, the earth from which they grow is the ground on which the celebrants act; it bears, as it were, the grasses and mountains the sunlight touches, that gangly, shifting creature the human bodies compose for the nonce, and three rivers (the trout feed in one, the heat spreads another, and there is the delta of human cheer). The modes of light augur an additional dimension. There's a gentling and integration, too, of the predatory and competitive aspects of survival, even of its implicit violence; the chicken fight is a sort of primitive, dancelike ritual, as the tableau of the winners' last "turn" may be seen to suggest. It's a poem of inveterate renewal, of "good nature" in an inclusive, complex sense, or is intended so. I also mean it to be an instance of art responsive to Friar Francis's request (in *Much Ado About Nothing*) that "wonder seem familiar."

On the heels of that modified praeteritio, I *can* say that writing the poem felt like the dream labor of giving; experiencing it now feels like an engagement with a gift. I'm not sure who to thank, especially and primarily for the music it makes, this skinny ode with its slant rhymes — tucked sometimes close together, sometimes stretched almost too far over space for the ear to make out — with its varying syntax tuned across its two- and three-beat lines.

These glimpses come, as Yeats wrote, "For one throb of an artery," and recede into the unconscious, or into the lamp of the spirits, or into Augustine's word (or Word, which he cared more about) waiting, or into some other form of forgetfulness. I don't know. I do know that, like listening, active waiting often feels like prayer, though undirected, inconstant, and incomplete, like one's life. It is an effort to keep open the way to one's center and is as delicate and easily lost an art as making the poems themselves, a sidelong glance toward the face we love most and would not scare away. Time is the dimension in which such opportunity occurs. Labor is both the curse of the Genesis story and the form through which we realize opportunity. It is to our self (and soul) as the work of the organs is to the body, natural and necessary. All this is complicated, of course, by the challenge of recognizing the rhythm work makes with idleness, exertion with rest, attention with the wandering mind. But the basic trick is to find the appropriate labor so that in engaging in it we celebrate the gift of time, become its harvest.

THOMAS SWISS

On a Stanza by Rilke

Difficult, isn't it?, to love these high-topped
foul-mouthed teens, this baggy threesome
in shorts and T-shirts—a torn one screaming,

as though it were informative or funny, Eat Me!
Sure, each was somebody's baby once—
this Beavis rough-housing with his Butt-head

buddies: chunky look-alikes, wanting
nothing more in the world right now
than to kick some ass in a game of fast-

break Two-On-One. Sometimes energy
has an odor and takes up a lot of space.
Thunk: somebody hits one. And immediately

a single gut-propelled syllable—Yes!—
spins through the gym, then echoes upward,
as if this voice meant to swallow the ceiling

that's higher than a steeple's. Next door,
in fact, they're actually building one—
or trying to. There's a half-done shell

and, on the grass, a huge bell by a sign
that says: Future Home of Grace Church.
Curiously, the makers are also believers:

I overheard one of them at a garage sale,
telling how he'd brought his family from Texas
to give his "brethren" a hand. They're not

the only ones, either; when I see them all
out there, during the day, measuring or carrying
or pounding on something, the parking lot's

crowded with silver trailers and cars
with out-of-state plates. Yes, the man said,
they were happy here thus far. So in that

they're like these boys: still strangers
to their grown-almost-to-adult-size bodies,
but pleased, why not?, with what

they've learned. Like the best way to hang
from a rim without snapping it, to slap the creaking
backboard as they test their new-found strength.

Do they feel like Supermen? Well, good for them —
but something still urges me to invoke the rules,
report them on the sly the way I did some-

times at practice: how else to get back at the one
who bullied me, the one who threatened
to piss in my mouth during showers?

Well, life's vulgar, I hear my 8th-grade coach say.
And isn't it? In the training room,
I put on the headphones that sing to me:

relax, and later, *pump up!,* and then a group
of preschoolers wanders into the gym,
assembled under watchful eyes. Whose?

—Camp-leader's? Baby-sitter's? Teacher's?
The hoops to these kids are higher than heaven,
so they roll a ball on the floor. And the teens

go off hungry to raid the machines,
to bang on the TV stashed under a counter
in the so-called supervisor's office: it's hard

not to judge them harshly, though my own son's
almost their age. There are too many people
in the world. As for the faithful, raising the church —

who'll struggle soon with that bell it takes
a two-story crane to lift—is it true what we
like to believe? That *for them existence*

is still enchanted. Still beginning
in a hundred places. A playing of pure powers
no one can touch and not kneel to and marvel.

Rilke Unplugged

Creating a history for the composition of a poem, even a brief history like this one, is tricky business. There's the need to search backward in memory, of course, in order to appraise and attribute meaning to things that at the time seemed like . . . well, just *things*. That's the pleasurable part, the part most like writing the poem itself. What's hard (and risky) is the subsequent work of lining these things up—entities, objects, people, relationships—to establish a sense of causality. Piecing together a provisional framework . . .

I wrote "On a Stanza by Rilke" in 1993, a year that in advance I had hoped would be (and sometimes was) a kind of heaven. I was on sabbatical leave, living temporarily in Iowa City, and for the first time in years I had sufficient time to read and write, to get lost in bookstores, music stores, libraries. But it was also the year of tremendous flooding in Iowa, and we'd had the bad fortune of renting a house that was located 50 yards from the Iowa River. When the rains came—and came over two months or more—the house nearly went under. After an all-day vigil on July 4th, fizzled fireworks on the porch that night and board games to pass the time while the water kept rising, we reluctantly moved out after midnight. Each of us, my wife and two sons, carried a garbage bag of belongings as we waded through knee-deep water to a friend's waiting car parked outside the flood zone. Though we did not know it then (it would be another week before it was clear the house was uninhabitable) we were about to move from Iowa City, a university town, to a nearby city that was both less familiar and decidedly tougher. A "townie" town.

Moving in the middle of a flood means taking whatever place you can get. And what we got was a cramped duplex a block away from the local Community Center. It was what you'd expect—a place for retirees to come in the mornings to exercise; for families to stop by in the evenings for a swim; for kids to play ping-pong and pool; and for those who could tolerate the close-in odor of sweat in order to lift a few weights or ride one of the rusty exercise bikes in a room with no windows (and no fans) that looked out into the gym. Because our living quarters were so tight, and because we knew nobody at all in town, the Center became a kind of second home to my preteen sons and me that year, a place that figured almost daily in our lives.

"On a Stanza by Rilke" is set in the Center. My worksheets show that the poem went through eighteen drafts, more or less, some quite different from others, but all of them starting with an image of three boys, probably in early high school, playing roughly with a basketball. What was it about them that interested me, these composite kids made up from the dozens of boys like them that came to the gym to roughhouse after school each day?

> Difficult, isn't it?, to love these high-topped
> foul-mouthed teens, this baggy threesome
> in shorts and T-shirts—a torn one screaming,
>
> as though it were informative or funny, Eat Me!
> Sure, each was somebody's baby once—
> this Beavis rough-housing with his Butt-head
>
> buddies: chunky look-alikes, wanting
> nothing more in the world right now
> than to kick some ass in a game of fast-
> break Two-On-One.

Why pick these guys out to start a poem? The answer has to do in part with the criticism I'd been reading in preparation for a new course I'd be teaching when my leave ended. Though I had no syllabus yet, I'd titled it "Youth Culture and Music." The course, as I was developing it, would work from the basic assumption that popular music provides not only entertainment, but a cultural space for the personal, social, and political experiences of young people. That is, the class would be more about music's social context than about music itself. Popular music, particularly rock and roll, had once worked for me in that way. Now, at forty, I wanted to understand more precisely (and to be able to articulate, to theorize) not only how some of my own interests and sensibilities had been shaped by music, but—more urgently—how those of my students and my children were in the process of being shaped.

Thus I'd been reading fairly widely across two intersecting areas, sociologies of youth and studies of popular music, focusing for the most part on two kinds of writing: academic essays and cultural journalism. But my preparation increasingly involved, too, close listening to recent music, reading magazines intended for teens, and viewing scenes from films that represented the experiences of youth in a musical context. Youth culture: impossible to generalize about because the meaning of youth is complicated and often contested. Young people are endlessly analyzed and categorized (hoods, hippies, punks, preps, burnouts), marketed to (the young as avid consumers), alternately thought of as "immature" or "idealistic," "creative" or "problematic." The reality is that being an adolescent is increasingly hard: teens in the 1990s are underemployed and overpoliced. They have a high suicide rate, a tendency toward depression; they have few safe gathering places, fewer civil rights. The youth population of runaways, drifters, and throwaways has been on the rise for more than a decade. And yet . . .

Like many adults, I find it difficult to be long in the company of teens-at-play. That's where the poem begins—close to the noisy and very physical activities of three boys in a gym, represented in the poem by MTV's "Beavis and Butthead." Cartoon characters known for their less-than-articulate responses to life in general and social responsibility in particular, these fantasy teens are most adults' worst nightmare because they embody adolescent "stupidity" to the nth degree; they are impenetrable to reason. What attracted me to the boys in the gym? My vague intolerance, signaled by the tone of the first stanzas. Eventually the tone changes somewhat as the poem opens out to a moment in which the height of the gymnasium ceiling is compared to that of a church steeple. Indeed, something like a steeple was being built just a few lots away from the Center.

Walking around our neighborhood, as I often did the spring I wrote this poem, I watched the workers—sometimes joined by friends, spouses, even children—putting in hard hours to finish the project of adding a structure to the church that already stood there. Friendless myself in this town, I admired their sense of community and common purpose, which was something they also shared—and here, perhaps, is the biggest "leap" in the poem—with the teenagers at the Center. Not to say that there weren't deep and obvious differences between these two groups. For starters, there was the fact that the church-builders in this working-class, churchgoing town were welcomed everywhere and talked to at length by passersby, while groups of teens (at least those I saw) seemed largely confined to the Center after their daily internment at school. What few adults were in the Center at that time ignored or tried to ignore them. Yet it seemed to me in the context of the poem that the teens' play was quite obviously their work, and that this peer culture of display and spectacle—"hanging out," "bumming," "chilling"—invited the scrutiny of adults even while remaining largely autonomous. The critic Andrew Ross talks about these kinds of youth activities as "schooling": learning the art of socialization on terms not wholly governed by adult sensibilities. It is, he writes, "part of a dialogue with adult practices."

This idea of a "dialogue" on these terms interested me, the awkward ways in which young people and adults communicate certain messages to each other—even when they are not aware of it. And it's surely what brought me in the poem back to a scene from my own adolescence— a scene in which I reported an act of bullying to an adult teacher only to be neither noticed nor understood, but simply "instructed." Life is cruel, he said.

O.K., but now where was I? The idea had never been, as far as I was conscious of it, to write a poem that ended with my own experiences as a teen (no matter how metaphoric), but to answer instead the question posed in the first line of the poem: how do we find a way to love those who strike us as unlovable? After several more drafts and several wrong turns, I returned to the poem's present moment and to the exercise room in the Center:

> . . . I put on the headphones that sing to me:
>
> *relax*, and later, *pump up!*, and then a group
> of preschoolers wanders into the gym,
> assembled under watchful eyes. Whose?
>
> —Camp-leader's? Baby-sitter's? Teacher's?

At this point, I felt I knew where the poem might be headed. The introduction of the preschoolers, late in the poem, had somehow opened another perspective, another way of thinking about my first question. Not an answer to that question, of course, but a chance to see the teens' behaviors in a new light. A chance to ask myself new questions about my own sourness and the fact that these teens were only older versions of what my own kids might soon become. Versions, too, of what these preschoolers would be like in ten years?

Sentimental questions for the most part, I suppose, they nevertheless brought me at last to Rilke whose poems I had been reading again after several years. Rilke who always seems to be calling readers away from the smallness of their lives, whose poems so often have to do with longing but do not admit any easy idea of transcendence. More than once, Rilke defined love as two solitudes that border and greet and protect each other. Not that this process is without roughness or resentment— love nearly always involves both. But in what measure? The anger in my own poem, the judgments, the multiple solitudes, all felt like they needed to be spoken to once again, but I didn't feel I had the words to do so. Following the image of the church bell, which juxtaposes the "music" of adults with the "noise" of the teens, Rilke helped supply that language.

Three years after writing this poem, I see it as another kind of preparation for the course I later taught—like the notes I'd been taking from my readings, the syllabus I eventually developed. But I also believe "On a Stanza by Rilke" was preparation for the life I'm now leading with two adolescent children who are busy creating their own social lives, only half in the light of their parents' knowing.

SUE ELLEN THOMPSON

What Happened After

The day it happened they found me
submerged in a quilt on the sofa watching
t.v. Why is she all covered up
on such a warm day? they must
have wanted to ask. Instead,
they sat in the room and watched with me, together
my husband and daughter and I watched men
playing golf, their shirts dots of citrus
when seen from above, in a tree so green
and vast it seemed they could never fall.

Why doesn't she eat? they must have said
to each other as dusk fell and they scraped
the glazed food from my plate. It is
so long ago now I cannot recall
how many hours I lay there, my eyes
perpendicular to their concern, saying
nothing, wondering when I would feel the strength
return to my bones, when I would rise
from my bed and walk, feel the grass pushing up
from the earth and the green coming back to where

it had always lived in me. For how many days
did I cling to my husband like a woman pulled
from the wreck? When he stopped to buy gas
I would brace my body against his back while he
pumped, I'd feel the fuel moving through me
and think, *You're going to live.* Everywhere
he went I went with him, the stripe of his sleeve
pinched hard in my fingers, my steps the shadow of his
and he never asked why. You won't read about me

in the papers. I'm the child who was lost
and found his way back before his parents
missed him, whose ferocious embrace
confounds them, who breaks every night
under the knowledge of where he has been.

Writing the Unspeakable

L̲ike a child who grows up to resemble neither of his parents but who is unquestionably a distillate of their traits, "What Happened After" is one of those poems that I look upon with curiosity. I recall little of its composition and cannot say how many drafts it went through or how long it took to complete. If I remember anything, it is that the poem was a breach birth: The closing metaphor arrived before most of what precedes.

Even now, it is a difficult poem to read in public because it is so overtly autobiographical. "The day *it* happened," the poem begins. Sitting down to write, I knew immediately that this was a poem about silence—a *willed silence* within the family, something that its members had tacitly agreed not to discuss. This in itself was a challenge for me: I was so accustomed to saying everything I could about a subject when I first drafted a narrative poem, then paring away the excess. But reticence, this time, was essential. I had to say as much as I dared about as little as possible—without sounding coy in the process.

Whatever "it" is, the title of the poem makes clear that the event has already taken place. Subsequent uses of the indefinite pronoun ("it seemed they could never fall . . . It is / so long ago now I cannot recall") continue to float, unanchored in experience. The pronoun appears to take on some definition by the time the second stanza leads into the third:

> . . . when would I rise
> from my bed and walk, feel the grass pushing up
> from the earth and the green coming back to where
>
> it had always lived in me.

But even the antecedent, "green," is a somewhat abstract concept, referring to a life force so diminished in me at this point that I am incapable of describing it more concretely. Every "it" seemed freighted to me as I wrote the poem—to the point where I abandoned the pronoun altogether at the start of the third stanza.

I wanted this poem to "weigh" a lot, to embody the burden of the experience from which it had been drawn. I didn't want to present it in easy-to-digest couplets or quatrains. In a sense, I was exhausted before I'd even begun writing, so I wanted the form of the poem to somehow reflect that diminution in energy. I started out writing in big, heavy, ten-line stanzas. But when I got to the third stanza, I had to break after nine lines in order to "set off" the closing metaphor—a final exhalation of only five lines. It made such an odd and unsatisfying shape on the page. But this time I knew better than to struggle for a more symmetrical structure.

The central difficulty that writing this poem presented was how to describe the emotions associated with an experience about which I did not feel free to speak. It seemed there were no images equal to the task. In the first stanza, all I could offer was the odd and, I fear, not altogether successful image of "men / playing golf, their shirts dots of citrus / when seen from above, in a tree so green / and vast it seemed they could never fall." Lying on the sofa watching t.v.—an activity I'm certain I've never mentioned in a poem before, but one that seemed suited to my state of stunned withdrawal—I remember feeling much the same distance from normal family life that the cameraman must have felt, looking down on the tournament from the treetops. The golfers in their sherbet-colored shirts were no more than ornaments on a field of green—the same "green" whose loss I mourn at the end of the second stanza. Still, "it seemed *they* could never fall." The emphasis here is mine, and I'm not entirely sure the average reader would place it there. It implies that if they, the golfers, were immune to a fall, there is someone else who was not.

There are, in fact, a number of such clues—for example, the fact that for days I clung "to my husband like a woman pulled / from the wreck," that "When he stopped to buy gas / I would brace my body against his back while he / pumped, I'd feel the fuel moving through me / and think, *You're going to live.*" This tells the reader that whatever "it" was, it made me more dependent than I'd ever been on my husband's sheer physical presence. I craved anything that made him more tangible—even the "stripe of his sleeve / pinched hard in my fingers." The pulsing of fuel in the line from the pump was enough to remind me that the blood still moved through my veins, that I was alive—whether I wanted to be or not. But dropping clues was not the point; I didn't *want* anyone to guess what had happened to me. I wanted to portray a state of mind that I imagined was common to many difficult and tragic situations.

Although I am normally rather sparing in my use of assonance, the string of harsh *a* sounds in the second stanza ("as they scraped / the glazed food from my plate") seemed to capture the raw state of my nerves. I was also suffering from great physical exhaustion, and the little puffs of air emitted by words like *nothing, strength,* and *earth* were significant. It would take a miracle—I would have to "rise / from my bed and walk"—to bring back my energy and enthusiasm for the life that patiently awaited my return. Even if the poem could not describe that miracle, it could at least stand as evidence that such a miracle had occurred.

The closing metaphor was a gift, the kind that comes rarely. I remember jotting it down in my notebook fairly early on in the writing of the poem, consciously saving it for the end, when my limited powers would be spent. I'd been thinking of a story my mother used to tell, about how she'd come across a sodden pile of winter clothing in the basement belonging to my then 10-year-old brother. Apparently some years elapsed before he confessed that he'd fallen through the ice in a nearby pond and had somehow managed to pull himself to safety and sneak back into the house through the cellar door. I wanted an image for the secrets we all harbor without really wanting to, for the burden that withheld information represents.

"You won't read about me / in the papers," the poem says, meaning that the reader won't ever get the full story, no matter how often or how carefully the poem is read. "I'm the child who was lost / and found his way back before his parents / missed him"—how willingly I embraced the masculine pronoun, wanting to distance myself from the entire experience, wanting to enter the universality of the metaphor rather than dwell on specific events. But of course this isn't a poem about what happened; it's about "what happened after." All that can be found on the page are the physical and emotional aftershocks of an experience, not the experience itself. Even though my intent in approaching the writing of the poem was to conceal, I wanted to reveal *everything* about the physical desperation and the emotional desiccation that often follow a soul-shattering event. And the "ferocious embrace" with which the poem ends is a metaphor not only for the gratitude I felt for my survival but also for what I hoped the poem itself would achieve, which has little to do with understanding and everything to do with love.

ERIC TRETHEWEY

Scar

Hunting along the logging road
swamped through to Pockwock Lake,
we stopped beside the spring to drink—
startled a drowsing snake.

I must have been fourteen that fall,
still young enough to prove
on a dare the limits of my nerve.
Before the snake could move

from sight, I'd picked it up, my grip
hard back of the swiveling head,
clamped tight in fear of its flicking tongue.
I'll lop 'er off, Bob said,

hold still. The knife rose in his fist,
and knowing's ancient form
writhed in mine, twined its length
along my held-out arm.

The snubby head swung left, swung right,
the blade came down—but wide.
The big woods breathed and circled in.
Bob raised the knife, he tried

again to gauge that narrowest gap,
to echo as act what's known
by the eye. A snake slithered in the leaves
as he cut me to the bone.

Cutting to the Bone

I had been sitting at my desk, thinking about scars. Raising my eyeglasses with my left hand in a meditative gesture, I rubbed with thumb and forefinger the slightly deformed bridge of my nose, broken several times during a boxing career. As I did so, the following thought occurred to me: the inception of all genuine existential knowledge is invariably memorialized by some kind of scar, either physical or psychic, sometimes both. I wrote the thought down, realizing as I did that it was not a new conception, certainly, but rather, just one more restatement of what has been thought and said many times before.

As I wrote, my gaze settled upon the forefinger of my right hand, the hand I write with. Just behind the knuckle, slanting at an angle back from it, is a keloid and a knot of scar tissue that deforms the joint in an immediately noticeable way. Putting my pen down, I performed an inventory of my hand: the keloid on my wrist larger than the one on my index finger; the hump at the first joint of the second finger (sign of an old break); the thin white scar running from the humped joint to the second knuckle; and the obvious disfigurement at this knuckle where the part of the finger below it begins to rotate at least ten degrees from the axis. Each of these scars was a memorial to physical and sometimes psychic trauma that had accompanied me through time, a lasting reminder of one way of knowing in the world. Each had a tale to tell, and for a long time I sat there musing, reinhabiting old events until I was moved to try to retell the story of the scar on my index finger that initially had invoked the inventory.

I was fourteen or fifteen years old at the time. My friend Bob Brooks and I had hatched a plan to go on a hunting trip, spending a couple of nights in a fishing and hunting cabin that his father and several of his father's friends had built. In those days, the 1950s in rural Nova Scotia, it was not unusual for fourteen-year-olds to go off in the woods with rifles, unsupervised by adults. I had been hunting alone from the time I was twelve. Sometimes we would hunt on our way to and from the one-room schoolhouse we attended, leaving our .22 rifles and shotguns propped in a corner behind the teacher's desk while class was in session.

The hike into the camp near Pockwock Lake was approximately four miles along the main road from home, and then another five miles along an old logging road through the woods. Packs on our backs filled with grub, we glided along the logging road in mid-afternoon, alert for movement or other signs of game. I can remember yet some of the bends and hills along that road, stretches of high ground where the trail wound through fir thickets, and patches of low, marshy terrain where what was left of an old corduroy roadbed snaked between the stands of alders crowding up on either side.

At one point, about half-way in to the camp, there was a small spring on the left-hand side of the trail. It was always perfectly clear and icy cold even at mid-summer. We never passed without stopping to drink. This time, when I kneeled to scoop water in the tin can that served as a makeshift dipper—and that each user was expected to return to its place hanging from a nail in the maple beside the spring—I noticed sudden movement in the grass. It was a snake, a common brown snake, a couple of feet long at least. For some reason, bravado perhaps, I stood up, forefinger holding him tightly, just behind the head, so that he couldn't turn back far enough to get his jaws on me. I held him aloft for Bob's approval.

My friend had his skinning knife out by this time. "Hold him steady," he said. "I'll lop his head off."

He took one swipe and missed. On the second swipe, overcompensating for the miss, he hit my finger. The snake, needless to say, escaped unscathed. Blood welled out of the wound. Suddenly, I was in pain and a long way from medical assistance.

That was the end of the hunting trip. We bound my finger as best we could with a handkerchief cut into strips the width of a bandage. Soon, it was soaked through with blood. My hand throbbed with pain. And in that state, we began the seven-mile tramp back home. Bob kept apologizing for what had happened, but I knew then as well as I know now that the fault was not his alone. I told him I didn't blame him.

By the time we made it back home, the bleeding had stopped and the pain had abated somewhat. After my mother had cleaned and dressed the wound, I went to bed with a lot of aspirin. By then it didn't seem to make much sense to get the cut stitched, and besides, there was no car available to take us to the hospital twenty-five miles away. The wound healed eventually, but it took a long time. It was many weeks before I regained the full use of my hand.

Sitting at my desk some thirty years later, rehearsing this event in my mind, I decided then and there to write a poem about it, beginning by jotting down words and phrases that came to me and by sketching out the story. Before long, I had a rough draft of a poem entitled "Hunting."

By the time I returned to it a few days later, I had decided that since the poem was basically a simple, straightforward narrative with folk-tale overtones—the snake, the rural setting, the bloody scene—I would try to shape its lines into the form of a ballad stanza just to see what might come of the attempt. In retrospect, I think it was a good decision because the demands of meter and rhyme pushed me into verbal and allusive felicities and economies I otherwise would not have come to. It encouraged me to compress the narrative I have presented above into but six four-line stanzas.

The first thing one will notice is that in the new title I have returned to the triggering conception of the poem, the idea of scars. "Scar" as a title also better suits the controlling idea of the poem as it emerged in the process of composition, and which first surfaces in the lines describing the snake in stanza 4: "Knowing's ancient form / writhed in mine, twined its length / along my held-out arm." Though I had not known exactly where I was going when I began, apart from my intention to tell a story about what to me was an interesting, if painful, experience, I now discovered that I was writing a poem about initiation and about knowledge. Of course, it is all but impossible to write about a snake in the context of the Western literary tradition without invoking echoes of the serpent in Genesis. The allusion was there quite naturally. It only remained to articulate for myself and for the poem the most significant point of correspondence between the Genesis story and the central event of the poem.

I have for a long time understood the account of the fall in Genesis as, on one level at least, a parabolic representation of the archetypal movement most of us experience individually as the change from innocent adherence to cultural imperatives into the frequently painful experiential knowledge that comes as a consequence of testing or violating those imperatives. It is one thing to know about things notionally, to be adept at giving voice to various ideas about the world, and another to take upon oneself the risk and responsibility of trying to act in accordance with what one believes: "to echo as act what's known / by the eye." The difference between what we might more or less wish to do and what we are capable of achieving at any given time is a powerful reminder of the human condition: our weakness, our fallibility, our need for forgiveness. I didn't want to say all of this in the poem, but I hoped that the allusive resonance of "knowing's ancient form" and the alliteratively formulated statement of the ethical dilemma the poem presents—"to gauge that narrowest gap / to echo as act what's known / by the eye"— would suggest some of it to the discerning reader.

When I realized that the poem was becoming an account of initiation, a sort of ritualistic scarification, I wanted to include some clue that would further suggest a ceremonial dimension to what was happening. The line "The big woods breathed and circled in" does this I think by implying the image of a group of elders gathering close to witness the action. I can imagine all too readily one kind of reader who would object to this line as a commission of the pathetic fallacy. My only defense would be to point out that the experience of feeling that the deep woods is a living, observing presence, somehow participating with us in consciousness, is common enough and widely attested to in our literature. Whether or not the forest actually behaves in this way is far less significant to the poem than the fact that the speaker feels that it does.

There are two other points worth making perhaps, about the composition of the poem. One has to do with diction. As I wrote and revised I was conscious of looking for words that would create a tone suggestive of the rural culture out of which the poem emerges. Such colloquial expressions as "swamped"—to clear through bush—"hard back," "lop 'er off," "snubby," and "big woods" do this I hope, serving to counterbalance the more literary language used to evoke the central theme.

The other point has to do with meter. Having decided to write in ballad stanza, I needed to avoid the monotonous dogtrot of uninterrupted iambs, while nevertheless remaining true to the basic pattern of alternating four- and three-stress lines. How well I have done this remains for others to judge. However, I must confess to being pleased with certain effects: the sudden trochee, "startled," that begins line 4, evoking by the shift in stress pattern what the word denotes; the twin amphimacers divided by caesura—"writhed in mine, twined its length"—that slow down the tempo and create emphasis in line 3 of stanza 4; the arresting spondee of "hold still" at the beginning of stanza 4; and the enjambments between stanzas 2 and 3, 3 and 4, and 5 and 6.

As a teacher of literature and of writing, I am obliged to remind my students repeatedly of the deadly consequences of using clichéd language in their writing. So I am particularly sensitive to the hoary cliché that concludes "Scar." Do I get away with "cut me to the bone?" If so, I think that, apart from the phrase being both used literally and figuratively, it is because of formal considerations: the clause "as he cut me to the bone" ends the poem at the climactic moment of the narrative and arrives as something of a surprise on the heels of two enjambments—"he tried / again to gauge"; and "to echo as act what's known / by the eye."

Indeed, the central thematic idea of the poem—the epistemological distinction between merely knowing and knowing and doing—is itself a cultural cliché. As well as being a commonplace, however, it is also part of the permanent wisdom of our culture. That is why, I suppose, we persist in worrying the issue and try endlessly to articulate it in moving and memorable language.

CHASE TWICHELL

To Throw Away

A smudge of flame takes the twigs,
the dry sisters of the leaves.
It's time to ask for the teachings.

From this high rock I can see
the granite faces of the mountains.

My thoughts are like the smoke
that begins in a heap of oak twigs
and ends diffused in the sky.

There's a Japanese expression,
"to throw away the world."

I can smell the balsams,
resinous in the first long cold.
In my mind I walk out into them.

The sound of boots in light frost—
my breath, feeding the fire of my question.

"To Throw Away"

About a year ago, I did something dramatic: I impulsively destroyed fifteen months' work. One morning I sat down at my desk and looked at the poems I'd written since *The Ghost of Eden*, and realized that they disappointed me. Way up here in the mountains, we have to pay for our trash disposal by the pound, so everyone burns their nonrecyclable paper. In the yard, my husband was burning ours. With the thrill of rashness, I dumped the sheaf of poems into the barrel, then erased them from the floppy disk and the hard drive. All this took less than two minutes. I actually broke into a light sweat, but it was a sweat of exhilaration, of freedom—I was back at the blank page, the threshold of the unknown. Since I hadn't yet articulated what it was I next wanted to know, I'd been writing poems that hadn't taught me anything and that ultimately bored me. So I burned them, and never thought about them again.

For several years, I'd been studying Japanese zen, eventually entering a monastery as a lay student. I was also reading Japanese poetry and studying its history. With the failed poems out of the way, I suddenly saw something their presence had obscured: I *had* identified the new frontier, but had been keeping it sequestered, as if the study of the self—which is what zen is—were a parallel inquiry instead of the only inquiry. When I say that zen is the study of the self, I'm not talking about introspection. Rather, the discipline is concerned with *what*, rather than *who*, the self is. In this way it's more closely related to philosophy and psychology than it is to religion, as is commonly supposed. The challenge became how to approach this enormous question in the poems. What kind of poem could sidestep the rational and logical mind that obscures what zen seeks to reveal?

I began to experiment with Japanese forms, particularly the tanka and the renga, because their psychological structures are alien to me, and force me to work without my familiar tools, my little linguistic reflexes and logical assumptions. It's fun to keep throwing away those familiar responses, which amount to the old way of working, and to try to do something that makes me feel like a beginner again. It's like finger-painting—I can make lots of fast, trivial messes and then crumple the cheap, ephemeral paper. Gone! Not important! And every once in a while I really surprise myself, and write something that suddenly throws light on the mystery. In order to do this, I've had to make some rules for myself. One: don't save drafts. I used to cling to all the false starts and apparent dead ends in case some gem might be embedded there. I still believe that the unconscious knows valuable things that I don't, but most of what it knows is useless stuff. Two: if a line isn't working, start again from scratch. Words aren't precious. If I lose a promising trail, so what? *Unless* I'm willing to lose it, how can I get to the next one, and the next? I think I used to stop far too soon, letting whatever happened to be there on the page command my attention, instead of asking myself what else could be there in its place. What is this myopia but a reflection of my self, which likes to fix broken things and which would rather not think painful, self-annihilating thoughts? Thus the third rule: there's only one question—what is the self? Until it's answered, keep asking it. Then, who knows?

"To Throw Away" is a renga, or rather a simulation of a renga since by definition the form is a collaborative effort in which several poets take turns writing stanzas of three and two lines. The renga is a bastard child of the five-line tanka, split into two separate miniature worlds. In *Japanese Death Poems*, Yoel Hoffman says,

Most tanka contain two poetic images. The first is taken from nature; the second, which may precede, follow, or be woven into the first, is a kind of meditative complement to the nature image. Tanka produce a certain dreamlike effect, presenting images of reality without that definite quality of "realness" often possessed by photographs or drawings, as if the image proceeded directly from the mind of the dreamer. . . . The tanka may be likened to a person holding two mirrors in his hands, one reflecting a scene from nature, the other reflecting himself as he holds the mirror. The tanka thus provides a look at nature, but it regards the observer of nature as well.

The psychology of the tanka intrigued me, but because I wanted the poem to replicate the way the mind can detach and study itself, I wrote it as a renga (remember that the renga is a fractured tanka), with each stanza both belonging to and distinct from the whole, like a vase that's been glued back together. It went through hundreds of permutations before I settled on its final one. Each decision came to me independently of the rest, an isolated sharp moment, and I let those moments determine the relation of the separate parts. In this sense the poem feels to

me as if it had been written by more than one mind, and I can honestly
say I don't know how I did that, because there's no history or evidence
of the work. All that survives is the words in the poem. I should also
say that "To Throw Away" is part of a long, linked sequence. I really
can't judge how well it stands alone. My interest lies not in its power
or completeness as a single poem, but rather in how it reveals the mind
changed by its mission.

To be brought from the bright schoolyard into the house:
to stand by her bed like an animal stunned in the pen:
against the grid of the quilt, her hand seems
stitched to the cuff of its sleeve—although he wants
most urgently the hand to stroke his head,
although he thinks he could kneel down
that it would need to travel only inches
to brush like a breath his flushed cheek,
he doesn't stir: all his resolve,
all his resources go to watching her,
her mouth, her hair a pillow of blackened ferns—
he means to match her stillness bone for bone.
Nearby he hears the younger children cry,
and his aunts, like careless thieves, out in the kitchen.

Kyrie

$\mathbf{M}$y father was the oldest of five, and his mother died six weeks after the youngest was born. The children were sent away to live with relatives—my father to an aunt and uncle (who, I found out recently, were only twenty-one and nineteen when they inherited this eight-year-old boy). For four years my grandfather mourned and looked for a wife. Once he'd found one, the family was reassembled, all but the baby, left to grow up with her adoptive parents down the road.

This was family data, as familiar as our name. There was no story, no enlargement or detail: just the fact of the grave, which we visited every Sunday, on the way home from my other grandmother's house, the rest of us waiting in the car while my father stood beside the stone, wiping his eyes. And the fact of a great aunt, several hours away, hunched and shortened by arthritis, who called my father "my little Lloyd." And the fact of a slender, pinched woman—"Miss Sallie" is what my father always called *her*—who lived with and outlived my grandfather in his brooding house. Data is bloodless. The force of my father's experience—that he was, after all, orphaned—wasn't quite real to me until after his death, by way of my own son from age eight, which is when ribs and collarbones poke through babyfat, to age twelve, which is when my father was moved back not into the house but to an unheated shed, like the fieldhand he was expected to be.

After I've finished a book of poems, the dangers of reiteration, and mannerism, have seemed so strong, I've willfully devised, each time, some new formal project as a way to begin again. *The Lotus Flowers* (1987) emerged from a practicum in narrative, *Two Trees* (1992) from two years' worth of antinarrative fragments, exercises in tone, the same haystack seen in differing light. As a productive habit, however, this has lost vitality over time. When I had proofed the galleys of that fourth book, and mailed it back, the "next thing" remained a series of prohibitions (no more open-verse fragments, no more references to myth, no more autobiographical "I"), and vague instructions (move lyric closer to dramatic structure, investigate character through voice, develop a stronger sense of irony.) Nevertheless, trusting that a writer thinks most clearly when writing, and to avoid paralysis, in the fall of 1991 I started work on a short symmetrical lyric, familiar data from a new point of view: child beside his mother's deathbed.

No doubt the open-ended "variations" of *Two Trees*, which had weaned me from any lingering fidelity to formal conventions, at the same time plumped an appetite for a fixed form's discipline and resolution; what it seems I wanted was dramatic compression, and a loosely structured unrhymed third-person sonnet was one way to get it. But the fourteen-line restriction excluded from this new piece associations uncovered and now ripening on a back lobe of my brain, one of them a family story.

My grandfather's second marriage, and the return of four-fifths of the children, occurred in the fall of 1918, during the Spanish influenza's brutal second wave. Within weeks of their reunion, the lot of them—new bride, grieving husband, bruised children—fell ill. It was a dreadful winter, in Virginia one of the worst and earliest on record, with drifts to the eaves and blocking the doors. The story featured Dr. Gilmore Reynolds, for whom my father was given a middle name, who had presided over all my grandmother's deliveries and her death. Its thrust (for my father's stories always had some moral) concerned the insufficiency—even unto folly—of modern science. With so many sick and dying to attend, this particular housecall was the last in an exhausting day of them. Admitting he had nothing in his bag of the least help, he asked my grandfather slyly, "Rob, have you got any corn?" A jug was produced; Dr. Reynolds took a swig—then divided the moonshine among everyone present, children and adults. Here my Baptist father liked to pause before delivering the punchline: "And all of us survived."

Typical for his era, miraculous home remedies—and preventions—were among his favorite topics, ranking somewhere between ghosts (he hadn't seen any but knew others who had) and pragmatic farmlore (i.e., kingsnakes nibble a little weed, which makes them immune to venom, before attacking a copperhead.) But I was caught up less by narrative pull than by one odd detail: when the country doctor came by on his horse, they let him in through a window. From this developed a poem of 30 lines, spoken by my reinvented "Dr. Reynolds."

I can't remember exactly when I conflated the events of the two poems, when I diagnosed the death in the sonnet as an early case of influenza (although it was well before I learned the first signs of epidemic included an increase in childbed fever). Within months I was hearing other voices from that time, that affliction:

"In my sister's dream about the war,
the animals had clearly human faces. . . ."

"A large lake, a little island in it.
Winter comes to the island and the ice
forms along the shore—"

"How we survived: we locked the doors
and let nobody in."

"Who said the worst was past, who knew
such a thing?"

"Oh yes I used to pray. I prayed for the baby. . . ."

Shortly thereafter, I divided the doctor's poem into two more unrhymed sonnets, and began to posit a sequence flexible enough to accommodate all the voices. Research—historical, medical—came later, and proved more a check on the authenticity of what I imagined than the impetus for new poems: information was hard to locate, and the language of statistics lacks resonance. Later still, when I'd come to understand "the story" belonged to the illness itself, there would be decisions about the length and scope of the sequence, about structural and narrative obligations, about pattern and variation, about what readers already knew or would need to be told.

I hadn't set out to write about 1918, or the pandemic (it was in fact worldwide), but about individuals in extremity. But in time I realized, for most people—even those my age, whose parents or grandparents had most certainly lived it—that extraordinary year (twenty-five percent of the United States acutely ill) was not included in either their family data package or family stories. The records show my Vermont county, with its granite workers already encumbered by white lung disease, had the highest influenza mortality rate of any other in the state; yet my neighbor, who has lived here all her life and at eighty-four remembers perfectly the weather of the past fifty years, can recall only a cousin with the flu in the Service. A *Kyrie* reader who asked her grandmother about the epidemic was given a moving report of watching the great-grandfather die. "Why did you never tell us?" "It was so awful, I wanted you spared." And spared we usually were—even, I learned, by historians and novelists—although shaped by its effects nonetheless, like the man who told me recently, "Influenza killed the woman who was supposed to be my mother."

It was the willed silence that I increasingly wanted to counter, in what became a book-length poem—because my father's life shared a plotline with millions? Because modern medicine had rescued my own two children when they were small? Because of our current AIDS epidemic? Because the opposition of individual and community is thematic material I return to over and over? Because I was obsessed by how to balance received literary form and idiom, how far the *volta* might be effaced or relocated, how to displace or amplify end-rhyme with internal or slant rhyme or anaphora, how to get patterned syntax to do the work of meter, how many distinct personae a reader will tolerate, how narrative may be suggested through repetition, juxtaposition, and sequence?

Because a single poem opened a door.

RICHARD WILBUR

Bone Key

He used to call his body Brother Ass . . .
—St. Bonaventure, *Life of St. Francis*

You would think that here, at least,
In dens by night, on tawny sands by day,
Poor Brother Ass would be a kingly beast.
So does the casuarina seem to say,

Whose kindred haziness
Of head is flattering to a bloodshot eye;
So too the palm's blown shadows, which caress
Anointed brows and bodies where they lie,

And Angel's Trumpets, which
Proclaim a musky scent in fleshly tones.
Yet in this island soil, that's only rich
In rock and coral and Calusa bones,

It's hardihood that thrives,
As when a screw pine that the gale has downed,
Shooting new prop-roots from its trunk, survives
In bristling disarray by change of ground,

Or the white mangrove, nursed
In sea-soaked earth and air, contrives to expel
From leafstalk glands the salt with which it's cursed,
Or crotons, scorched as by the flames of Hell,

Protectively attire
Their leaves in leather, and so move to and fro
In the hot drafts that stir the sun's harsh fire,
Like Shadrach, Meshach, and Abednego.

Becoming Subtropical

Even the most guarded people have their moments of merging with what we call nature—moods in which they enjoy "ecstatic identities with the weather," or states of mind in which human life seems but one crop and compost of the fruitful earth. For the most part, however— though Wilde went too cleverly far in saying that "Nature is our creation"—we see in the natural world not Being or biosphere but particular bushes, fields, birds, and rocks that are implicated in our walks and labors, our dwelling places, our human loves, imaginations, and memories. It is natural, in the sense of not surprising, that I should recall with intensity the ruddy-barked cherry tree to the south of my parents' house in New Jersey, or the fox I saw as a child near the giant sassafras at the edge of Armitage's woods. It is also natural that long residence in rural New England should have accustomed me to boulders and sweet fern, small cold rivers, shadbush, deer, hemlock, partridgeberry, woodchucks, crickets, rock maple, lilacs, and the rest, and that I should know these things both in themselves and in their overtones and associations. As I write this, the larches along Route 9 in Windsor are getting ready for their annual splendor. They are fascinating trees—tall, pyramidal, northern conifers that shed their needles in the late fall. They grow clear up to Hudson's Bay, and their wood is so strong that it was formerly used in the building of battleships. Most of the year they are inconspicuous, but there comes a time in November when their tufted or fascicled leaves change color, and they suddenly stand forth from the surrounding bleakness in fibrous gold. They are one of the wonders of the year for people who live in this region, so much a part of their lives that it would seem no impertinence to invest them with human value, and see in their epiphany some human meaning, or a glimpse of Being, for that matter.

If New England "nature" is interwoven with the lives and feelings of its inhabitants, so is the nature of every other place, and that can lead the outsider to skewed perceptions. Back in 1965 or so, when my wife and I first started to spend some part of the long winter in Key West, I confess that I looked at Florida palm trees with an unjust eye, seeing them as belonging to garish postcard art, or to that banal dream, peddled by annuity salesmen, of retirement to an ocean-view condo called Windermere Arms, and a life of perpetual golf. If Key West—not then so resort-ridden and gentrified as now—delighted us by its anarchy, its jumbled population, and its atmosphere of comic acceptance, we were not unaware of cultural poverty, tackiness, and squalor, and my sense of the island's natural beauties was colored by those things. That is to say, I initially saw Key West's glorious sunsets as tinged by bad taste, while its flamboyant orchid-trees and allamandas struck me as a sort of botanical persiflage. Or camouflage.

It has taken me a long time to modify those impressions, as it might take someone a long time to dissociate poinsettias from Christmas. After thirty winters, I still see Key West's human and natural worlds as an ensemble, but differently now, and I know more about the subtropical "environment" than I did. It embarrasses me to acknowledge how long it was before I could read the signs of seasonal change; how long it was before I learned that mint (for instance) does poorly in the Keys for want of cold nights, and shook off the notion that the subtropics were a kind of Eden hospitable to "All Trees of noblest kind for sight, smell, taste," regardless of their climatic range. In time I came to know, from talk and books and experience, that the flora of Key West are sorely tried and hard beset, and so could transfer to them the respect I feel for the toughness of larches, and write a poem that says that, though the island is associated with self-indulgence, life is challenging, there as elsewhere, to plant or man.

The name "Key West" stems from Spanish "Cayo Hueso" (Bone Island), which may or may not derive from intertribal Indian warfare, the final massacre of the Calusas, and the littering of the island with their bones. The casuarina, a feathery tree that takes its name from the cassowary bird, has an aptitude for growing in seacoast sand, and is also known as the Australian pine. Angel's trumpet is a poisonous, narcotic tree of the genus *Datura*, and is sometimes called Brugmansia. "Screw pine" is a common name for the large Asiatic shrub pandanus. White mangroves and crotons are well known, and so, I hope, are Shadrach, Meshach, and Abednego.

Robert Frost once owned an orange grove in Florida, and spent much time in Key West, yet had nothing to say in verse about—or by way of— that part of the world. Though I have now taken up legal residence in Key West, I think I am like Frost in that it is the New England landscape that I do my feeling in. Still, it pleases me, after all these years, to have written a Key West poem.

Questions My Son Asked Me, Answers I Never Gave Him

1. Do gorillas have birthdays?
   Yes. Like the rainbow, they happen.
   Like the air, they are not observed.

2. Do butterflies make a noise?
   The wire in the butterfly's tongue
   hums gold.
   Some men hear butterflies
   even in winter.

3. Are they part of our family?
   They forgot us, who forgot how to fly.

4. Who tied my navel? Did God tie it?
   God made the thread: O man, live forever!
   Man made the knot: enough is enough.

5. If I drop my tooth in the telephone
   will it go through the wires and bite someone's ear?
   I have seen earlobes pierced by a tooth of steel.
   It loves what lasts.
   It does not love flesh.
   It leaves a ring of gold in the wound.

6. If I stand on my head
   will the sleep in my eye roll up into my head?
   Does the dream know its own father?
   Can bread go back to the field of its birth?

7. Can I eat a star?
   Yes, with the mouth of time
   that enjoys everything.

8. Could we Xerox the moon?
   This is the first commandment:
   I am the moon, thy moon.
   Thou shalt have no other moons before thee.

9. Who invented water?
The hands of the air, that wanted to wash each other.

10. What happens at the end of numbers?
I see three men running toward a field.
At the edge of the tall grass, they turn into light.

11. Do the years ever run out?
God said, I will break time's heart.
Time ran down like an old phonograph.
It lay flat as a carpet.
At rest on its threads, I am learning to fly.

The Dialogue of Question

and Answer

ANSWER: Now, about Nancy Willard's poem, "Questions My Son Asked Me, Answers I Never Gave Him." She doesn't really answer his questions. If her son had asked me, "Do gorillas have birthdays?" I would have given him a straight answer.

QUESTION: Wait! What was Rilke's advice to the young poet?

ANSWER: Love the questions.

QUESTION: But which questions? Aren't the questions different for each poet?

ANSWER: What do you mean?

QUESTION: Isn't "Tyger, tyger, burning bright in the forests of the night, what immortal hand or eye dare frame thy fearful symmetry?" a different kind of question than "Oh strong-ridged and deeply hollowed nose of mine! what will you not be smelling?"

ANSWER: Of course they're different. William Carlos Williams is celebrating his nose. Blake is standing in the invisible footprints of God confronting Job: "Hath the rain a father?" and "Has thou entered into the treasures of the snow?" I often wonder why God didn't just tell him the truth. "You have not entered into the treasures of the snow. You do not know the source of the rain."

QUESTION: Do you really think Job would have listened to God? He would have said to himself, "Oh, I'm nothing but a mote in the Creator's eye." No comfort there. No relevations to shake a sullen spirit. Nothing to lift Job out of his sorrow. Why do you think the Zen masters gave their disciples riddles to meditate on instead of precepts to memorize? I'll bet you don't know any riddles.

ANSWER: Hah! What's black and white and read all over?

QUESTION: Everybody knows that one. What is the sound of one hand clapping?

ANSWER: Silence.

QUESTION: But clapping is never silent. You can't answer that kind of question with a yes or no. You can only let it lead you to a place where yes and no are no longer opposites.

ANSWER: You're losing me. Give me some questions I can answer.

QUESTION: All right. Take another look at the questions Nancy Willard's son asked when he was four and five years old. "Can I eat a star?" "Could we Xerox the moon?" "If I stand on my head will the sleep in my eye roll up into my head?" Do you have the answers?

ANSWER: One answer will do. It's *no*, to all of them.

QUESTION: In the world of common sense, the answer is no. But in the world of uncommon sense, the sky is the limit. The moon speaks: "I am the moon, thy moon. Thou shalt have no other moons before thee." The poet prophesies: "Yes, with the mouth of time that enjoys everything." A question turns itself into an answer: "Does the dream know its own father? Can bread go back to the field of its birth?" The common sense answer is the one most people agree on. But in the realm of uncommon sense, the answer is different for everybody. The question leads to metaphors, to questions, to stories.

ANSWER: We were speaking of poetry, not stories.

QUESTION: We were speaking of questions and where they can lead you. What is the story of Adam and Eve and the serpent but the answer to the question, "How did death come into the world?" The Hottentots answer that question with the story of how the hare, carrying the moon's promise of eternal life, garbled it and turned it into the assurance of mortality. The same question got both stories rolling before it discreetly disappeared.

Take away the question, "Do the years ever run out?" and you have the story of what's left after God lets the universe wind down. The poet probably heard that story for the first time in church: "And the heaven departed as a scroll when it is rolled together." I beg of you never to forget that questions open doors and answers close them.

ANSWER: And I beg of *you* never to forget the last words of Gertrude Stein: "What is the answer?"

QUESTION: That's not the whole story. When no answer was forthcoming, she laughed and added, "Then, what is the question?"

Adjusting to the Light

—air—air! I can barely breathe . . . aah!
Whatever it was, I think I shook it off.
Except my head hurts and I stink. Except
what is this place and what am I doing here?

Brother, you're in a tomb. You were dead four days.
Jesus came and made you alive again.

Lazarus, listen, we have things to tell you.
We killed the sheep you meant to take to market.
We couldn't keep the old dog, either.
He minded you. The rest of us he barked at.
Rebecca, who cried two days, has given her hand
to the sandalmaker's son. Please understand
we didn't know that Jesus could do this.

We're glad you're back. But give us time to think.
Imagine our surprise to have you—well,
not well, but weller. I'm sorry, but you do stink.
Everyone, give us some air. We want to say
we're sorry for all of that. And one thing more.
We threw away the lyre. But listen, we'll pay
whatever the sheep was worth. The dog, too.
And put your room the way it was before.

The Writing of "Adjusting

to the Light"

I don't like poems that seem to say, "Guess what I mean." And I don't much like symbolist poems, in which people and things are standing in for the real subjects, who for some reason are absent. I also don't care for surreal or impressionist poems that assume a reader wants to help interpret the poet's dreams.

This is not to say that I think everything in a poem should be on the surface. Not at all. It's simply to say that there should *be* a surface, a place for the reader to stand. Young journalists used to be taught to answer the questions *who, what, where, when,* and *why* in the first compressed paragraph of a story. I would go so far as to say that the first four of these ought to be answered in a single reading of most poems.

But this is only a starting place. Because the question to ask is not, finally, "What does a poem mean?" but "How does a poem mean?", as John Ciardi tried to make clear in his textbook by that name.

Look from this perspective at the poem "Adjusting to the Light." The dramatic situation is clear enough. Lazarus has just been revived. He speaks, and then his sisters speak. He is understandably confused. He is told—though he may not be paying much attention—that his return from the dead is going to call for a lot of adjustment on the part of several people, including Lazarus himself.

But it would be wrong, in a sense, to say that the poem is *about* Lazarus. A young woman recently noted in an interview with me that she could see in my poetry influences of my father, who was a Methodist minister. When I asked for an example, she referred to this poem, "the one," she said, "about resurrection."

"That poem," I said, "is only incidentally about resurrection. At heart, it's about questioning. It questions the simplicity of the story as we have it in the Bible, and the happy consequence of miracles."

Nearly every poem, at heart, is a questioning, a way of saying, "We don't have the whole story," or "We may not have been looking at this thing in the right light," or "Let's check behind this curtain to see if there's somebody else in the room."

Browning's "My Last Duchess," Eliot's "The Love Song of J. Alfred Prufrock," Bishop's "The Fish"—each is a way of questioning what we have thought.

In its own small way, so is "Adjusting to the Light" a questioning. So what does it mean? It means that the stories we hear and tell are more complicated than we usually allow, because people's lives and deaths are more tangled up in one another than we want to realize.

How the poem means calls attention to a number of other matters.

Its way of meaning is to invite the reader inside to take part in its making. All poems have to do this, if they work. They do it by appealing to the reader's senses, imagination, emotion, and intellect. A poet brings all this about by the manipulation of language, its ambiguities, its echoes, and its rhythms.

I don't consciously write in identified feet, but in counted stresses (though English being what it is, the lines are usually iambic). Frequently I write not in a rhyme pattern, but with scattered rhyme. Both elements of style lend themselves to the conversational, a quality that I'm comfortable with in my poetry. I will cast a poem in regular rhyme if I want to take it further from plain talk.

Everything a poet does in a poem has the effect of moving the experience of the poem closer to that of conversation or of ritual. Anglo-Saxon root words, contractions, enjambment, lack of rhyme or slant rhyme or irregular rhyme, all make a poem more conversational; Latin-root words, end-stopped lines, regular and true rhyme, all make the experience of a poem closer to that of ritual.

The poet's medium is language as the sculptor's is stone. A poet can't do much to change what words mean, but can do a great deal to change the way they rub up against one another. A part of what we go to poetry for is the soundplay—not only rhyme, but a poem's rhythms and the way consonants knock together and vowels wrap around them.

And I should also say something about what I hear as a *line* of poetry. A ragged right margin obviously does not turn a piece of prose into a poem. The right margin is uneven because a poem is written in lines, and lines are self-defining; we can't decide where we want them to break. A line of poetry is at its best a unit of sense, syntax, and rhythm all at the same time. (Note that the unity of sense is violated once in "Adjusting to the Light," in the third line, which breaks after the first word of a new sentence to suggest the confusion of the speaker.)

All of the elements I've mentioned can, I hope, be seen at work here.

As the poem opens, Lazarus has just come back to life, disoriented and unaware that he was dead. His sisters—Mary and Martha, as we know them to be—are concerned and solicitous.

One speaks in the second strophe, the other in the third, and one of them—probably the first—speaks in the final section, as they break the complex truth to their brother.

Generally, I prefer poems that could be played out on stage. I like to think that anyone, reading the poem aloud, is naturally going to assume three different voices, one for each of the speakers.

Now a closer look at the shape and direction of the scene:

The alliterative "Lazarus, listen" is intended to focus not only the attention of Lazarus, but of the reader, a way of saying, "Those six lines were the introduction; now that you know where we are, let's get on with it." And then the line announces "things" to follow, raising expectation and sending the reader forward. Or, again, I hope so.

Then we learn that Lazarus, not having lost his life, has lost his sheep, his dog, his sweetheart, his lyre, and probably his entire place in the scheme of things. All the while, we move forward from lines like "Rebecca, who cried two days, has given her hand . . ." (to whom?) and discover the answer in a line that ends with "Please understand . . ." (understand what?), taking us to the next line to find that answer in turn. Sometimes the expectation is subtler, as in "give us time to think" (about what?) or very explicit about what is to follow, as with "We want to say," though, and "one thing more."

Not every line can raise such questions, of course, and in any case it's not something one needs to be conscious of during the reading. But the continual raising and filling of expectations in this way creates a sense of forward motion that is part of what moves a reader through a poem.

Rhyme is absent as the words of Lazarus open the poem. I don't think I could believe his gasping confusion were it expressed in rhyme. The explanation by the sisters becomes increasingly marked by rhyme as they choose their words carefully and look for an order they don't quite find. It slips away from them as the rhyme slips away, never falling into a pattern until the closing strophe, when they apologize and promise to make amends and welcome Lazarus back as best they can; here the terminal rhymes tumble over one another, suggesting, perhaps, that there is still a way to fashion some sort of desperate order here.

Still, Lazarus and the readers both see that he can never truly be at home again. Not as he was. And that every player on the stage has lost something. Time has moved in the wrong direction and will now always be out of joint. Maybe the poem says that miracles are not something to hope for, after all. It is meant to be, in any event, a questioning of what we have taken for granted.

The poem closes with several resolving moves in the final lines. "We threw away the lyre" returns to the earlier listing of losses, and the cata-log—"lyre," "sheep," "dog" recapitulates most of that list; "Listen" hear-kens back to "Lazarus, listen;" the promises to make things right—or as right as possible—come as unambiguous assertions; the "room" echoes, in both sense and sound, the earlier "tomb." Perhaps the strongest sug-gestion that the poem is coming to an end is the interruption of the conversation by a sister's address to the crowd standing about the recent corpse ("Everyone, give us some air") followed by a shift of focus back to the subject at hand. All these—reaching back to an earlier element in a poem, returning to an interrupted line of thought, the making of unqualified statements—are ways of signaling to a reader that a poem is about to close.

Barbara Herrstein Smith noted in her study entitled *Poetic Closure* that it's the business of every line in a poem to raise the expectation of another line to follow, except for the last line, which has to change that to an expectation of nothing to follow.

Otherwise, when a poem ends, we feel that we've been hung up on.

So what does the poem mean? It means a number of things in a number of ways. A part of what and how it means will depend on who reads it, because a good reader takes part in the completion of a poem; whatever a poem is, finally, belongs in part and separately to each of its readers. The poet James Whitehead and I were invited to Plains, Georgia, in 1981 to help welcome home from Washington Jimmy and Rosalynn Carter, and were asked if we would each write a poem for the occa-sion. After we read our poems to the Carters in the presence of their assembled family and friends, Mr. Carter accepted presentation copies and spoke briefly. As well as I can recall, he said this to us:

"Rosalynn and I will always keep these poems on our closest wall so that we can read them over and over until we find what is to be found there. Now, what we find may not be only what you put there; it may also be what we took there, because that's what good poetry demands and allows."

I was impressed, first, that we had had a president who was capable of having and framing such thoughts. And then I was impressed by how much of the nature of poetry he had captured.

I have read "The Love Song of J. Alfred Prufrock" many times, but I have never read it twice as the same poem. This is because part of what it is I bring to it, and as I'm never quite the person who read it before, I never bring quite what I brought before. This is what Mr. Carter under-stood.

So the meaning of "Adjusting to the Light" depends in good part on my co-author—the reader—who will bring to it memories and associations that are not mine, other attitudes toward myth and religion and nature, and perhaps a different sense of irony. A poem is not complete until the reader has contributed to it, so I will never see this as a complete poem; only the reader can do that. And, if the poem works, it will not be exactly the same poem for any two who read it, as no one is quite the same person to any two friends.

CLARA YU

Little Purple

I still dream of you, Little Purple,
My childhood playmate, friend, teacher,
Who, on that warm August night 25 years ago,
Gathered up her dirndl skirt into a tight knot
And walked into the dark Tan River,
Determined not to rise like a flower.

When the village match-maker and
Your parents announced their choice,
You didn't sing a song of madness,
But quietly said,
Without true love
Life would not be worth living.

Everyone laughed: What a silly notion—
To pick your own mate, without the blessing of
Clan elders, family, the entire neighborhood.
One hundred generations of women
Had acquiesced. What could you, shy, little,
Sixteen year old Little Purple, know, or do?

So the next morning, when they dragged you
Out of the river, all empty-eyed village wives
And hollow-cheeked widows
Came out of their bamboo-fenced houses
And encircled you in silent awe:
You had a smile on your face no one could wipe away:

For some reason,
The river fish had eaten your tender lips,
So you looked a little slaphappy,
Your perfect teeth exposed, turning
Heads away with your
Ferocious triumph.

A Destitute Time

A
... and what are poets for in a destitute time?
—Hölderlin, "Bread and Wine"
n anthology of poets writing about their own poems asserts by its existence that a writer actually might have something to say about his/her own writing that is interesting to a reader. To the writer, though, it is a precarious undertaking. What might I have to say that could engage a reader yet avoid interpreting my own poem, thereby limiting its suggestibility?

I consoled myself with the thought that perhaps I could fall back on my own cultural heritage. After all, the scholar-poets of old China considered it both pleasure and "business," indeed the central occupation of the literati, to gather and compose poetry, to talk and write about their own works, and engage in witty and exuberant discourse, often with flashes of intoxicated genius, on others' compositions. Later readers have delighted in reading these accounts, not only because they provide a clear context for the creative process, but also because the readers become privy to the personages as well as the art, to the creative as well as the critical process.

The deliberate creation of intertextuality is also something in which Chinese authors have traditionally indulged, sometimes extravagantly. One could argue, for instance, that Cao Xueqin wrote his monumental novel, *Dream of the Red Chamber* (five volumes, 1200 pages of text when rendered into English by David Hawkes and John Minford), as a prose elaboration of the collection of 12 short poems, known as "Songs of the Twelve Ladies of Jinling."

Cao's novel, often compared by Western critics to *Remembrance of Things Past*, rests on one persistent rhetorical device. The inscription over the gate to the "Land of Illusion," which the reader enters at the beginning of the story, reads:

Truth becomes fiction when the fiction's true,
Real becomes not-real when the unreal's real.

Thus forewarned, the reader progresses through the work, realizing that every yarn from which the rich tapestry of the story is woven has two worsted strands, the imaginary and the actual. For generations of *Red Chamber* scholars since the mid eighteenth century, their primary enterprise has been to tease apart these strands.

Having ventured somewhat into that very enterprise, in an exasperated moment, I promised myself that if I ever wrote creatively, I would strive for simplicity, following both the example set by the Tang poet Bo Juyi, and the admonitions of Henry James. Legend has it that Bo Juyi tested his poems by reading them to an illiterate, elderly woman. If she didn't readily understand a poem, he would rewrite it until she did. Henry James declared that the only reason for the existence of a literary work is that it attempts to represent life. James also believed, of course, that "It is art that *makes* life, makes interest, makes importance," bringing to full circle the relationship between life and art.

What follows, then, is an interior journey through the experience that led me to write my poem, "Little Purple." I will write around the poem, leaving it undisturbed.

It is difficult to describe the mental state of the generation of Chinese who grew up in the wake of the second World War and the retreat of the non-Communist Chinese from mainland China to Taiwan. Unlike the postwar baby boomer generation in the United States, we were not a generation that was prosperous, victorious, or confident. There was no euphoria because Japan lost the war—for in the end, we lost China, our homeland. We were the children of the exiles. We were silent, cautious, and uncertain of the meaning of our existence. In retrospect, we have been labeled the "lost generation"; there is even a category of literature that has been given that name. But if we were lost, we were also at a loss for words. Much was unspoken, or spoken in understatements. Conversations with new acquaintances would often go like this: "How many brothers and sisters do you have?" "Four, but there were seven of us in the beginning. You know." "What does your father do?" "Nothing. But he was such-and-such back in the mainland." When some of us behaved poorly, our parents needed only to look at us ruefully for us to feel the sting of shame. The reproach was silent, and potent: "You are lucky to be alive; the least you can do is be less of a pest." When we saw grown-ups act lost or despondent, we understood: "How else could they behave, having lost their country, jobs, possessions, members of their family?"

My father, for his part, retreated completely into a world of fictitious warfare: the world of the game of Go. The only books in our household were Go manuals and Go magazines—*The Best Games of Go* and the like. It was with astonishment and incomprehension that I discovered, upon entering school, that there were books that were composed of text only. I had thought, from my experience at home, that all books contained grids and depictions of the ubiquitous black and white stones, strategically positioned for silent sieges and clever maneuverings to decimate the opponent. As I grew older, my fascination with my father's devotion to the game gave way to contempt. It did not require special talent to detect his obsession with Go as an escape. But I felt my father was particularly spiteful and spineless in his choice of this form of escape. In choosing this traditionally high-brow game, he attempted to disguise his escape as a devotion to an ancient art form, a pastime that demanded higher intellect than could be mustered by other fathers, who merely got drunk, or went completely insane.

But it was women whom I lived with and observed, women who got up in the morning, swept the perennial dust off the scanty pieces of furniture, struggled with the little coal stoves to serve up ingenious meals the ingredients of which came largely from bartering and borrowing and what little the small gardens yielded, and tackled the daily laundry with washboards and home-made soap until their hands cracked like parched earth. The daily chores were so overwhelming that their lives took on a kind of frenzy that filled every minute. Yet astonishingly there were occasional laughter and sighs of contentment at the end of the day, when they laid their bodies down on the lumpy cotton mattresses.

My mother, a woman of small stature and iron will, guarded her dominion of work with the ferocity of a lioness. Study, she would say, pushing me out of our little kitchen, that's your job, your *only* job. What I could not tell her was that I wanted not so much to take work away from her as just to be close to her, to inhale the coal-smothered air with her, so that I could endure it better when I heard her coughing at night, to soak my hands, too, in the wash water laden with lye, so that when I saw her hands I would not have to hide my own, my perfectly protected hands with delicate skin. We lived a simple life in material terms, but one destitute in spirit. In that life, all but the barest essentials were a luxury, and therefore excluded from consideration or discussion. Thus excluded were expressions of love, pity, and all questions that are abstract and existential, questions such as personal choice, free will, happiness—the meaning and pursuit thereof.

With my adolescent friends, I slouched around, my eyes downcast, my feet dragging behind me. I created an invisible shield around me, which gave me a sense of fogginess and indifference. I now realize that it was probably very close to being drunk or being on drugs. I didn't probe, didn't ask questions, didn't think. I lay low. I took whatever came to me with resignation. I was vaguely aware of various social conventions, social contracts that you didn't enter into deliberately, but were rather born into, and that you accepted as the way things ought to be. Take, for instance, marriage. I didn't know a marriage that was happy. Not in my family, my friends' families, my neighbors'. Happiness was irrelevant. Love was irrelevant. In my young mind I had separated married life and love completely. Marriage was something you had to endure in order to sustain the existence of your family, your clan. It was an obligation, much like study, or work, or caring for aging parents. It was a social security system, complete with prospective children who would care for you in your old age. Love, however, was something that existed in fiction and imagination. It was reserved for the few upon whom fortune smiled. It was there for fantasizing, and perhaps, if you were very lucky, experimenting. But it had nothing to do with hard reality.

Then came Little Purple into my life, crashing my gray world. She was older than I, perhaps by three years, a native Taiwanese girl who for some reason didn't continue to go to school. I was fascinated by her. Nothing seemed to have touched her—not history, not tradition, nothing dark or heavy or old or bloody. She laughed a great deal, at just about anything. She seemed to have just sprung from a magical stone and stepped into this wonderful paradise of the Taiwanese countryside, and couldn't contain her glee. I would blink at her radiance, in total disbelief. I envied and adored her. We were some pair. She was light in spirit, I, heavy. She saw colors where I saw gray. She made herself ruffled skirts in pretty prints in which she twirled, while I moved cautiously, always in black and white.

Then she confided in me. She was in love. There was a boy, whom I never met. I was sworn to secrecy. There wasn't much to tell, really. Only Purple's giggles, and her darting back and forth uncontrollably and unpredictably, like a colorful fish in glad water. Then her family decided that it was time for her to marry, to someone the family thought was appropriate, a good match.

I didn't see Purple for days. I learned later that her family had kept her under lock and key after she refused to go along with the arranged marriage. But then the story was that she had acquiesced. She was let out, "freed."

I remember vividly the morning Purple came to visit me. I could see her coming now, through the gate, crossing the threshold, in slow motion. This movie has played itself in my mind so many times, voluntarily and involuntarily.

It must have been a holiday, for our modest house was full of relatives and visitors when she came. She walked into the main room of the house; she saw me; she made a sound that was like nothing I had heard before or after. Then she flung her full skirt up, covered her face with it, and cried. There was a sudden hush, as everyone in the room stared. She was now standing with her skirt lifted over her head, exposing her white, shapely legs, thighs, her faded white underpants, in plain sight of everyone in my family, male and female, old and young alike. I knew that everyone else was shocked and embarrassed. But she was oblivious to it all. Her action wasn't improper or obscene; it was natural. I later mused on the truly improper and obscene, but all I could think of then was to get her out of the room, out of the astonished gaze of so many. (I realize that in my poem I have omitted this part of the story, an omission that mirrors my intention to shield her chaste body from strangers.)

The next moments have become less distinct in my mind. I must have rushed over and taken her away to the room that I shared with my sisters. She cried silently. I held her in my arms. Gradually, her supple body tensed up, and she pulled away from me. I remember feeling rejected. I later realized that from that moment on, she no longer needed anyone, not even me. Throughout the whole time, the usually bubbly Purple did not utter a single word. Words, words, words were insufficient, superfluous.

The skirt she had on when she was laid out on the river bank was tightly knotted around her legs. I did not know whether it was her doing, intended to resist buoyancy, or was some rescue worker's idea of modesty. But the image I had of her was one of clean-edged resolve. Unmermaidlike she sank, a well-sheathed sword. I did not get close enough to see her face clearly. I could not verify the story about her lips having been nibbled away by fish. What I saw, for a moment, and forever etched in my mind, was what looked like a wide smile on her white face.

I did not see her family, or the family she had been betrothed to, or the boy with whom she had been in love. There were almost no men present at the river bank. Would their presence have been deemed shameful? I don't know. But the women turned out, weeping. I looked around and saw a huddled mass of gray, bent bodies—bodies that ordinarily at this time of the day would be carrying baskets of laundry or bent over the family stove. But they seemed to have been hollowed out, and at this moment unable to bear even their own weight. There was hushed murmuring. "She is happy now; just look at that smile." Years later, when I heard Yeats' recorded reading of his "Song of the Old Mother," I remembered those contorted figures. His raspy voice whispered, drawing the poem to its end: "And the seed of the fire gets feeble and cold."

Quickly, life went back to normal. The only thing that lingered long in the village was speculation about what had attracted the fish to Purple's lips—whether she had eaten candy or put on lipstick. To me, however, Purple came in dreams, in flashes, always laughing, dancing, her skirt flying high. The sharp images of these dreams invaded my wakeful moments as well. It was as if Purple had lifted a corner of the gray, foggy backdrop against which my life was to play out. I began to see the unjust, the unexamined, the unlived. To hand over one's best friend to death at such a young age was not so much a terrifying as a liberating experience. It made death touchable, if not intimate.

How do we know that something is perfect? It is perfect when anything added or taken away will make it less. How do we know when a life is perfect? A life is perfect when nothing that can happen to it is more beautiful than death. For some this comes early. For some this comes with a smile. For Purple, her choice of death was probably a natural choice, perhaps the only choice. I have learned to respect that. Nevertheless, I wish I could swim against the stream of time. I would like to have that morning back, with Purple in my arms. Whenever I pause to appreciate a sunset, a breeze, silvery ripples in a lake, or hold a child in my arms, I wish Purple were here to share the joy with me. Failing that, I have lived my life as I imagine Purple would have, had I been able to restore that day to its zero moment. It turns out that there is an advantage to looking at life in that light. There is probably no greater fear than the fear of death. When that great fear is removed, every other fear retreats from the horizon. You can take life in your own hands, and play with it seriously, lovingly, lightheartedly. In my mind death and I are old acquaintances that show mutual respect. In the end it would be a fairly negotiated deal, a happy conclusion.

In response to Hölderlin's question, Heidegger writes, "To be a poet in a destitute time means: to attend, singing, to the trace of the fugitive gods." But I like Hölderlin's own words better: ". . . the philosophical light around my window is now my joy."

PAUL ZIMMER

In Apple Country

A year begins with marriage in apple country,
Immaculate drift of lace in light crosswinds,
Consummation of dusts, caverns of blossoms,
Endless circles forming and expanding.

As a child I drew circles for hours,
Arcing the compass around its point
To feel the pleasure of circumference,
Roundness conjoined, swallowing, embracing,
Shoebox full of buckeyes in their husks,
Baseballs, acorns, bags of marbles,
Tulip bulbs, yo-yo's, dandelions—
But ripe apples sliced across always
Made the most perfect circles of all.

Late in harvest good pickers wear gloves
To keep their fingertips from frostbite,
The delicate twist and pluck—
A hundred and fifty bushels a day.

Do apples die when they are picked?
When they tumble from baskets and bags,
Bruised, crushed, slithering under bootsoles?
When the first bite is taken,
Sweet death dribbling onto the chin?

In truth they triumph and abide.
If all the apples ripening
On one fall day and all the circles
Ever grown in these orchards
Draped across the driftless hills,
Were counted by a great master,
They would total the number of stars
In western skies on an autumn night.

I lean back in my garden chair and watch
The great harvests turn slowly in vast distances—
Red, yellow, green, their blemishes and tiny wormholes
Revolving in the October sky all the way
Out to the round ends of the universe.

Apples

When I was a child both my parents worked six days a week in retail stores in Canton, Ohio, and on Saturday nights they came home too weary to prepare a dinner. We would go out to the Fulton Tavern where, without fail, I ordered salisbury steak and a large Waldorf salad. I always liked this time of the week. I had played all day and was tired, too. Each Saturday I took the same seat in the restaurant because just outside the window next to my chair extended the long rows of a large apple orchard. I could look out and dream while my parents recouped from their drudgery and discussed their adult business. The orchard was owned by one of my father's old school chums and so sometimes after dinner we would go next door for a visit, or to buy apples, and I would run around amongst the trees.

I remember that our parish men's club always put apples in our gift boxes at their annual children's Christmas party. Once on the playground Joe Moledor blackened my eye with an apple he had thrown. My friend Pat Mylett and I would sneak up into his neighbor's tree with salt shakers in our pockets and eat the early green apples until we had to make a run for it. When I was sick my mother would give an apple along with my medicine. When I was well she put them into my lunch bag.

Then, when I got older, there were the literary apples. Whitman's rich apple-blossomed earth, Yeats's silver apples of the moon and golden apples of the sun, the apple that Eve gave to Adam, Frost's apple picking, Shakespeare's goodly apple rotten at the heart, or the apple boughs under which Dylan Thomas was young and easy. Perhaps the best work in my first book three decades ago was a poem called "Apple Blight." I begin my selected poems, *Crossing to Sunlight*, with it and conclude with "Apple Country."

A few years ago I discovered a lump under my arm and showed it to a doctor. A friend of mine had recently died rather suddenly from lymphoma. The doctor sent me quickly to a surgeon who, after examination, gravely arranged an appointment for me to have it removed early the following morning.

I had to go home and tell my wife about the operation, but before doing this I wanted to calm myself. I was numb with anxiety, aimlessly driving the streets in my pick-up. Finally, out of no real process of deliberation that I can recall, I found myself sitting in the parking lot of a grocery store, eating a large apple I had purchased. It was what I instinctively chose to do to comfort myself. This story, I am happy to say, ended benignly.

But apples have always had large significance for me. I even like the sound of the word. I love to say it—the short a, the pop of the p's, and then the lilting el—kind of like the sound of an apple when you bite into it.

Several years ago we bought a small farm in southwest Wisconsin, set in the middle of the Kickapoo Valley apple orchard country. The little towns nearby have annual celebrations called Apple Fest and White Blossom Festival. In the autumn the area becomes vibrant with the apple harvest. I guess I have always wanted to make poems about apples, and now I have come to a place where their imagery abounds.

I began working on this poem by nudging some thoughts about plentifulness—necessary grunt, like "one grows used to opulence in apple country," and romantic stuff about how apples are "reminders of Paradise." But then one evening as I gazed up at the autumn stars I began thinking about Yeats's silver apples. My symbolism does not run deep, nor do I have a cabalistic "system," but certainly I could sense those apples up there, rounding in the Milky Way over the orchards on the nearby ridges.

So I began first by noodling this imagery, which I thought might start the poem. I also made a few stabs at bringing in applewood as fuel for fire, but this didn't really fit the scheme and eventually I dumped that idea. I obviously wanted to concentrate on apples and circles. I wanted memories and actions, some good lists and some questions that would resolve themselves "poetically" in the end.

I kept pushing the old verities around—the deeper images of childhood, marriage, sex, death. I tried to start the poem with the apple/stars imagery, but realized after a while that this was my natural conclusion. I threw away a lot of tweedle-dum and tweedle-dee about wind and rain, sun and miracles.

As always, I was relearning what it is to make a poem (that excruciating, wonderful, exasperating, renewing process), learning again how to be patient, look carefully, and trim the branches. Finally I decided that marriage would be the beginning, with some memories of boyhood brought in. Next I wanted to speak of how the apples are harvested and raise the question of whether they die when they are picked. Then I wanted to tie their ripening and harvesting to the stars.

As always, I wanted my lines to be either units of sound or units of sense. I wanted about five hard beats in the lines, but didn't want them to be overbearing, desiring a kind of rhythmic relaxedness to go with the flow of the imagery. Yet I wanted tension, too, a regularity, and I wanted the sounds to be resonant. Finally, I wanted the whole thing to be "beautiful," to contain some of my childhood apple orchard dreams, to give the kind of comfort and pleasure that round things give to the hand and eye—balls, flowers, stars, toys, fruits—apples!

NOTES ON CONTRIBUTORS

SANDRA ALCOSSER is the author of *A Fish to Feed All Hunger* and *Sleeping Inside the Glacier*. She teaches at San Diego State University.

JULIA ALVAREZ teaches at Middlebury College and is the author of *Homecoming* and *The Other Side*, two books of verse, as well as three novels.

A. R. AMMONS teaches at Cornell University and is the author, most recently, of *Brink Road* and *Garbage*.

DAVID BAKER most recently published *After the Reunion* and *Sweet Home, Saturday Night*. He teaches at Denison University.

PETER BALAKIAN teaches at Colgate University and edits *Graham House Review*. He has published several collections of verse and *Theodore Roethke's Far Fields*, a book of criticism.

MARVIN BELL has published thirteen volumes of poetry, including *The Book of the Dead Man*.

PHILIP BOOTH lives in Castine, Maine, and has published numerous volumes of poetry, including *Selves* and *Relations*.

ROSELLEN BROWN is the author of numerous works of fiction and poetry, including *A Rosellen Brown Reader*. She teaches at the University of Houston.

TERESA CADER is the author of *Guests* and *Paper Wasps*. She lives in Lexington, Massachusetts.

CARL DENNIS teaches at the State University of New York and has published many volumes of poetry, including *The Near World*, *The Outskirts of Troy*, and *Meetings with Time*.

MARK DOTY teaches at the University of Utah and is the author of *Atlantis* and other volumes. His memoir, *Heaven's Coast*, was recently published.

RITA DOVE teaches at the University of Virginia and was recently Poet Laureate of the United States. She has published numerous books of poetry, including *Grace Notes*, and won a Pulitzer Prize for Poetry.

STEPHEN DUNN recently published his *Selected Poems*. He teaches at the Richard Stockton College of New Jersey.

JOHN ENGELS teaches at St. Michael's College in Winooski, Vermont, and has published many volumes of poetry, including *Walking to Cootehill: New and Selected Poems, 1958–1992*.

CAROL FROST has recently published *Pure* and *Venus and Don Juan*. She directs the Catskill Poetry Workshop at Hartwick College and is the recipient of two NEA fellowships.

ALICE FULTON most recently published *Sensual Math* and *Powers of Congress*. She teaches at the University of Michigan in Ann Arbor.

PAMELA WHITE HADAS has written a book on Marianne Moore and several volumes of poetry, including *Designing Women* and *Beside Herself*.

DAVID HUDDLE teaches at the University of Vermont and has published many books of fiction, poetry, and essays. These include *A David Huddle Reader* and *The Writing Habit: Essays*.

RICHARD JACKSON has just published his third book of poetry, *Alive All Day*. His books of criticism include *Dismantling Time in Contemporary American Poetry*.

ERICA JONG lives in New York and has published many well-known novels and six books of poetry, including *Becoming Light: New and Selected Poems*. Her memoir, *Fear of Fifty*, appeared recently.

X. J. KENNEDY most recently published *Dark Horses: New Poems* and a reprint of *Nude Descending a Staircase*.

MAXINE KUMIN is an award-winning poet, novelist, and essayist. Her books include *Looking for Luck* and *Nature*. She lives on a horse farm in New Hampshire.

GARY MARGOLIS is a psychologist at Middlebury College. His several volumes of poetry include *The Day We Still Stand Here* and *Falling Awake*.

PAUL MARIANI teaches at the University of Massachusetts in Amherst and has published numerous volumes of poetry, including *Salvage Operations: New and Selected Poems*. He has written biographies of William Carlos Williams, John Berryman, and Robert Lowell.

WILLIAM MATTHEWS teaches at the City College of the City University of New York. His recent collections include *Time & Money* and *The Mortal City: One Hundred Epigrams from Martial*.

LYNN MCMAHON has published her poems in numerous periodicals and has published several books.

J. D. MCCLATCHY edits *The Yale Review* and has published several collections of poetry, including *The Rest of the Way* and *Ten Commandments*. He has also published a book of criticism, *White Paper*, and edited *The Vintage Book of Contemporary World Poetry*.

CHRISTOPHER MERRILL has, most recently, published *Watch Fire*, a book of poems, and *The Old Bridge: The Third Balkan War and the Age of the Refugee*. He teaches at Holy Cross College.

JOYCE CAROL OATES teaches at Princeton. Her recent books include *We Were the Mulvaneys* and *First Love*.

CAROLE SIMMONS OLES is the author, most recently, of *The Deed* and *Stunts*. She teaches at the California State University, Chico.

ROBERT PACK is College Professor at Middlebury College. His recent books include *Fathering the Map*, a volume of new and selected poems, and *Minding the Sun*.

JAY PARINI teaches at Middlebury College. His collections of poetry include *Anthracite Country*, *Town Life*, and *House of Days*.

ROBERT PINSKY teaches at Boston University and has just published *The Figured Wheel: New and Collected Poems, 1966–1996*. He has also translated Dante's *Inferno*.

STANLEY PLUMLY has published many volumes of poetry, including *Celestial Summer* and *The Marriage in the Trees*.

WYATT PRUNTY directs the Sewanee Writers' Conference and has published several books of poetry, including *The Run of the House* and *Balance as Belief*.

LAWRENCE RAAB teaches at Williams College. His two most recent books are *What We Don't Know About Each Other* and *Other Children*.

BIM RAMKE edits *Denver Quarterly* and has published five books of poetry, including *Massacre of the Innocents*. His first book won the Yale Younger Poets Award in 1977.

HILDA RAZ edits *Prairie Schooner* and teaches at the University of Nebraska. Her books of verse include *The Bone Dish*.

IRA SADOFF teaches at Colby College. He has published several collections of poetry, including *Emotional Traffic*, and *An Ira Sadoff Reader*.

ROBERT SIEGEL teaches at the University of Wisconsin at Milwaukee. His recent books of poems include *In A Pig's Eye* and *White Whale*.

KATHERINE SONIAT teaches at Virginia Polytechnic Institute and State University. Her poetry has been widely published.

DAVE SMITH edits *The Southern Review* and has published many books of poetry, including *Cuba Nights* and *The Roundhouse Voices*.

W. D. SNODGRASS has published many volumes of poetry, including *Heart's Needle*. He has won the Pulitzer Prize for Poetry and many other awards.

MARK STRAND teaches at Johns Hopkins University. His numerous books of poetry include *The Continuous Life* and *Dark Harbor*.

DABNEY STUART has published numerous volumes of poetry, including *Narcissus Dreaming, Second Sight: Poems for Paintings by Carroll Cloar*, and *Long Gone*.

THOMAS SWISS teaches at Drake University and has recently published *Still Measure* and *Rough Cut*, as well as *Mapping the Beat: Popular Music and Contemporary Theory*.

SUE ELLEN THOMPSON has recently published *This Body of Silk* and *The Wedding Boat*.

ERIC TRETHEWEY's poetry, fiction, and essays have appeared in numerous magazines. His most recent book is *The Long Road Home*. He teaches at Hollins College.

CHASE TWICHELL has published several volumes of poetry, including *Perdido*. She teaches at Princeton.

ELLEN BRYANT VOIGT has published five collections of poetry, including *Two Trees* and *Kyrie*. She has won many awards for her work, including the Emily Clark Balch Award and the 1993 Hanes Poetry Award.

RICHARD WILBUR has published his *Collected Poems*. He was a recent Poet Laureate of the United States.

NANCY WILLARD has most recently published *Swimming Lessons: New and Selected Poems*. She teaches at Vassar College and writes novels and books for children as well as poetry.

MILLER WILLIAMS directs the University of Arkansas Press and has published twenty-six books, including *Living on the Surface: New and Selected Poems*.

CLARA YU has most recently published *To the Interior*. She teaches at Middlebury College.

PAUL ZIMMER is currently director of the University of Iowa Press. His books of poetry include *Big Blue Train* and *Crossing to Sunlight: Selected Poems*.

Introspections

.SITY PRESS OF NEW ENGLAND publishes books under its own imprint

.s the publisher for Brandeis University Press, Dartmouth College, Middlebury

.ollege Press, University of New Hampshire, Tufts University, and Wesleyan

University Press.

Library of Congress Cataloging-in-Publication Data

Introspections : American poets on one of their own poems / edited by
Robert Pack and Jay Parini.
p. cm.
ISBN 0-87451-772-9 (alk. paper). — ISBN 0-87451-773-7 (pbk. : alk. paper)
1. American poetry—20th century—History and criticism—Theory, etc.
2. Poetry—Authorship.   3. Poetics.   I. Pack, Robert, 1929-   .   II. Parini, Jay.
PS325.I58   1997
811'.509—DC21   97-19542